Dear Clanger (?)
Now

BUSHELL'S
BEST BITS

Great to
meet you
and fantastic
display from
the Gurkha Dave's
band

[signature]

BUSHELL'S
BEST BITS

EVERYTHING
YOU EVER NEEDED TO KNOW ABOUT
THE WORLD'S CRAZIEST SPORTS

MIKE BUSHELL

JOHN BLAKE

Published by John Blake Publishing Ltd,
3 Bramber Court, 2 Bramber Road,
London W14 9PB, England

www.johnblakepublishing.co.uk

www.facebook.com/Johnblakepub facebook
twitter.com/johnblakepub twitter

First published in paperback in 2013

ISBN: 978-1-78219-012-7

British Library Cataloguing-in-Publication Data:

A catalogue record for this book is available from the British Library.

Design by www.envydesign.co.uk

Printed in Great Britain by CPI Group (UK) Ltd

1 3 5 7 9 10 8 6 4 2

Papers used by John Blake Publishing are natural, recyclable
products made from wood grown in sustainable forests.
The manufacturing processes conform to the
environmental regulations of the country of origin.

Every attempt has been made to contact the relevant
copyright-holders, but some were unobtainable.
We would be grateful if the appropriate people could contact us.

For Lucy, Isabel and Sophie

CONTENTS

CONTENTS

INTRODUCTION

A MOUSE AND AN OWL

'Hey, morning, how's your dad?' It was an odd question at 7.30 am in the shower block of a Dorset campsite. Half my face was covered in shaving foam, and my eyes were still hibernating.

'He's...err...fine thanks'. Perhaps the chirpy Cockney standing next to me had joined us at the campfire the night before, but a combination of the dark and cider had blurred my memory.

'I have heard so much about his time at Chelsea, does he still go?' came the next question, revealing the true reason for his curiosity. It certainly wasn't the first time I had been asked about 'Dad's' time at Stamford Bridge. It happened whenever I was mistaken for Chris Hollins, my former colleague at BBC *Breakfast*. His father John did used to play for Chelsea. However, my dad, also John, has been involved in education throughout his career. He still is.

Now Chris and I are roughly the same size. We both have two ears, two eyes, and our own hair, but that's about it.

Nevertheless, I have lost count of the number of times I have been congratulated for Chris's ballroom success on *Strictly Come Dancing*. Despite my insistence that I am more Bambi on ice, I have had drinks bought for me and even been patted on the back at a party by a member of the *Strictly* casting team.

It also blew a date, when a chap who had met Chris at Ascot the week before was practically aggressive in his insistence that I was Chris Hollins, in front of the lady I had met for dinner. She started to wonder if I was a spy, or a serial liar who had a different identity for every date. I never saw her again.

It is of course flattering to be mistaken for Mr Hollins (not sure he feels quite the same when he gets called Mike…) but this was the first time there had been identity confusion in a shower block.

'My dad, oh yes, well he's still in education in Yorkshire, thanks,' I replied with a smile. I could have predicted the next line, but it makes me giggle every time: 'Ah yes, of course, sorry mate! You're the guy who does all those different sports! My wife wakes me up every Saturday and says "come and see what he's doing this week". Me and the kids love it. It's Mike, isn't it?'

By the way, it's always comforting to know that other people get up on a Saturday morning and enjoy their breakfast with us on the BBC. So please never hesitate to say hello.

As I wiped the last fluffy cloud from my chin, the man told me how he had tried indoor skydiving with his sons, having seen the feature I had done. He'd also bought himself a mountain bike.

'We can't believe what you get up to,' he continued, 'but you're not very good at most of these sports, are you?'

We continued chatting as we gathered our toilet bags and tiptoed into the daylight, as the smell of cattle straw ushered our senses back to the holiday I was having with my daughters on Norden Farm at Corfe Castle. It was a fair question. Others have asked me: 'Why are you rubbish at some of these sports you feature?'

I answer that beginners don't normally excel at a sport in their first lesson. It can be a painful and humiliating baptism of fire. My role is the medieval everyman: your average bloke off the sofa. I realised at a young age that I didn't have the size or balance to make it as a professional sportsman, or at least that's what I was led to believe. However, that shouldn't stop anyone from using the immense power of sport to enrich their lives. Lack of ability should never stop anyone from having fun, from playing, from getting involved and enjoying the enormous health and social benefits of whatever activity it may be.

Some people shy away from the pitch or sports hall because they feel ashamed, embarrassed, or out of their comfort zone. I hope this book will break down this barrier, and show that there really is something out there for everyone. If I was good at everything I profiled on a Saturday morning, it would appear horribly arrogant. I am merely the guinea pig lucky enough to represent other beginners, showing what a particular sport is like at first: reporting on how easy or difficult it is: how steep the learning curve may be, and whether there is any pain involved. I usually join other pioneers, often youngsters trying a sport for the first time, to get their perspective, and they would agree that compared to the experts and professionals, we do look complete amateurs.

Another aim of the Saturday morning pieces is to showcase how good the dedicated athletes, who have mastered their art, really are. So who cares if this presenter is not a natural at first? Giving something a go gives you the most liberating feeling of fun and excitement as you push the boundaries of your own personal world, and discover those muscles you never knew you had. Plus come on be honest, how many of you really enjoy seeing me with egg on my face, when taking a battering from a 13-year-old Muay Thai champion in Cornwall.

So, no apologies if some of the sports have challenged me and I have ended up flat on my face. Surely if a middle-aged bloke who likes a pint can get involved, so can you. I promise there is a sport for all.

Before we go on a journey of discovery beyond the world of sport you may know, the other common question I get asked is how I ended up doing what I do. There is no set way into broadcasting, because people come from all walks of life. I have worked with former teachers, policemen, lawyers, and actors who have made the switch. So there is no one answer, but I hope the following will be useful for those harbouring journalistic ambitions.

Are you nosey? That's the first thing to ask yourself if you want to be a journalist. Are you interested in what others are doing? Do you care? Do you also get an enormous buzz from telling your friends in the playground, on the bus or down the pub all about it? If so, then perhaps there is a dormant reporter in you.

What you like when you were seven years old? The famous quote from St Francis Xavier, 'Give me the child until he is seven and I will give you the man', certainly rings true in my case – not that I had a clue at the time. I was adamant I would be a farmer, if I was turned down by all the top football clubs.

Like many seven-year-olds, I had an imaginary friend – Sammy Mouse. My sister Jane had Cumsiarbar, Alley Dorby and Heffer's wife, so mine felt rather mundane in comparison, which is probably why the stories I wrote about him were never published. So by the time I was eight, I realised that if I wanted to get anything in print, I would have to do it myself. Many youngsters get a job as a paperboy or girl, delivering the morning news, but I decided to make my own publication to deliver. It was driven by an obsession with telling people things they didn't know. On FA Cup Final day I would display the latest score on the front window, even though we lived at the end of a cul-de-sac and only a passing cat would ever see it. So it seemed perfectly natural to spend my spare time writing and printing the *Daily Owl*, with the help of my old mate Derek. He was a duplicator I got for Christmas when I was nine. I have no idea why I called him Derek. She could equally have been a Deirdre.

For those too young to remember, the duplicator was the great uncle of the printers we rely on today. I can tell you that one of my early thrills came from threading in the carbon paper on which I had typed my stories, and then turning the handle to make the copies fly off the press. This was Ashwell though, a village in Hertfordshire, rather than Wapping, and the *Daily Owl* had a circulation of just eight. Despite this I like to think it had a loyal readership and they were well rewarded, especially if you entered the weekly competition. With only eight readers you stood a great chance of winning. Not that Mum was very impressed when Gary McCormick turned up to collect his prize, which happened to be the Leeds United football shirt I had just got from Father Christmas. However, he had won the competition fair and square and so we had to hand it over.

Like a couple of the national papers, though, the *Daily Owl* was eventually consigned to history. I still remember how I wept when, aged 11, I was told we were moving away from the cosy Hertfordshire village to Yorkshire. 180 miles away from all I had known, from the girls I hoped to marry, and from friends I had made for life. But Dad had a new job, and so in 1977 we moved north, and fate took me closer to the world of extreme and bizarre sporting challenges.

That desire to report, to tell a story – the driving force behind the *Daily Owl* – had followed me to Yorkshire. But now it wasn't just print I was interested in. At the age of 13, I broke into the world of broadcasting – not that anyone else knew it. I took a tape recorder onto the school bus and recorded the teenage banter. I kept it in my bag for a whole day in lessons and even assembly. When the Chemistry teacher thought I was reaching into the bag for a pen, I was really flicking the pause button from off to on. Soon I had a 30-minute montage of sound-bites from a day in the life at Harrogate Granby High School.

My cover was blown when another teacher caught me whispering away into my rucksack. I was doing a piece of voiceover commentary, but he thought I was disrupting class. I was sent to see the headmaster, who listened to the recording as I fidgeted nervously, gazing out of the window and picturing the cane landing on my hand. Thankfully though, there was nothing malicious or offensive on it and so instead of getting a detention, the fly-on-the-wall documentary was played to the whole school. These days there are many opportunities to make radio and television programmes at schools, and you will end up with a far better result if you discuss it with your teachers first!

On other occasions I would follow the sound of a fire engine on my bike, all the while talking into the tape recorder. I didn't know or question why. It just seemed normal and if you have the same symptoms, a career in journalism is the only cure. It has to be a passion, an interest, and it was the same when I got to King Alfred's College for my drama and television degree course. I ended up presenting the weekly TV programme *Pulse* and writing the college newsletter.

Sports-wise, though, through those formative years I was always overlooked. It can't just have been my size. After all there are plenty of 5'5" sporting heroes and heroines. So I concluded that it was because I am flat-footed, which still means I don't quite have the touch of a Messi. I am also bow-legged: and have often been accused of impersonating John Wayne. However I was determined to make up for this oddity with sheer determination and belief.

As I settled into life in Yorkshire, I couldn't get into the football team. Even the five-a-side tournament was beyond me, as I was told that I was too Southern: too soft. This is where the Jack Russell gene in me, which I think I get from my Mum, kicked in. I had threatened to 'run home' to Hertfordshire numerous times, but it was still a shock when one day Dad's patience snapped and he said 'Go on then, do it, run home'.

So a year later I did. 175 miles in six days. I had great company in Simon Wild, a friend from school who for some bizarre reason had also thought it seemed a good idea to run over six marathons in as many days. Not many other 15-year-olds would have seen the point of it, but Simon was an inspiration: the driving force behind each cold winter training session.

By now the idea had snowballed way beyond a stroppy teenager's foot stamping. We were running to raise money for the International Year of Disabled People. Simon's father Malcolm had come on board, planning the route, sorting out a support car and arranging for the mayor of each town to roll out the red carpet. It was a first taste of being on air, as we were interviewed and had our departure covered live on BBC Radio Leeds.

So it was, that after six days of blisters bleeding, of dogs barking and sometimes chasing, of sleepless nights in dodgy B&Bs, of Simon's father shouting the test match and Open golf results, we got our first taste of sporting champagne. It flowed down our red cheeks at the finish line in Ashwell, and the blurred image of familiar old faces cheering, hangs like an oil painting in my mind, a permanent reminder of what can be achieved. This was the moment I was bitten by the adrenalin rush you get from a sporting challenge. It had shown me that you don't have to be talented, or blessed with the Pele gene, to get the most out of sport. Our own goals and challenges are not just about winning, or even competing.

I have learned that it's the adventures you have, that enrich your understanding of this complex, rich tapestry of life that count for as much. Sometimes you have to follow your heart, go with your instincts and take a risk.

For example my early steps in journalism meandered more than the yellow brick road. Having left King Alfred's College in Winchester with a 2:1 degree, I got a job as a newspaper reporter on the *Hampshire Chronicle*. My extra-curricular interests at college had proved to be worth their weight in gold, and demonstrated my enthusiasm for the profession. The editor did take me down a peg, though, saying that the only other applicant had been a woman who had sent in a picture of herself topless. I was fully clothed, so the job was mine.

Local newspapers are still seen as the best way into the media by many in the business, because of the training they give you, not just in writing, but in law, local and central government, shorthand writing and the ability to tell a story. If you can get to the bottom of a dog show and make it into interesting copy, you won't have much trouble reporting on something much meatier higher up the food chain.

The *Hampshire Chronicle* sent me on a 10-week journalism course in Portsmouth, but I didn't complete my two-year indentures, because I joined a band with other journalists Marion and Nigel and his friend Dave, and the following summer we set off on a tour of Europe. It was a tour ended prematurely by thieves in Amsterdam and mechanics in Spain, but the Spinal Tap gang would have been proud, and the experience gave me something to talk about as i got a job on a daily paper in Derby.

That New Year I was travelling again, as Nigel persuaded me to spend New Year's Eve with him, ringing in 1990 on the Berlin Wall. It was just months after it had started coming down, and the atmosphere was uneasy at times as thousands of revellers from both the East and West, all tried to get onto the wall leaving decades of misconceptions and tension on the ground. I wrote about the experience for the Derby paper and it was this, more than anything else that persuaded Steve Panton and Henry Yelf to give me my first job at the BBC just a few months later, on Radio Solent in Southampton.

The early days at the BBC were all-consuming. My enthusiasm is still the same. It's not like a job, it's my passion and I didn't mind staying into the night to edit a radio report. I was there at two in the morning, slowly cutting bits of the reel-to-reel tape with a razor blade and sticking them back together in a different order to tell the story.

I was posted to the Isle of Wight to be the correspondent there, running the office in Newport where I produced my radio and TV reports for BBC South. On the Island, getting the stories was all about mixing with as many people as possible – at the quaint, quirky pubs, at the supermarket, or on the bus. The more people I talked to, the more stories I would hear about. The Isle of Wight had so many tales to tell, and it was here that I had my first introduction to the more bizarre stories that now I love telling. There were the escaped prairie gods tunnelling under farmers' fields, the shire horse that drank at its local pub, and come to think of it, there was a fox that liked a pint in Ventnor as well. There he was sat on the bar stool, sipping a pint of real ale. I am sure there was a broadsheet newspaper and packet of pork scratchings as well.

What I realised manning that office, day in, day out, was how important the BBC is to people at a local level. I was front of house, their first port of call, and people would come in to talk about all sorts of television and radio matters, or sometimes just to share their problems. There was one elderly gentleman who always announced his arrival with raucous, smoke-grated laughter. Did I want to meet his friends, Barbara and Ken, who couldn't agree about the 1992 general election? Barbara was a conservative, but Ken was a liberal democrat. It was only later that I discovered they were both snakes. I saw from my little window on the world the company that BBC local tv and radio provide people. They feel it belongs to them.

Having covered news on the Isle of Wight and then in Reading for BBC South, my natural interest in sport was calling, so I joined the BBC's sport department. This eventually led me to joining the BBC News channel and going to the World Cup in France in 1998 and the Athens Olympics in 2004.

But my passion went beyond just being a spectator and reporting on what was happening. My 180-mile marathon from Harrogate to Ashwell had shown me what an average person could achieve with a bit of training. I thought that if we could push the boundaries of people's self belief and get more involved, we would bring a whole new audience into the sporting family.

The BBC and in particular *Breakfast* has given me the creative freedom to explore the world beyond mainstream sport. Since 2006 as well as presenting sport bulletins on BBC *Breakfast*, the BBC News channel, and BBC World, I have been on a mission to broaden the audience and to entice in viewers who wouldn't necessarily consider themselves to be sports fans. So each week I profile a different sport or activity which doesn't normally get much exposure and which sometimes people won't have even heard of. Or, I might also take a different look at a high-profile sporting event or do a feature showing another side of a well-known sports star. Or sometimes it's a report on a new initiative by a mainstream sport to get more people involved.

I have lost count of the number of people who have said 'I didn't used to watch the sport, I would go and make a cup of tea, but now I wait for your feature to come on'. Imagine the feeling I had when I got a letter from Susan Tilford, received over a year after I did a feature on Horse Trek – orienteering on horseback. She wrote: 'I was smitten by a thunderbolt! You opened a whole new world to us. It has been fun and exciting, and educational, a tremendous confidence-booster. This is such a wonderful, no-pressure sport, but then at the end of last year, I decided it was high time for me to take on a real challenge, and seriously compete. I'm 64, and my pony is 27. I cannot find words to adequately express my appreciation for doing this feature.'

It makes every ounce of effort worthwhile. I do believe the Saturday features have a very important role. It's not just getting people more active, joining in and having a go; it's about getting people playing. The word 'play' is sometimes tarred with the notion that you are not taking a sport seriously. Yet all sport begins with play, with the time and space to experiment and make mistakes, to do something just for fun.

There are leading academics who believe that play has been schooled out of children, and that as a result they not interacting with others and stretching their imaginations as they used to. Times have changed. Whether it's because of more traffic on the roads, the perception that our streets are now not as safe, or due to the rise in computer games and hand consoles, play has been in decline over the last generation.

So on Saturday mornings, I have been trying to get people playing again, trying something new for themselves. Some are more extreme for the adrenalin seekers, but others are simply activities that get people of all ages interacting together. What's more, if Bushell can do it, then nearly all of us can. The features have opened doors for me and the programme as well, with many top sportsmen and women telling me they like taking part because it brings variety to their training – or because they like seeing a sports reporter suffer! More importantly, though, many of the professionals like giving something back.

It's been a wonderful seven-year journey, and I am so grateful to the BBC, to the Saturday *Breakfast* team – including for a long time Julia Barry and Katie McDougall – for running with the idea and helping me broaden the sporting spectrum. I am also grateful to sports news editors, like Nick Dickson and Richard Burgess, and to David Kermode and Alison Ford on *Breakfast*, for giving me the space, time and freedom to continue this mission: to carry on this campaign to get play, back into the heart of our communities, and our society.

INTRODUCTION

Over the last seven years the number of school sports on offer to students has more than doubled, and beyond the school gates the opportunities to go out there to find the sport for you, have never been greater.

By increasing the number of people participating in sport, we might well find the next Dame Kelly Holmes, but above all else it's not about making the first team, it's about enriching your lives with the enormous benefits taking part brings, in physical, mental and social development. So even if it's worm charming, don't knock it, because like any activity, it will have changed some people's lives, and this book is about finding the sport that can do it for you.

SPORT OR SPOOF?

Before you get stuck into this book, test your knowledge of some of the lesser known sports out there. Get everyone in the room to put up their hands. Then read out the various sports or spoofs below. If people think they are genuine activities, it's hands on heads. If they think it's completely made up, it's hands on behinds. Those who guess correctly stay in the game. The winner is the last person standing. The record when I have tested this out in the past has been 15 – no one in my experience has ever got past that point. Good luck and no cheating!

1: Horse-boarding
2: Oofball
3: Stool heron
4: Aunt Sally
5: Worm grunting
6: Husband dragging
7: Haggle ball
8: Sid Heslop 'in the net'

9: Rolf
10: Nurdling
11: Pole climbing
12: Floorball
13: Bat and ball
14: Singobat
15: Tambournelli
16: Rabbit showjumping
17: Udder-ball
18: Finger jousting
19: Shin kicking
20: Mantis Secto

(ANSWERS: 1, 4, 5, 6, 9, 10, 11, 12, 13, 15, 16, 18, 19 are organised sports and activities with governing bodies and rules. Numbers 2, 3, 7, 8, 14, 17 and 20 are as far as I know completely made up)

HOW IT ALL STARTED – A SHAGGY DOG STORY

In life you don't know when fate is going to come and bite you on the behind, and give you a gentle reminder of which path to take. I was at a crossroads of footpaths and speckled sunlight was ping ponging off giant conifer trees.

I heard the noise first. A crackle of fern, a stutter of stones and then the crunch of wheels on gravel, twig and pine needle matting. 'Hike on, hike on' is not something you hear in many British forests, but a burly, bearded man was bellowing this out to his teammates, which were two Siberian Husky dogs. It's what you expect to see in the Arctic circle, rather than a Berkshire woodland, but whistling past me was a rider, stood in a sled, with two dogs pulling him along. What's more there wasn't a speck of snow in sight.

I had to pinch myself to believe what I was seeing, but I had stumbled across the latest event in the UK's Sled Dog racing calendar. There were hundreds more like him, arriving later that day, in huge motor homes: team camps on wheels, with velvet lined apartments for the stars of the show, the dogs. Lack of snow is something of a drawback in the UK, so instead the dogs pull carts on three or four wheels. They are known as rigs.

I had stumbled into a whole new sporting world, into the premier league of sled dog racing, and I could see this was a whole way of life for these people, taking up their weekends from November to May. One couple told me they had just spent eight thousand pounds building a special hot tub and Jacuzzi in their garden just so they could keep their top dogs cool and fit in the summer months. This was serious. This was dedication to sport like you see on the Kop, or at the Millennium Stadium.

There was no financial reward in this, no long-term career, and the main physical prize was a bronze statue of a dog to take pride of place on the mantelpiece. The real attraction ran far deeper. It was the great sense of togetherness, the camaraderie, the fun, the thrill of working day in day out with your dog so that when it comes to your moment, you can pit your wits against the clock and beat other teams from across the land or even the globe. This was their world, in which they could be champion, and this meeting was a chance to mix and to share a drink with others who felt the same.

They couldn't wait for me to experience the rush of the 'mush', which used to be what sled dog drivers shouted in Alaska. So I took charge of a beginner's rig, with two very experienced dogs straining to give me the ride of my life.

Let me tell you, you haven't lived until you have hurtled along behind a team of huskies, and you certainly don't have to go to Greenland or Alaska to experience the thrill when you can shake, rattle and roll your way through the British countryside, twisting and turning and ducking the branches as your dogs get you through the tightest of angles.

It takes strategy and training to keep your team in peak condition, and to be able to work your sled dogs in harness on

Forestry Commission land you have to have a permit, which you pay for. There are only a limited number of permits available in each area, and such is the sport's popularity now that there is a long waiting list for permits in some regions. Some enthusiasts have to wait years. What's more when you do get a permit, all your training on this Forestry land has to be done, either after dark or 8pm, or before 9am, when there are fewer members of the public around. It certainly requires dedication, travelling and training at the crack of dawn and at night, but as I jolted and wobbled on my rig as we careered through the trees, the river of adrenalin running through my veins convinced me of its appeal.

I even started to kid myself that I was in control and that my four-legged team members were actually listening to my voice command, 'Hike on, hike'. We must have covered a mile: a mere sprint, but I felt like I had been in a tumble dryer. It would take more fitness training to build up to the longer races, like the Iditarod, the biggest event in the dog-sled racing calendar which covers 1150 miles, and takes anything from 10 to 17 days. This one is on snow, and in the UK they do race on the white stuff when it's thick enough – the Siberian Husky Club of Great Britain have done this on several occasions in the last few years. On the whole though, it's wheels and a rig, and a much bumpier ride. They welcome new members so for more information go to the website www.absasleddogracing.org.uk

This covers mainly the South of England, so other useful groups that can help include, Siberian Husky Club of GB, SDAS Sled dog Association of Scotland, BSHRA British Siberian Husky Racing Association, AMWA - Alaskan Malamute Working Association, and Snopeak – this lists all sled dog events for the whole race calendar covering all organisations.

While the most common dog used in dog sled racing is the

husky, it's said that between 1988 and 1991, a team of poodles competed in the famous Iditarod race. If you can't afford to build a cart, or sled, then other variations include bike joring, when a dog or team of dogs pulls a bicycle, but for obvious reasons don't try this yourself at home! There is also scooter joring, which involves the rider pushing along on a scooter which is being pulled by their dog. Finally if you want the minimum of equipment or fuss, then the sport of CaniX or Cani-cross could be for you. In this growing sport across the UK, you are harnessed from your waist directly to your dog. This does require a level of fitness and understanding with your companion though. Your dog is going to help you set a personal best for sure by running faster, but if you can't keep up with them or hold them back, you will end up in the bushes or being dragged along the gravel. It's proof that four legs are always faster than two. There is more on this in the chapter on animal sports.

My first encounter with the dogs was to have a lasting impact. I had been lucky enough to glimpse into a sporting world that I didn't know existed. A sport whose results never appear on the back pages of the newspapers, or get a mention on the TV, and in the years that have followed it has been a privilege to lift the lid on hundreds of other similar sports.

After hearing about the huskies in their Jacuzzi, I thought if there's that amount of dedication in this sport, what else is going on? What other stories of passionate sporting commitment deserve recognition?

If there are hundreds doing this in the forests, what else is going on behind closed doors, over hedges, in our lakes and on our seas?

So it began: a journey, a mission to broaden our sporting

horizons, to uncover the events and activities that make this country the diverse and unique place it is. I thought it would be a journey that would last a few weeks, maybe months. I could never have imagined that it would be a marathon to outlast that Yorkshire to Ashwell voyage.

Some of the sports and activities I have encountered hadn't even been conceived when I started. Rock-it-ball, for example, which aims to make school sport more inclusive for those children who were left on the sidelines in mainstream sports, hadn't been invented. Now it's played all over the world.

It's this explosion in sporting opportunity that has fuelled my mission, and lifted me up, every step of the way. No matter how daft or bizarre or trivial an activity may seem at first, there is always a story to be told, a tale of how sport has enriched people's lives.

First came the huskies, then a Frisbee and Octopush. Not the inky creature wallowing in the sea, but underwater hockey, to give it another name. Over the following chapters I hope you will find something that grabs you by the legs and leaves you gulping for air, or bites you in the way the huskies did to me in that Berkshire forest.

1
ANIMALS

And they're off. If it's got four legs and can move, it's fair game. Animals have been involved in our sporting pursuits ever since the first game was played. Today the Grand National, the Cheltenham Gold Cup, the Derby and Royal Ascot are highlights of the sporting calendar, and horses are also the stars in prestigious polo matches all over the world. Dogs can also claim to be main players, while in contrast cats are too cool to get involved in such mindless activities. This section looks at some of the main sports involving animals that I have come across. Thankfully barbaric so-called pastimes like cock fighting and bear baiting are no more on these shores, and I won't be covering ferret-bagging either, but there should be plenty of surprises and we will discover why some animals more than others seem to relish that 'back of the net' feeling.

DOGS

I was on my way to meet some British canine stars at their training camp near Worcester, and I started thinking about that old saying, 'never work with children or animals'. I learned years before joining the BBC that you have to treat our four-legged friends with the utmost respect.

I had a job with the Winchester tourist board as a Roman Centurion, on their guided walks of the city walls. My role was to leap out from behind a wall brandishing my sword, in a very short tunic. Over the course of a week I had been mocked by a group of punk rockers, who goaded me from the garden of a pub with their mangy looking dogs straining on the end of bits of string. One day, with the latest tour party still down the path and around the corner, the dogs moved into position. They had been let out of the pub garden and gathered on the gravel by my wall. Hearing what I thought to be the crowd of tourists, I jumped out with my sword held high, shouting my lines, but instead of intrigued faces reaching for their cameras, the audience consisted of three rows of gnashing teeth.

I recognised one breed to be a border collie and was pretty sure the others had horns and forked tails. I wasn't sticking around for a picture and hot-footed it in my sandals the other way up the path. I vaulted up some steps, onto a bridge and past King Alfred's Statue. The snarling of canine jaws was never far behind, until I came to a pelican crossing and realised that stopping at the lights was a police car. Huffing and puffing, I asked if the officers would do me a favour and arrest the gang hounding me. 'The dogs, the dogs...' I panted...the dogs which had now disappeared. They had given up the chase, probably realising there wasn't much meat on the bone. Remarkably the policewoman kept a straight face as she reassured this pathetic excuse for a Roman and agreed to go and have a word with the dogs and their owners.

Thank fully over the years man's best friend and I have settled our differences. I no longer dress up as a Roman Centurion, and there are numerous sports which are guaranteed to bring you and your dog together.

DOG AGILITY

There aren't many sports in which an 89-year-old can beat a 16-year-old, but dog agility is one. Mary only got into sport at 80, but nine years later in a field near Farnham she was giving us all a lesson, beating teenagers and myself in a warm up for the UK championship to be held in Eastbourne. It was then on to the world championships in Norway. Think show-jumping, but it's your dog going around the obstacles, chasing a clear round, and although Mary wasn't riding her dog, she was instrumental in the outcome.

'Stay, go, weave!' she bellowed as her border collie raced up and down steep narrow ramps, before leaping a two-foot pole. Then it was through a long tunnel, over some hurdles, and then faster than the eye could follow, it darted through a series of poles. 'Go on, weave, weave!' Mary shrieked as she followed the route around the course, waving her arms, dipping her shoulders, pointing her fingers, whistling and nodding her head.

It's not just the dogs that get the exercise and Mary's team got a clear round. You get penalties for fences you don't clear, and for any refusals.

'I get nervous, yes very nervous, but wow when I go, I love it, I love it', Mary said, roaring with laughter. This sport has obviously taken years off her, because she could have passed for 60. The 16-year-old lad who'd been out-thought and out-fought was equally enthusiastic. 'It's an unusual sport, but it keeps me fit. There's a lot of running around and I like showing off our skills to my friends and family in the garden.'

I had taken my faithful old mutt Basil along, who at 12 had lost most of his agility. He was part Labrador, part Lurcher and could have got acting work as a calf. But he was reasonably fit in the autumn years of his life, and would do anything for food. His black tail wagged furiously as we went around the course, his eyes were bright and his silky coat gleamed in the sun, but it was me who was eight feet up in the air at the top of the ramp, and I ended up crawling through the tunnel, jumping the hurdles and climbing through the hoops. I thought that by showing him he might follow, but my hand signals, shoulder shimmies and voice commands were all wrong, and his sole contribution was to go for a wee. I had almost got a clear round, but of course it didn't count.

My theory that Basil's age had cost him his agility didn't carry weight for long either, because the following February he managed to get my daughter Sophie's birthday cake off the back of a kitchen unit during the night. It was way out of reach of his paws, and either he had help from a cat or he did still possess that old showjumping magic.

In truth it can take months to build up the voice commands and body signals that enable you to get your dog around the course, and many go at first just for the social side, greeting each other like long-lost friends and having picnics after the competitions. Now that was something Basil excelled at.

Dog agility started in 1978 when a committee member at the Crufts dog show was challenged with entertaining the audience between the regular competitions. He got together with a vet and they decided to show off the dogs' natural agility and speed. By 1979, some dog clubs then started offering training and a year later the Kennel Club recognised it as a sport. Now there are competitions all over the world.

As breeds go, Basil would have been a natural in his heyday, with his Labrador and Lurcher genes, but there were all sorts there, from Jack Russells to Corgis and an Otter Hound. There are different rounds for different sizes, and all I can say is, may the course be with you.

For more information its www.ukagility.com and http://www.thekennelclub.org.uk/agility

FLYBALL

Flyball is all about speed. It's a sprint relay for dogs, with hurdles along the way. The dogs also have to collect a tennis ball, which they release by pressing on a spring-loaded pad. Then it's back to the starting line where another dog on the team sets off to repeat the sprint. It started in California in the 1960s as a way of keeping energetic breeds of dog fit. It's one of the few dog-and-owner team sports that doesn't involve hunting.

I didn't have a dog with me when I went to a Flyball meeting near Northampton. Basil had barked his last woof, but in his pomp he would have been quick down the course, although mentally challenged by the tennis ball. However, you can just turn up as a beginner, and get paired up with a team member when you arrive. I got a Jack Russell called Spike. He was coaching me rather than the other way round. I was distracted by the noise and the passion as owners and trainers screamed encouragement and dogs strained on their leads, yelping with frantic excitement as they waited their turn.

The course is 15.5 metres long and all four dogs have to run the length of the course and back, collecting the tennis ball on the turn. There are penalties if any dog drops the ball, or if there is a foul on the changeover – for instance if the next dog in line goes off before the previous runner has crossed the starting point.

That was the problem with Spike. He really was champing at the bit to go, rearing up on his back legs, tail beating like a helicopter blade with anticipation, and it took all my restraining powers to keep him back until his moment arrived. Spike didn't even look at the four hurdles on the course as he skipped over them like a skimming stone, and I hadn't even got to the end of my first 'Come on Spike!' before he was back.

Jessica Ennis would be very proud, because the world Flyball record is 14.690 seconds. That's over a total distance (for all four dogs) of 124 metres, and it was set by the Touch and Go team in Las Vegas.

After the first Flyball tournament was held in the USA, a Flyball box was brought back to the UK for use by the Kennel Club in 1987, and this was followed by a competition at Crufts in 1990. It has now spread to all corners of the world, and the European championships were held in the UK in 2012.

This sport means every dog can have its day. The ragged-looking mongrel gets a chance to mix it with the pedigrees. One of the competitions is specifically for mixed breed dogs, and winning teams in the main races often have mutts running one of the legs. Although border collies and whippet-like dogs dominated the line-up at the tournament I attended, all the teams included a smaller breed like a Jack Russell. This is because the height of the hurdles is based on the size of the smallest dog. They are known as the 'height dog' and are essential for any top side, who want to avoid large obstacles.

The only problem for some smaller dogs is getting enough weight on the pad at the end to trigger the release of the tennis ball from the hole. Spike though had developed the funniest technique: leaping into the air with all four paws flying, Kung Fu Panda style.

In truth there are many funny sights in dog agility and Flyball – as anyone who has seen a Corgi hurdling will know. For more information go to www.flyball.org.uk

TO THE RACES

Going to the dogs was once seen as a poor relation compared to a day at the races. But recently greyhound racing has undergone a transformation.

It started in earnest in the UK in 1926, after American Owen Patrick Smith had invented the mechanical hare which could lure dogs around the track. He'd come up with the idea 14 years earlier, hoping to stop the killing of jack rabbits.

Greyhounds are one of the oldest breeds of dog known to mankind, and are said to date back 4,000 years. They are referred to in the Bible and have been celebrated throughout history. They were the dog of the Pharaohs in Ancient Egypt, of rulers of Ancient Greece and of the landed gentry in England. So much so that for hundreds of years in Britain it was regarded as a crime for a peasant to own such an animal, since they were thought of as the sole property of the aristocracy.

During the reign of Queen Elizabeth I (1533–1603) hare coursing rules were introduced. The winner of the race was the dog that caught a live hare and this was the first form of greyhound racing. The sport was quick to exploit the fact that spectators were keen to lay bets on the winning dog, and this quickly attracted bigger crowds to the meetings.

Modern greyhound racing began in the UK at the Belle Vue

Stadium in Manchester on Saturday 24 July 1926. The first race was won by a dog called Mistley. The sport was an instant hit, with interest spanning the length and breadth of the British Isles. It appealed as much to lords and ladies as it did to the working classes. Leading up to the Second World War it was very much in vogue to be seen 'at the dogs'. Some hounds, like Mick the Miller, became national superstars. There was a big boom period which lasted right through the 50s and into the 60s, but then high street bookmakers and televised broadcasts of live horseracing caused gate numbers at greyhound stadiums to drop.

During the late 1960s and 70s the sport went through a lean period, and by the time Ballyregan Bob set a world record of 32 consecutive wins in the 1980s, the sport had gone into decline. However, the tracks continued to invest in facilities and went on to benefit from the sport's resurgence in the 1990s. Indeed, track-based greyhound racing is now a world away from that day in 1926 when it made its first appearance.

There are 26 venues across the country and according to the sport's governing body it is still one of the most popular spectator sports, with over two million people a year going to watch the live races. The stadiums feature restaurants and bars, corporate entertainment facilities and private boxes, all geared to watching the athletes deliver an adrenaline-packed night out, and the greyhound still stands tall above other breeds. They are the fastest dogs, reaching a top speed of 45 mph compared to humans at 28mph. They are the leanest breed: they have the best vision and are able to see clearly for half a mile, and they are officially the fittest: with a larger heart, lungs and more red blood cells than other canine breeds. In the air, they also have a 'double suspension gallop' (to you and me it means they run more like a cheetah than a horse). Indeed greyhounds spend

80% of their time in the air. It's as close to 'flight' as a land mammal can get.

For more information contact the Greyhound Board of Great Britain, at www.thedogs.co.uk

AFGHAN RACING

If it's not speed you are after, but dog racing with a twist, then Afghan hounds certainly offer that. They may not be quite as fast as the greyhounds but they are beautiful to watch with all their hair flying in the wind. Around the Ellesmere Port Dog Track, they maybe around six seconds slower over 260 metres, but they do have unique appeal and offer something a little different.

They are a sociable and playful breed, and in the training race I witnessed near Winchester in the mid-1990s, some of the dogs stopped along the way for a play fight. One of these paw scuffles then turned into something far more amorous, and the measly hare suddenly lost its appeal as love was in the air (and their hair).

Amanda Reed from the Ellesmere Port Afghan racing club said: 'They do sometimes cut across their lanes and occasionally will stop for a play fight. Others may just stop and there's one really fast dog who gets near to the finish line every time and then jumps over the barrier, so we can't record his time. People do come to watch and have a laugh, and while it is about what time the dogs do, we don't all take it too seriously'.

To add extra colour the dogs wear fancy dress rather than just their normal race jackets. It certainly makes for unpredictable racing. However, while there are still clubs up and down the country, due to reduced track access the future for the sport has become less certain. The annual season begins in March and for more information, go and see for yourself by contacting the Afghan Hound Association.

DOG DANCING (HEELWORK TO MUSIC)

First things first. We shouldn't call this 'dog dancing'. This makes it seem like something out of a circus and that couldn't be further than the truth. It may be what people think it's called, but the official name of this sport is heelwork to music.

It's why I was crouched forward, microphone in one hand and a piece of sausage in the other. I waited rather uncomfortably, having seen the trainer's bite marks around her fingers. There was a whistle, the music played, and the patter of feet behind me was followed by the prodding of paws on my shoulder. A border collie had come in to land. She was inch perfect and had taken the sausage without me feeling a thing. My relief was greater, because we were live on air, on *Breakfast*, and back in the studio Charlie and Louise were applauding the daring dog routine. It was part of a feature on the rise of 'dog dancing', or rather heelwork to music. It's *Strictly Come Dancing*, or *Dancing on Ice*, for you and your dog. After Pudsey and her owner Ashleigh became famous across the world for their routine which helped them win *Britain's Got Talent* in 2012, interest surged. But it's actually been a recognised canine sport since the 1990s.

It's why I was on the quayside outside the gleaming new studios at Media City in Salford, at 9.30 in the morning, with a border collie panting proudly in my right ear as it balanced on my shoulders. It was an honour because these weren't any old paws, they were the talented feet of Fly, who along with trainer Karen Sykes was part of the British team that had just won the European championships in Denmark. I had interviewed Karen live and she had shown me a bit of the routine that had helped lift the title.

Now you might reasonably question whether this is a sport, so with this in mind, I went along to one of the weekly training sessions held at a centre near Northampton, run by the UK's queen of heelwork to music, Mary Ray. She worries that calling it 'dog dancing' will alienate people and make it seem like an act that can't be taken seriously. Watching Mary and her dog Levi in full flow put such concerns to bed. The communication between the two was telepathic, as Levi fetched items, sat, weaved and displayed pathos and comedy with paws and expressions, all in perfect time with the music.

'It's very competitive,' Mary stressed, 'and it is that way all over the world now. The choreography is the hard part. Anyone can put music on and just work the dog, but the difference with Torvill and Dean was that they choreographed their routine to fit the music. At the time they stood out from everyone else, and that's what we have to do. We want to be taken seriously, if for no other reason, than as a way of promoting good dog training.'

Mary Ray started the sport in 1990, strictly as heelwork training, but with music playing in the background. Then as the sport progressed and became popular, choreography became more important, and gradually the need to add variety and a greater repertoire of moves naturally evolved. The first HTM show was held in 1996, and by then the sport was already established in a number of other countries.

The freestyle element of the sport has helped to re-establish the popularity of 'trick training' in pet obedience clubs. Team GB became the new European champions in 2012, and thanks to the TV exposure classes are now inundated with new recruits.

'It really helps to keep you fit, mentally and physically,' said Jenny Deakin, who has made the final at Crufts. 'It's like any good aerobic exercise,' added Sandra Hallam, who was struggling to keep up with her St Bernard, Alice. 'We both have to stay really fit, to be able to do a whole routine in the ring for three and a half minutes, especially with Alice who certainly goes for it.'

My daughters Isabel and Sophie, who have a Parsons Jack Russell called Lilly, had come along and were transfixed. Beginners who turn up are given an experienced dog to work, and Sophie had Ozzie, a Sheltie – or officially a Shetland Sheepdog – who was weaving through her legs, rolling and trotting backwards within minutes. In contrast, I was nearly taken out by poor Ozzie, who got entangled around my legs. Mary got me to make a circle in the air with my hand, holding a tiny bit of sausage. As I went around with my arm, so Ozzie's head followed, spinning on the spot like Dill the dog from the TV programme *The Herbs*.

'Dogs don't get dizzy,' Mary reassured me and it seems she was right. Ozzie didn't put a step out of place, as I tried to walk forward with my arms tracing a figure of eight between my legs. I used my head, voice and shoulders as well as my arms to guide Ozzie through. The little dog was now skipping in and out of my step and around the back so fast that I felt dizzy watching him. 'You're walking like John Wayne!' laughed Mary. My gestures were far too exaggerated. This is a subtle sport, where style and elegance counts for a lot. Once you have a routine, you can start introducing props. Mary's included a broom, a washing line and laundry basket. No doubt if I had tried this with Basil, it would have been me in the basket by the end!

For more information contact www.heelworktomusic.co.uk or www.mary.ray.co.uk

HORSES FOR COURSES

AT THE RACES

This section is all about how we harness the power of horses, whether it be to chase a ball, ride a board, or simply race and jump. The top jockeys have to among the toughest, most disciplined athletes in any world sport, whether it's the diets they have to stick to, or the pain they suffer when they fall.

Think of the Christmas dinner you enjoy every year. Most people consume up to 6000 calories on 25 December. Top jockey Tony McCoy has revealed he has taken on board just 597 calories even on Christmas Day to keep himself in peak condition. It starts with tea and two slices of toast. Then it's a hot bath to sweat out four pounds, followed by the main feast, which is often just three thinly-sliced pieces of turkey, a spoonful of cabbage, three Brussels sprouts and a splash of gravy. It's important when you're racing at Kempton Park on Boxing Day. I met Tony once at Ludlow racecourse. He had just arrived by car from Wiltshire and for him this was another day at the office, and I was amazed how they take this sport of extremes in their stride.

Horse racing provides excitement for millions of people every week, whether on a day out or just trying to pick a winner at home, but it's not one of those activities which we can personally understand what the jockeys go through. To get anywhere near the saddle on a racehorse takes a lifetime of dedication and hard work.

I did get a taste myself of what the Grand National riders experience, when I rode the course – albeit a virtual one, a wooden horse simulator, known as an Equiciser, in the jockeys' changing room at Aintree, alongside former winner Richard Dunwoody. I couldn't believe how demanding it was on my legs as I crouched over my mount's ears, trying to keep my bottom low as the excruciating pain seized hold of my knees. All the time, I was having to move the reins up the horse's mane, pushing with each stride along the wooden neck.

'Remember to keep your head still, that's crucial!' shouted Richard, who wasn't even out of breath.

'What do I do when I come up to the fence?' I panted.

'In your case, Mike, I would just close your eyes,' was his reply.

So I did and imagined what it must be like sandwiched between other flying mountains of muscles all striving to get over The Chair or Becher's Brook. My eyes were fully open again, eyelids propped up by nerves, as I paraded on a real racehorse, Ryes-dale Lad, later that day. He was different from any horse I had ever been on: his back was so hard, and I was told not to squeeze with my legs, as this would be like pulling a trigger. As I got used to holding the reins in a different way, I could feel how the slightest of twitches would cue the explosion of speed poised between my thighs to take off.

It was like sitting on a giant firework. If he went I would have no hope of gripping with my legs like the professionals and trainer Oliver Grennall was taking no chances, tightening his grip on the reins as we walked around the training track.

This was as far as I went on a racehorse, but for more information on all horse racing matters go to the website of the British Horseracing Authority, www.britishhorseracing.com

HORSEBOARDING

Let's get one thing clear straight away. This is not a banned form of water torture for horses, and it's not an advert for an equine bed and breakfast service.

This is for those of us who have aspirations of being a roman centurion riding along in a chariot (in my case Mikus Maximus) but who don't have the finances, or armour, or historical setting to do so.

What's more Horseboarding is a team sport that really is open to people who have never ever sat on a horse and never intend to do so.

What you do need is strong arm and shoulder muscles, good balance and plenty of nerve. As the horse is led out, you pull on your knee pads, elbow protectors, goggles and helmet. You limber up, stretch those muscles and get ready to ride, like a water skier or wake boarder, but instead of waves there is a muddy field and instead of a boat there is a horse who is straining, rearing, waiting to bolt.

Daniel Fowler-Prime first came up with the idea whilst visiting friends in Cornwall in 2005. They had originally tried horse surfing, a craze that started on the beaches of America and which involves a horse towing a surfer through the shallow breaking waves on a beach. Some surfers in Florida have also started standing on the backs of horses as they walk and swim through calmer, deeper water in sheltered bays. The cost of horse surfing made it restrictive at the time for Daniel so he focused on the land version, horseboarding. The first time he did it was in Maidenhead and the first centre opened in Seisdon near Wolverhampton. There are also now clubs in North Wales, Scotland and Australia.

It has caught on to such an extent that there are now national championships every year. It's no surprise that Daniel was the champion for many years. Well he is a professional horse rider and has appeared in many films such as *Kingdom of Heaven* and *The Da Vinci Code*. He lost the title last year though, to – of all people – his brother, Thomas Kilroy.

The start of a race is a majestic sight: a chariot race from the days of the Romans. Daniel settled his feet into the board as his rider Katherine revved on the reins. The horse, Rohan, was restless and ready to go. Katherine pulled back on the throttle and with Dan signalling down the rope that he was ready, the hooves thundered into action. The slack was taken in a split second and the rope became a live wire, electrifying Dan into life. If Dan hadn't put in all the training to develop his upper body muscles, he would have been a twisted mess of limbs. Instead he rocked and rolled around the 400-metre training track maintaining a steady speed.

Dan needs the horse to start at a gallop to reach 36 miles per hour. Most races are between two teams over 100 metres, and the world record is a time of 8.22 seconds, set in 2011. There is also now a slalom race in which the teams have to weave their way through a series of markers.

'If anything, it is the modern version of chariot racing,' Daniel said as he folded his massive biceps across his chest: his upper body muscles glistening like armour. 'There is a raw surge of natural power that you wouldn't get from any other sport, but it's really all about the team: it's you, your board, your rider and your horse. You all have to get it exactly right. If any one of you makes the slightest mistake it will cost you the race.'

Katherine Wynn is in charge of the riding his horse. 'It's my job to push on when Dan wants me to, and to steady back when I need to ease up. I have to make sure the starts are quick and easy and that we're going the right way. It helps to know your team, so you can communicate more easily as you are hurtling along.'

The start is the biggest challenge. Even for a beginner at trotting or walking pace, the moment the force of the horse grabs you, snatches you by surprise. You will lose your balance and wobble, and maybe fall off. It doesn't matter if you don't have any experience with horses, but it does help to come from a background of snowboarding, skateboarding or mountain boarding. It's a sturdy board on four wheels with two straps to fit your feet into. You begin by being towed by someone on foot before then hooking up just a few feet away from the bottom of your horse. The most important thing to remember is to let go of the rope if you feel yourself losing your balance.

This is why I was able to roll to a sudden stop, rather than being dragged head first through the grass. By my third go around, I had worked out that if you think of it as water skiing and get into a rhythm at the side of the horse, the balance and speed feels more under control. I was whooping with pride as we got up to a canter.

It may have felt like we were going at 50 miles per hour, but it was probably 20. However, I was getting a little bit of air over some of the muddy bumps and started to feel like I was riding the wake from a boat. I was grateful to Katherine for noticing me coming alongside the horse at one point and for pushing on slightly faster so that I wasn't pulling the horse, rather than the way it's meant to be, and we made it around in one piece. I hadn't got up to a gallop, because new horse boarder Dan Wild had told me 'I have found a whole new world of pain'. Falling off has been compared to getting out of a car at 30 miles an hour. 'But I love it,' he added. 'I have always been around horses, but wanted an extreme adrenalin sport which tapped into that, and also my love of board sports.'

There can't be many cooler sights than seeing a boarder hit top speed behind a galloping horse which is kicking up a confetti of mud and grass. That's why they wear the goggles, but unlike in water skiing if you do come off, you are not going to be soaking wet, and you can be surfing the soil again in seconds.

To give horseboarding a go, or to marvel at the roman riding skills then visit the website: www.britishhorsesurfingassociation.com

POLO

First of all I have to apologise to the people enjoying a picnic, or queuing for an ice cream on a gloriously sunny day at Hurtwood polo club in Surrey, in 2008.

It was a charity polo day to raise money for the Mark Davies Injured Riders Fund, and there were teams made up of professionals, celebrities and novices from the media. I was on a team captained by Kenny Jones, the former drummer with The Who and talented polo player. Other stars who were proving they could swing it with their mallets were Katie Price and Matt Baker.

I had been given some lessons by Kenny's son, and he had built a few foundations, so that I could even trot and hit the ball at the same time. Word about my 'ability' spread and to my horror, on the big day I was paired with the best, most decorated polo pony there: a high goal stallion who knew the game inside out.

However, that was the trouble. He did, and I didn't. In my defence, it is such a different form of riding. For a start it's one handed, and I was told to grip the reins as if holding a steering wheel on a go-kart. Push the reins forward, then back, and side to side to steer. It seemed simple enough, but my 'Champion the wonder horse' wasn't going to listen to my cautious instructions. He had pride; he was king of the pitch and was intent on showing it.

My efforts to restrain him with tweaks of the reins and polite croaks of 'whoa!' only seemed to confuse the poor athlete, who took a canter towards the ice cream van. With just a white line of rope and tiny sideboards separating the charging Bushell from picnic hampers and children, the crowd started to scatter with panic, saving whatever they could. But just as I was about to be the flake in a 99, my majestic mount averted any carnage by banking around to the right. He took us back to the horse boxes, where he could replace me with a proper polo player. He had given the crowd a glimpse of what he was having to put up with, and we were both relieved when we swapped partners.

I spent the rest of the match on a retired grey who loved the fact that I didn't have the conviction to get him out of a walk, and we gently turned in the middle as the action stormed past us like a tornado. Play whizzed past one way, and then by the time we'd turned our bewildered heads, the whirlwind came back in the other direction.

What I did see close up was how physical top polo can be. It's no wonder it has been described as rugby on horseback. There is another sport which fits that description and has similarities with basketball, and that's Horseball, and a date with the British team is pencilled in for the future. As for polo, don't be fooled by the chink of champagne glasses and polite country chatter. This is raw, physical and played at a thunderous pace. The sight of thoroughbred juggernauts putting on the emergency brakes and turning on a few blades of grass, while potentially colliding with others doing the same, is spine tingling. They reach 40 miles per hour as the high-speed scrums flow from one end of the pitch to the other.

It's no surprise that the top polo players have to be like gladiators, because the roots of this sport are in war. Alexander the Great is quoted as saying that he represented the stick, while the ball was the world he intended to conquer.

There's doubt over when polo actually started, with different sources claiming there was a game played by Persians in the 5th century BC, and in China even earlier. The word polo comes from the Tibetan word 'pulu', which means ball. According to the website Indiapolo.com, it seems that at first, polo was a way of training mounted troops for battle, with as many as 100 on each side. It became the national sport of India under the Mughal dynasty until the end of the 16th century, and India has often been seen as the home of the modern game. By 1870 it had spread throughout British India, where serving army officers and high ranking officials had ponies to hand. As word got around, one officer who'd read about the game in a magazine tried to set up a game with walking sticks and billiard balls. Needless to say he didn't get very far. Thankfully if you go to a match today, the balls and sticks are much more sophisticated and the players have the skills to match.

Even after a few lessons, my full polo debut had ended in personal humiliation. I like to think I played a crucial midfield holding role on my grey though, because our team, led by the talented Kenny Jones, won the tournament. It seems the drummer is a wizard whatever shape of stick he's holding. I could and should have ended my polo career with my head held high, but then a version of the sport came along that really does enable relative beginners like me to get involved without any danger of putting ice cream vans out of business.

ARENA POLO

If you thought polo was out of reach, well 'Arena' is doing what five-a-side has done for football and making it much more accessible. It's on a much smaller pitch, 300 by 150 feet, and there are high walls all around, so your horse can't gallop off out of control. The balls are bigger and softer and if you do fall, you are guaranteed a soft landing because instead of grass, it's played on rubbery mulch.

'You can see the ground is nice and soft,' Phillip Meadows of the Royal Berkshire Polo Club assured me, 'and you feel safer and more comfortable in that protected environment. It's when you take people outside onto the full hard grass pitches that they tense up.'

He was right. I joined a game with another novice polo player – Nathaniel Parker, the actor, who I had met on the set of *Merlin*. He is very experienced on horses and does most of the riding himself when filming. He's also a huge racing fan, but this was the first time he had been on a polo pony.

'This is so different. It's forward, back, left and right, and these horses are so well trained they know more about it than we do. I was out there and I had missed the ball, and the horse was thinking "ah, he's done it again", so he turned around and went back to get it,' he remarked.

It's true, the arena polo ponies do all the work which is why beginners are able to trot around and get involved after listening to just a few instructions. Indeed after five minutes on the pitch I had forgotten about being on a horse and my main frustration was timing and trying to get to the ball before Nat and his team had smashed it up the other end.

At the top level, arena polo keeps the professional players active during the winter months when the grass pitches are unplayable. England captain James Morrison reckons it's more physical than the summer game, because all the action is squeezed into a much smaller, enclosed area. 'It's more intense and I certainly get a lot more injuries in the winter when playing indoors,' he said.

Once a year, arena polo is now played in the O2. I took part in a media match there and once again in the comfort of an enclosed, soft pitched arena, my lack of riding experience wasn't to matter. The pony did all hard bits, cantering up and down while I clung on, trying to enjoy the ride and attempting to get the ball to teammate Kenny Logan, who proved if you can play rugby for your country, you can also cut it in a polo match.

So polo has come within reach. You no longer need your own horse or equipment to swing the mallet these days, and get a taste of the rumble of hooves and smack of ball. It's become a popular corporate or experience day for a group of mates. Even so, a session won't leave you much change from £100, but that's still peanuts compared to the price of some of the four-legged stars of this sport.

For information and to give it a go and for all your polo needs, its www.hpa-polo.co.uk

POLO CROSSE

Arena polo got me involved in the cut and thrust of this fast and furious sport, but it's fair to say that my time with the ball had been restricted to the odd touch. However, there is a polo game in which you can pick up the ball and run away with it. It was developed in Australia in the 1930s and is called Polocrosse. To get an understanding of this hybrid game, we first need to turn our attention to one of North America's first team sports, lacrosse.

I admit, that at first I had images of genteel jolly hockey sticks when I turned up for an introduction with some of the country's top female players at Berkhamsted School. I thought it would be a bit of a run around, throwing and catching the ball with my stick and its net on the end. How wrong could I be. My ignorance didn't last long and was quickly punished as they put me in the goal to show me the frenetic pace and aggression in this sport. Like a village thief in the stocks I was pelted with balls as they got in some target practice.

Out on the field, as sticks clashed and leaping bodies charged, I could see how this game originated from the American Indians, who used it to prepare for battle just like the early polo players.

In those days, perhaps as far back as the 16th century, the Cherokees called the sport 'the little brother of war' because it was seen as such effective military training. Sometimes there were hundreds, even thousands of players on a team, and the goals could be miles apart. It's no surprise then that a game could last several days. Imagine how long you could go without seeing the ball – so most players got bored and engaged in stick battles with their opponents while they were waiting. There are also reports that early on they used a human skull rather than a ball.

Originally the game was called 'Baggataway' or 'Tewaraathon', and over the centuries it was scaled down to 15 players on a team, with the goals 120 feet apart.

It was this game that French explorers found. They thought the stick looked like a bishop's crozier, which is 'la crosse' in French, and it seems this is where the name came from. Those early Europeans in Canada organised a team and the first club in Montreal was formed in 1844. It was one of the club members George Beers who rewrote the rules and fixed the teams at 12 a side for women and 10 for men. Thankfully today there are rules and it's much safer. The ball is still like a bullet. It's made of hard rubber and is similar in size to a cricket ball. So no wonder I needed protective pads and a helmet as I took that pelting in goal.

The sticks are like hockey ones, but with a net on the end. These allow you to scoop up the ball, catch and carry it, and then fire it out, like you are slinging your hook.

'Slide your hand down your stick,' I was advised if I wanted my shots to go faster.

It's still a game of immense athletic skill. It's non-stop running, while to outwit your opponents you have to be agile and mentally sharp as well. The game was originally only played by men and it's claimed that women's lacrosse stared in Scotland, much later at St Leonards School around 1890. It's ironic then that now, as Sam Patterson from the England men's team told me, it often gets generalised as a women's sport.

Men's lacrosse today is much closer to the original game. While in the women's version there is plenty of stick-to-stick action, but full body contact isn't allowed (although it is sometimes inevitable), in the men's game, all players have to wear protective armour and helmets, because full contact is permitted. It's like American football with sticks. It's one of the best team sports I have sampled. I can see why it's billed as the fastest game on two feet.

The number of players taking up this sport in all age groups has increased in the last few years, helped by Manchester staging the World Cup in 2010. The USA won and will be favourites to defend their crown on home soil in Denver in 2014. However on the European stage, England currently rule the roost. The men's team beat Ireland in the final staged in Amsterdam in July 2012, while England's women beat Wales in their final. There are clubs up and down the country, so to find your nearest, visit one of the following websites: www.waleslacrosse.co.uk, www.lacrossescotland.com, www.irelandlacrosse.ie, www.englishlacrosse.co.uk or www.insidelacrosse.com

So we have polo, and we have lacrosse, two of the roughest and toughest team sports. However, they are not enough for those who put them together to make Polocrosse. It's the challenge of lacrosse but on horseback, while for polo players it's a chance to chuck in a chukka, to scoop the ball up and run with it before unleashing a shot, not from down by the horse's side, but from up above the shoulders.

It's a team sport that is now played all over the world. There are six riders on each side, with three from each team on the pitch at a time, and they swap after every six-minute chukka to give the horses a rest. Instead of a mallet, each rider carries a cane stick with a racquet head on the end of it. It looks like a very long squash racquet but the net on the head is loose. The ball is made of sponge rubber. The other big difference from polo is that in this sport, players only use one horse for the duration of the match. They don't swap ponies during the game.

It is a bit like going onto a battlefield when you ride out in your helmet and the balls drop out of the sky like falling meteors. Scooping the ball off the ground while moving is also a challenge, but if you are a beginner like I was when I attended a Polocrosse centre in Kent, you play the game at trotting or even walking pace. It claims to be a sport for everyone. While at the top level it is physical and fast, at novice level it is played at a much slower speed. Regardless of ability you will be able to get the ball, and it is increasingly seen as a more entertaining way to develop riding skills. That's how it all started.

One of the UK's star players, Jason Webb, says the idea caught on at polo clubs because it was a way to spice up training sessions. 'You can only hit a ball so far, and back in the day a lot of the riding was done in schools, and so you'd only get to hit the ball once and it would be up the other end of the pitch, whereas in Polocrosse you can do so much more with it: you can shimmy it around and carry it,' he explained.

It's also more suitable for riding schools with limited space, and it appeals to beginners because you can pick the ball up and run with it, rather than getting just one swing at the ball before you have passed it by. It is now recognised by the Pony Club as a horse sport which improves riding skills.

There is a knack to scooping up the ball when moving on a horse, and I had just about got it when bang, another stick came in and sent a judder up my arm. My stick was elevated towards the sky and the ball was now sailing away through the air. You see your opponents can get the ball off you by hitting your stick in an upwards direction. This is when I needed my teammates around me for protection, and it's where the tactics come in to play. I did later catch a pass and at a snail's pace of a trot, moved forward and lobbed an underarm bouncer which hit the post and went in.

South Africa won the World Cup, staged in Warwickshire in 2011. It was the third Polocrosse world championship. On the previous two occasions Australia had won, with the UK team coming second in 2007. For more information visit www.polocrosse.org.uk – here you will find information about the UK's 16 clubs, from Scotland to Devon and from Wales to Kent.

PIGEONS

I end this chapter on my way to see the fastest long distance athletes of them all, those marathon travellers who are involved in one of the oldest sports, and whose place in our history is guaranteed. I am talking about the racing pigeon.

They may be the cousins of the feral mangy-looking ones that we see in towns and cities, which Ken Livingstone once described as rats with wings, but racing pigeons are very different. Many come from a long line of pedigree birds going back over 20 years. They are vaccinated against various diseases and parasites, and dine only at the top bird tables eating the finest food. You may well spot one in your garden at some point and as well as looking smarter, the racing pigeon will have a ring around one of its legs.

If you find one, you are looking at a remarkable bird – one which has made its mark on society throughout history. There is evidence that they were reporters for the ancient Olympics in Greece, flying the results out to the surrounding communities. But it's their subsequent use in wars that really underlined their heroic status. They were used by the ancient Egyptians in the siege of Rome. A racing pigeon brought news to England of the death of Napoleon after the battle of Waterloo, and over a century later nearly half a million birds served their country in the two world wars. They were a vital part of the war effort.

They had proved so effective at getting messages back home from the trenches in the First World War that at the outbreak of World War Two, some 7,000 of Britain's pigeon fanciers gave their birds to the military to act as carriers. The National Pigeon Service was formed and as a pigeon fancier himself, my Uncle Don was allowed to stay at home rather than being sent to fight. It was more important that he was supplying and training his pigeons. During the war, pigeon lofts were built at RAF and army bases and nearly a quarter of a million birds were used. All RAF bombers and reconnaissance aircraft carried pigeons in special waterproof baskets, and in case the plane had to ditch into the sea, a message was placed in a container on the pigeon's leg so it could fly back and report what had happened. Many more were dropped by parachute to help the French, Dutch and Belgian resistance.

The intelligence they ferried back saved thousands of lives at a time when using a radio was far too dangerous. Pigeons themselves though carried a risk. As their reputation spread, being caught with a racing pigeon meant death by German firing squad.

It wasn't just the British who had cottoned on to their value. The homing pigeon was also used by American, Canadian, and German forces all over the world. And their work didn't go unrecognised. Animals that served in the war were later awarded the Dickin Medal, commonly known as the Animal Victoria Cross. Horses, dogs and a naval cat were among those to have the medal hanging around their necks, some posthumously, but of all the 53 Dickin medals handed out for animal bravery, 32 of them went to pigeons.

One bird, GI Joe, was awarded the honour for saving over 1,000 Allied soldiers in one move. On 18 October 1943, an American infantry division called for a heavy aerial attack on a town called Colvi Vecchia in Italy. It was occupied by the Germans, or so it was thought. To the Allies' surprise, the Germans retreated from the town and a British brigade was able to secure the area that day. They would have become the victims of a friendly fire massacre, because radio signals were failing to get through to their base telling the Americans to call off the bombing. So GI Joe was released, with the lives of a whole division resting on his wings. He flew 20 miles in 20 minutes and arrived just as the American planes were on the runway. The mission was aborted.

Another pigeon, Winkie DM, helped rescuers find his stricken crew after their plane had crashed into the sea in 1942. And then there was White Vision. He flew 60 miles over stormy seas from the Hebrides off the north of Scotland, through thick mist and against a vicious headwind. Visibility was no more than a hundred yards for most of the journey and so rescuing her stricken RAF crew would have been impossible without precise information about where they were. Thanks to White Vision struggling against the odds, this crew was also saved. Even more recently, in the Gulf War pigeons were again valuable, because their messages weren't affected by electronic jamming.

Racing pigeons were already been involved in sport long before the world wars. Long distance racing grew with the spread of the railway system and was officially organised in 1897 with the formation of the Royal Pigeon Racing Association. The spread of the railways was important, because one of the ways pigeons find their way home is by recognising landmarks or lines on the ground, be it a railway line or road. That's not their only talent, because on their own, map reading skill wouldn't be enough to get them back home during 1,000-mile races.

Research is still being done to pinpoint exactly what it is, but it's thought they have an inbuilt ability to navigate using the position of the sun in the sky and the earth's magnetic fields. Some scientific evidence which is being studied by university teams suggests they have a magnetic receptor in their brains. Other research points to them using smell.

After the war, pigeon racing became fashionable, thanks in part to footballers. In the days before they earned huge amounts of money, they would own racing pigeons rather than racehorses. They made the sport popular with the masses. Some involved in football today have maintained their love for the birds. The former England football captain Gerry Francis was one of the big names involved, and he still has a loft. At the time of writing, he is assistant to Tony Pulis at Stoke City.

What attracted the footballers was that the birds were

cheap to buy, but were fast and unpredictable to race. What's more, according to Stewart Wardrop, General Manager of the Royal Pigeon Racing Association, you just never know what may happen.

'You can be a beginner or have a pigeon that has a pedigree you have nurtured for many generations, but everyone has an equal opportunity. No one knows if the weather is going to be right, or if the elements are going to be in your favour. You all have the chance to win the big race.'

Footballers may have moved on to horse racing, but the attraction is still the same. You can still become an owner for ten pounds, and in one race your bird could win you £20,000. You do pay a one-off fee, perhaps in the region of £100, if you want to keep your bird with a manager and trainer at a professional loft. Here it will be trained, and its natural instincts honed. Jeremy Davies is the manager of the One Loft near Malvern, where one of the big annual races is held and where 1,500 pigeons are housed. Jeremy gets birds in when they are around four weeks old. He then provides their health care and gives them the right nutrients and food to help them settle in. They learn to fly around the loft before eventually being taken for their first flight home. To begin with, Jeremy will take them a mile away. Then days later it will be two miles, and then he will release them from five miles and 10 miles, building up gradually to 50 miles. All the time, the birds are programming the map of the ground below into their brains. In races they will often track a road, even to the point of going around the outline of a roundabout in the sky.

'It's like managing a racehorse,' says Jeremy. 'You have to give them the right diet so they stay really fit and healthy. I take them out to increasing distances to train them so they get to know their way home, but it's all about them really and their natural ability to read the earth's magnetic fields and the sun. I make sure they have the right food, and make it nice here for them, so that they want to come home, to the hens and the cocks. These are all motivational factors to make them go that little bit faster. It's the love of home really.'

Jeremy's greatest reward is breeding a winning line that runs through several generations.

'I love the creating the true pedigrees, that give birth to offspring who then also go and win races. You get to know them all, and it's a great feeling when you see them come in from a long race.'

Not as many birds are making it back, though. 2012 was one of the hardest years on record for the sport, with 20,000 pigeons going missing. They have been hit by a triple whammy. According to Stewart, the sun's behaviour has changed. Solar activity has increased to a level that hasn't been seen for a thousand years. Its poles have switched for the first time in 11 years, and the resultant unseasonal weather has confused some birds.

Then there are birds of prey. Their population has been booming to such an extent that they have been moving into towns and cities where most racing pigeons are kept. Some have nested near to this free food source and even preyed on the pigeons in their own lofts. 'It's been an incredibly tough year,' mourned Stewart. 'To see 20 years of hard work disappear in a hawk attack is very upsetting, and it is driving people away from the sport.' The main diet of a peregrine falcon is racing pigeon, while sparrow hawks will join the feast if the supply of songbirds is running out.

According to the RPRA, when a sparrow hawk attacks a flock of racing pigeons, it's not just over for the one it choses for lunch, but the other pigeons will panic and scatter and their homing instincts are destroyed. Pigeon fanciers are bird lovers, so they insist they have nothing against the birds of prey, but they want help in protecting their sport. There used to be around 120,000 pigeon fanciers in the UK. Today there is half that number, with 45,000 association members. They are now working on ways to reduce raptor attacks. One is a £32,000 project at Lancaster University to develop ways of deterring the birds of prey. It may be in the future that pigeons carry bells or wear sequins, to make them less appealing.

The sport is now on a mission to get new people owning racing pigeons. The RPRA has started sponsoring keen youngsters to enter a pigeon in the name of their school. They want newcomers, like seven-year-old Heather Davies, Jeremy's daughter, to get hooked. 'I like the white ones, they're quite pretty,' she explained as she reached across the loft to prize her favourite from its perch. 'I love them coming home at the end of the race and once I came fifth. My friends think it's really cool that I am involved in the racing.'

I was invited to see the attraction too. I picked a bird called Louise who had recently won a race from France and was in top international form. I also thought it would appeal to my *Breakfast* colleague Louise Minchin, who would be on the sofa on the Saturday when the piece went out. I helped load the birds into a basket before they were taken to a table to be electronically recorded, ready for the race. Then it was into a car for a short journey into the picturesque Malvern Hills. I was allowed a quick pep talk with Louise through the slightly ajar lid of the basket. 'Just turn left at the trees, keep out of the wind and head in a straight line and think of what you did to the rest on the way back from France' were my words of wisdom, as Louise fidgeted and looked away. It didn't seem quite the right moment for the Sir Alex Ferguson hairdryer treatment.

Then I stepped back with the other hopeful trainers and held my breath for the liberation: the moment when the birds are released. The door to the basket flipped down and for a second, nothing. Then one bird – but not Louise – stepped tentatively into the sunshine. A quick look to the right and to the left, and having given the signal that it was safe to go, the leader was followed into the sky by the whole flock. A sweeping kite of grey and white was swallowed up by the blue and within seconds they were dots above the trees, veering off to the right at incredible speed. The average speed they get up to is 60 miles per hour, but they have been recorded doing 110 mph, with the wind behind them in Australia.

In reality we would never have made it back to the loft in time to see the even the slower birds finish this five-mile race. It is a sprint for them, a race for the Usain Bolts of the pigeon world. So the birds were released for a second time, and this time, in the race that mattered, I waited the whole time at the finish. I got the call to say they were on their way. Silence descended over the loft as we anxiously watched the skies.

Within minutes of them taking off, they suddenly came into view, a flying carpet of feathers circling the trees, getting lower and lower before a group of them started to descend towards the loft. Cries of 'come on!' had punctured the vacuum. 'That's it, Louise!' – I joined the clamour, pretending that I could tell she was in the breakaway group.

She was, as it happened, but this is where it can be interesting, and where your skills as a trainer are really tested. The pigeon has to cross the line and actually enter the loft if it's to claim the prize. Yet Louise decided to rest on top of her home along with three others. They were sunbathing, having arrived in the leading group. This can happen, even after they've travelled hundreds of miles, and races can be lost and won in these few critical moments. £20,000 can be gone in an instant and so trainers like Jeremy rattle buckets and use whistle and voice commands to coax their birds over the final few inches. This is where experience counts and I didn't have any. My calls to Louise just seemed to vex her. She eventually followed in ninth. Even though I had followed the advice and not fed her before the race, she still had no sense of urgency when it mattered.

I had seen what a lottery this sport can be, with a twist at the end that you don't get in any other sport. Imagine Frankel stopping to eat some grass or to admire the view a couple of lengths from the winning post. Punters would be tearing their hats into pieces.

It can even happen in the biggest race in the world, the Million Dollar race in Sun City in South Africa. As the name suggests, one million dollars is given to the winner. In some parts of the world like China where the sport has really taken off, some birds have sold for hundreds of thousands of pounds. In Europe the highest price paid was €300,000. The sport has become big business and yet for a tenner, anyone of us can still get involved.

For more information of the sport and if you want to join Her Majesty the Queen and become the owner of a racing pigeon (Her Royal Highness has a loft at Sandringham) then visit the website of the RPRA at www.rpra.org

What's more if you find a stray pigeon in the garden with a ring around its leg, it will be a racing one. It may be resting, but if it stays and looks lost, then get in touch with the RPRA via the website or via twitter on @pigeonracinguk and they can find its owner.

That's it for this chapter on our sporting animal friends, but bigger creatures also feature later in the book when we focus on unusual sports from around the world.

2

A FAMILY AFFAIR

These are sports which bring families together: to get all of us playing and to make sport more inclusive. Many of the activities featured have been created since I started my Saturday series and some have been invented by crossing two existing sports together. If you want to know how to play the love child of rugby and golf, read on. Others may be more traditional activities which are great for all ages, and these are the sports I have picked out which I found to be most family-friendly.

A NEW SPORT IS BORN

Strange noises were coming from the barn. A whirring, a bang, a thwack – and then silence. The door creaked open and a man in brown overalls, with hair styled by shock, stumbled into the sunshine, blowing at his hands, as the last flicker of flame retreated into his gloves. His face was speckled with the charcoal, sweat and toil that you might associate with his work as a blacksmith, but there were no horses today. A broad grin beamed through the vanishing smoke: it was more than just a smile of satisfaction that the fire was out.

This grin quickly realised its ambition to be a smile, and was then knighted into unbridled euphoria. For this was a eureka moment that could make this man's family life bearable again. He reached back into the barn to fetch a wooden ball, a four-pronged metal arch and a giant wooden hammer. This was his new baby, and it is what happens when sports are crossbred in a workshop. I have come across countless examples of these hybrids.

NET RUGBY

It was originally known as rugby netball and was founded in the late 1800s as a way to keep troops returning from the Boer war out of the pubs. It started on Clapham Common in South London and in its heyday in the 1920s there were dozens of teams playing in several leagues. It's now staging a comeback on the common with the return of a league, and a World Cup competition, held every summer. It's simple to play. Think of the flowing teamwork you get in football, but you can pick the ball up and run with it as well.

You don't need to worry about forward passes. They are allowed, but so are full rugby-style tackles, so the game won't stop for a foul. The final sport to throw into the mix is netball, because to score you have to throw or drop-kick the ball into huge nets hung on posts at each end of the grassy field. It's proved a useful way for rugby players to keep fit during the summer, and Junior – who played at the time for London Welsh – was keen to show me how physical it could be when I had a go, lifting me off my feet in a challenge when I was running in on goal. It's a wonder I didn't end up in the net myself. What struck me was how this sport is great for all round fitness. There were very few stoppages, so the action was non-stop which is why we needed rolling subs.

To get involved try www.netrugby.org

CANOE POLO

This crosses the paddling skills of canoeing with the ball handling skills of water polo and basketball. If you have a wicked streak in you, this could be the sport to bring it out, because the quickest way to clear your route to goal is to turn your opponent's boat over! You have two giant nets hung on poles two metres above the water at each end of a pool or outside water course. There are two teams of five players racing up and down trying to score from their canoes. It's a contact team game in which tactics and positional play are as important as the fitness and speed of the individual athletes, and it helps promote canoeing in a different environment.

Early records show a variety of canoe ball games being played in Great Britain in the late nineteenth century, but these were more novelty games played for fun. It wasn't until the 1920s in France and Germany that canoe ball games were first used in earnest to build up river skills and to get more people into the boats.

At the time it was difficult to attract new paddlers and spectators and this provided an exciting introduction to canoeing. It was contained and safer, and so in 1926 the German Canoe Federation introduced 'Kanupolo' as a way to attract new members. It also helped build more camaraderie and swelled the coffers. They also published rules of play. The ball can be thrown by hand, or flicked with the paddle, to teammates and towards the goals. Pitches can be set up in swimming pools or any stretch of flat water. Boats are specifically designed for polo and at three metres are shorter than typical kayaks, which gives them greater manoeuvrability. It also made an early bath for me inevitable when I tried this in Putney. It pays to perfect your Eskimo roll.

'It's like five-a-side football, but the goals are six foot in the air, and you're allowed to push people in,' said one of the players competing in one of the 100 or so clubs in the UK. 'I do it to completely de-stress from work. All the frustrations of the week get out of my system in just an hour and a half.'

Paddles are very light weight and designed with both pulling power and ball control in mind. Body protection, helmets and faceguards are all compulsory. World and European Championships are held every two years, and Great Britain is one of the world's foremost nations, with the British women the current World Champions. Within the UK there is a National League structure for all ages, and during the summer months a number of canoe clubs host large outdoor tournaments which attract teams from all over the country and the world. Just a word of warning though: be careful how you celebrate scoring a goal, because once my arms were aloft and punching the air, I lost the only balance I had and was upside down in the pool again!

For more information go to www.canoepolo.org.uk

DISC GOLF

The aim is to get a plastic disc around a course, aiming for metal baskets instead of holes. It's reported that the first known instance of anyone playing golf with a flying disc occurred in Vancouver, Canada, in 1926. A group of school age kids apparently played a game with tin lids. They called it Tin Lid Golf and played on a regular basis on a course they laid out around their school grounds.

The scoring and basics are the same as in golf. You aim to get birdies, by getting the disc into each basket in as few throws as possible. I played on a course at Croydon and getting the tee throws right was mind-boggling at first. The wind had me in suspense as it kidnapped my disc in mid-air and then teased me with the outcome, the disc hanging like a bird of prey above the park. Several times I read the wind's direction wrong and went hunting for my disc in the bushes and undergrowth. The putting throws require a delicate touch and I was surprised how far I ended up walking. Exercise without realising you're doing it, is always a winner. There are a growing number of disc golf courses, which are free to play, around the country – this might explain why there are strange wire nets that look like bins in some parks. For more go to www.bdga.org.uk

ROLF

This has nothing to do with tying a kangaroo down. Instead you drop-kick a rugby ball around a cross-country course of obstacles. The scoring is based on golf, so a par 4 hole might include kicking across a river, while the target at the end might be a car trailer or a wall that the players decide on beforehand. It was started by PE masters at the Monkton Combe school near Bath, who wanted pupils to get excited about rugby training on cold winter days when the snow was covering the pitch.

It's simple for anyone to play. You just need a rugby ball, and an imagination to decide on your course. It was the first time I had tried to kick a rugby ball from up a tree, and also from in the middle of a river. It does wonder for your kicking skills. For more it's www.rolf.co.uk

GOLF CROSS

It's golf and rugby crossed again in this one, but it's the former that's more dominant in this hybrid sport. I spent a day with the

Wasps team and Lawrence Dallaglio, playing on a golf course with mini rugby balls. You aim for nets mounted on miniature rugby posts. This sport, designed in New Zealand, certainly made the tee shots far more unpredictable, while chipping in had never been more satisfying.

'You've got a much wider target to aim for,' Lawrence told me, 'so for you and I it should come in rather handy'. Speak for yourself, Lawrence...! For more information go to www.golfcross.org

WALKING FOOTBALL

This is a great idea, started by Bury football club, and it's one that's spreading through the north west. It combines the beautiful game with a stroll in the park. Its aim when it started in 2012 was to get over-50s who had given up playing football through age or injury back into the game and into exercise. It's like five-a-side, but no one is allowed to run. Anyone who bends those knees and breaks into a trot is committing a foul and a free kick is awarded.

I had seen the benefits of walking when I tried race walking in Battersea Park. It was an organised five-kilometre race which I did in 50 minutes, alongside dozens of others doing the famous waddle. I saw how with the right technique, enhancing heel-to-toe speed, some of the top athletes can walk quicker than some of us can run, and there were a surprising number of young entries too. 'People ask me "why don't you just run?",' said one teenager who had just joined a club. 'I say, "this is harder so why don't you just walk?"'.

There are said to be many health benefits of walking and those apply for the pioneers of walking football too.

'It's an opportunity for people to play a sport that they used to in the past,' explained Joanne Shepherd from the Bury FC

Community Trust, 'but now feel they are not physically able to, at a competitive level. So we have brought it down to basics again, to make them feel comfortable doing it.'

At 81 Lawrence never thought he would be able to play football again. 'Very enjoyable but I am knackered,' he grinned, 'because I have had open heart surgery as well, so I am out of breath, but it's really good fun. It's amazed me, and I will be looking for a younger woman next,' he quipped. 'It's a night out too,' his younger teammate told me. 'Instead of being in the pub you are down here.'

Health improvement specialists like Stefan Taylor helped develop the idea. 'We know that men have this attitude of not exercising for 20 years, and thinking they can come back in where they left off, and undoubtedly they have aching knees and sore joints. You may run the risk of raising your blood pressure so it's important that this is a starting block in a safe environment,' he explained.

Under-50s can get involved too and I found it's much harder than it looks, because it's so tempting to leather it and then break into a run as you try to reach the ball first. It's helped improve players' passing ability too, and coach Ian Hughes who used to play professionally says there a spin-off for players of all ages, even at a professional level in training. 'The tempo of the game is changing now,' he said, 'rather than just 100 miles per hour. This takes it down a level to make sure players are looking to pass to feet.' The website is www.walking football.co.uk

STUNT BIKE FOOTBALL

Football played with giant inflatable balls, by riders on stunt bikes. Think spins, wheelies, the screech of brakes into the penalty area, wipe outs and dramatic headed goals. The match

I was played in was abandoned, though, after a second ball was punctured. They have since sorted this problem and internationals have been held.

CROSS FIT

The ultimate crossbreed sport is cross fit, which can include over 20 different disciplines in the same event or work out session. You turn up having to be ready for anything – squat thrusts, rope climbing, jumping onto blocks, swimming, weight lifting or running. The list is endless, and a growing number of centres offer this intense fitness class up and down the country. There is now a world championship.

RAT RACE

Another multi-discipline sporting event that offers adventures on your doorstep is the Rat Race. It takes you into the nooks and crannies of an urban environment and can involve running, cycling, climbing, kayaking, abseiling, scrambling and crawling in the most unusual places. For more information see www.ratrace.com

CROLF

And now we're back to our blacksmith on the edge of Dartmoor who had nearly gone up in smoke. The ball he was holding was wooden and slightly bigger than a cricket ball, with a strip of yellow tape around its middle. The metal arch with its three prongs was the size of a lion's paw. Robbie Richardson had the appearance of a zany professor, hair singed by a spark of genius.

If he could be declared a professor of anything it would be of play, because what he had set himself on fire for, the reason he had been banging and whirring, was for a new sporting challenge for the garden. Robbie has always loved to play games with his wife and three daughters, and was once given a croquet set for Christmas. However, it sat in the shed, abandoned. For a start, he always won, and the garden at their Devon home was too hilly and rough for a croquet lawn. The bushes, the trampoline, the garden swing, the tree stumps, the long rough undergrowth just got in the way. What's more, it had also been years since Robbie or his wife Sarah had found time for a round on the local golf course. So Robbie tried to solve the problem and combine the two sports he loved. He mixed the big tee shots of golf with the garden tactics of croquet. It's cross-country croquet – or golf in the garden.

So here I was watching Robbie Richardson teeing off on the third, keen to avoid the rusting trampoline and Lola the pet Labradoodle. A swing of the hammer and *smack*, a clean shot between the flower bed and tree stump.

'I wanted to get people exploring their gardens or nearby parks or countryside again as a family,' said Robbie, 'while at the same time getting more people into croquet and golf. Yes, serious golfers will still play golf, but at some golf clubs, they have now introduced this game near their club house, to help bring the children back. They used to just hang around or go elsewhere, but now when the mums and dads have their round of golf, the children have their game too.'

Crolf is also now played in 14 schools. It can be tactical and you can knock your opponent's ball into the rough with yours. In most cases beginners don't need any help to get their ball into the bushes, and once it's in the rough, there's no dropping a shot – you have to get in there and somehow fetch it out with a hammer strike.

I found myself in a jungle of rhododendrons which snared my ball for three hits until finally my frustration forced it free.

Then I hit it with such vigour that I smashed a treasured pot in the garden. The balls are hard and will break any ornaments that get in the way. I ended up under a tree stump and had to use a snooker-style shot with the end of my stick to poke the ball clear and get it nearer the 'hool', which is Crolf for hole. Unlike the one hoop in croquet, the 'hool' is a four-pronged arch so you can get it through from north, south, east and west, making a little bit easier for beginners.

It's hoped it will spread the great and underestimated sport of croquet to a new audience, while also helping new people onto the golf course.

'I haven't seen anything like it,' said amateur golfer Dave Lightfoot, who had been out walking his dog and who'd stopped for a swing. 'I can see how it can gets the kids involved and once they have done this they can pick up a golf club.'

I played a round of Crolf on the undulating grass alongside the river Dart, and got a hool in one. There must be something about these unusual challenges that bring out the best in me. If you are ever unfortunate enough to play a real round of golf with me, I apologise for the amount of time you will spend waiting at each hole, and it might pay to bring along the *Complete Works of Shakespeare*. However, in a warm up for the crazy golf world championships at Hastings I stunned the reigning world champion with a hole in one there, on the 18th. It was a perfect shot, which involved a trip up a ramp, through a castle and down the other side, all the way in. I was told not to attend the championships the following week.

Back in the world of Crolf, Robbie Richardson is not alone. Other versions of this hybrid have sprung up independently in other parts of the world, including Denmark, while the British Crolf Open, held at Ugbrooke Castle near Exeter every May, is now in its eighth year.

If you do ever have a game, remember the ball will have been made by a Devon blacksmith who might have set his eyebrows on fire in the process. For more information see www.crolf.co.uk

BLOKART SAILING

Tilly Carter tugged at the rope and glanced up at her sail, which now puffed its chest with pride, as it reared to the right. Like a puff adder filling its cheeks with air, the bulging canvas flapped and roared, forcing this brave seven-year-old to grip on even tighter. The turbo charged gust of wind that next caught her vessel, meant Tilly, was suddenly staring at the water. She was just inches from the silvery film.

Her next move would be crucial. If she could hold her line and maintain speed, the sunset was calling, but if she lost her nerve and surrendered to the wobble, she would be calling for help. She was after all alone with her sail. Tilly knew she was tipping over, and braced herself for the crash. The sail became her umbrella, her canopy shielding the sun. She was upside down and helpless. Like a beetle turned onto its back, she knew she would need rescuing.

But Tilly didn't have to wait for a lifeboat, because help came walking along. There was no danger of this beginner drowning, because the water was only a centimetre deep. She was on a vast stretch of wet sand on Pembrey beach in South Wales and her sail was attached to a land yacht – or Blokart.

I think this has to be the most fun you can have with your family when trying out a new sport for the first time. True, it's not going to be the most accessible activity every weekend, because you need to be near a suitable location (i.e. a stretch of empty beach or land) and the equipment isn't cheap. But in terms of picking up a skill, in a first session, everyone I was with, from child to adult, was soon using the power of the wind to get up to 20 miles per hour, on long adrenalin rides along the sand.

Blokart sailing is sailing on land. You are in a go-kart on three wheels, two at the back and one at the front. There is a steering handle, and then above you, your sail, which you control with a rope. If you have always fancied the idea of taking the family sailing on the high seas, but couldn't afford it, or you worry about the dangers of deep, cold water, this is a superb alternative.

Just like in sailing, Britain is becoming very successful in this sport. I had to come to South Wales to see the 2010 world silver medallist Tim Seed. He arrived with just a large holdall bag. The other advantage this has over sailing is you don't need a trailer for your boat. The Blokart will come apart and fit inside your car boot.

So Tim was changed and ready to go within around 20 minutes, and in capable hands like his, these land yachts can reach speeds of 60 miles per hour.

'It's great for getting the adrenalin going.' he said. 'It's very similar to sailing. You are looking at the wind, trying to read it all the time, and constantly checking the sails, making sure the tails are full, as we turn and tack.'

The children in the group of beginners I joined were in their own Blokarts within half an hour, after a tutorial on the sand. We sailed up and down, and every 200 metres we would try to turn, by adjusting the angle of the sail with the rope, and by moving a handlebar attached to the front wheel. It's a fine line, and all of us tipped over at times, when we misjudged the strength of the wind or simply got our hand movements on the rope and bar wrong. However, you are secured into your seat with a belt, and so while you may feel helpless, it doesn't hurt. With a helping hand, you are back on three wheels again in an instant.

'It's like riding a bike,' said one beginner, Lara Bell aged nine. 'It's scary when you tip over,' said Annabelle Gilborn, the youngest girl there. She was seven at the time and in 2012 she came third in the BLSA fun series. 'I have tipped over twice already, but the second time was quite fun,' she admitted. Her dad John hadn't fared so well in the adult competition.

Blokart is seen by the instructors as a valuable way to teach children the skills needed for sailing, before they can then try their hand at sea. Blokarts were first designed in 1999 in New Zealand, and because they are small enough to be packed away in the car, they are light enough for people of all strengths and sizes to manoeuvre. There are also double karts, which enable you to take even younger children for a ride. The wheels can also be replaced by blades, and the first Blokart ice world championships were held in 2010 in Lithuania. The main competition though is on wheels and the international championship is held every two years. While these events are staged on beaches, parking areas and disused runways are also used. As a hobby it can be done on any open area larger than a tennis court.

'Wahooo!' – I couldn't help myself making ridiculous baboon-like noises as I picked up speed with the wind behind me. I was only going at about 25 miles per hour, but it felt double that and every turn now was one smooth line. The learning curve had been climbed, I thought as I waved to the instructor…and then promptly flipped over like a toy, helpless in the hands of the ogre of overconfidence.

The price is similar to that of basic sailing. A new Blokart will set you back around £1,500, so the best way to start is to arrange a session for a group, via the the BLSA Blokart sailing website. They run taster experiences all year around depending on the weather and it's certainly ideal for a summer holiday activity in a number of locations around the UK. The sport is also working with the Army and their 'Battle Back' scheme for injured servicemen, and Sportability. In 2012 a team of 15 UK competitors travelled to the World Championships in Ivanpagh, and two of the squad were wheelchair athletes. One of these sailors, Chris Selway, a primary school teacher from near Bristol, came third in his class. To get involved the governing body can be contacted at www.theblsa.com

SAILING AND RIB RACING

If you want to experience actual sailing and are ready to go straight onto the water, then there are plenty of ways to learn how to do it safely. The Royal Yachting Association's Junior section provides training courses for beginners and upwards. Safety is paramount, with professional coaches helping every step of the way. The best way to get started, whether it be as a young sailor in a dinghy, or a junior rib racer in a starter powerboat, is to join a club. The RYA is the place to look, and their website is www.rya.org.uk.

Don't think you have to be near the sea, either. In 2008 after his gold medal winning performance in Beijing, I joined Paul Goodison and a group of beginners on a lake near Sheffield, one of the most landlocked cities in the UK. There was hardly a breeze which made his ability to read the slightest of ripples even more impressive.

STAND UP PADDLE BOARDING

Another water-based activity that is relatively easy to pick up is stand up paddle boarding. You jump up on your feet on a large surfboard and propel yourself along. In my first lesson, I was paddling out, and after the inevitable first few falls, it was a case of trying to steady myself on the waves as they brought me back in.

I tried this off West Wittering beach, where the most experienced boarders were paddling out to the Isle of Wight. They looked as if they were walking on water. It's a cross between surfing and punting, except instead of the large poles that you dig into the river bed, you just gain speed and direction with oar like paddles. It's become one of the fastest growing water sports in the world, after its rise in Hawaii in the late 1960s. There are now national and international competitions. It's growth is gathering more momentum thanks to inflatable paddleboards which make them more portable and accessible for lakes, and rivers.

www.standuppaddleboarding.co.uk is the place for more information.

BOOMERANG

Cue the resonant drone of the didgeridoo. Imagine you are tiptoeing across the outback, flattened stick in your hand, ready to flush out your dinner, and it will explain why I was in deepest Hertfordshire, looking for a man in a park. It's why my daughter and I had a Sunday morning we'd never forget in my original home town of Stevenage.

The boomerang has been used in hunting for more than ten thousand years and it's thought to have been a weapon used by stone age tribes. It is still a favoured method of some Aborigines, because of its ability to come back. The swishing noise generated by its movement and the way it can sweep around in a circle behind a clump of trees or a bush make it effective for flushing out prey. More commonly though, it is now used in sport, and boomerangs can increasingly be seen hovering in the skies above the UK.

Lucy and I had come to Stevenage for a session with Adam McLaughlin, one of the UK's finest throwers. He's been in the sport for 30 years and has competed all over the world. There aren't many cheaper, more accessible sports. The first thing that struck me was how different the colourful, light, carbon fibre boomerangs were compared to the large heavy wooden one I had been given by a friend on his return from Australia.

Some of the flyers had three arms, others two, and they were small enough for Lucy to get going straight away. They are not going to cost you much more than £10 and to get in some extra practise, the British Boomerang Society has tips on how to make free ones out of cardboard for use indoors.

Now, don't think for a moment this is just about how far you can throw. This is a sport which like the sky, knows no limits. Adam stepped forward, and like a javelin thrower, drew back his arm before thrusting it forward. With a flick of his wrist, the boomerang cut through the air. It raced to a height of around 200 feet, but then slowed as it started turning. It was like watching a bird of prey circling and hovering, before diving for its victim. It seemed to take an age for it to meander gracefully back down.

We watched in wonder as Adam sat down and rolled onto his back. He stuck his legs in the air, and having read the flight of his winged wonder perfectly, it came to rest on the soles of his feet.

Trick catching is one of the many disciplines in this sport. From the behind the leg catch, the under the leg, to the tunnel catch, eagle catch, Hackney sack catch and one hand behind the back catch. There are many ways to score points. Adam was like a ballerina: spinning, throwing, and jumping. This was the easy part. To up your game, you can throw two boomerangs at the same time and attempt a pair of catches. In competitions, you also score points for accuracy. The less you have to move from your throwing position to make the catch, the higher your mark.

At first, mine were doing their best to fly away for good. I narrowly missed a lady walking her dog, who was oblivious to the swirling stick stalking her hat, while another ended up in a tree. I needed to listen to Adam more carefully.

'Mike, you need to make your hand into more of a fist,' he reiterated. 'Then hold the boomerang in place with the edge of your thumb. You have to make sure you keep it upright too, as vertical as possible. Then take your right arm back, step forward with your left foot and throw as hard as you can.'

It's a magical feeling when the boomerang turns for the first time. It is as if you have trained your own raptor, and it's coming back because it wants to sit on your hand. Lucy and the other beginners were having to move even less to catch theirs. 'It's quite hard to judge where it's going to land, as it seems to change and slow up at the last minute,' said one girl, who added that it's really good for keeping you on your toes and moving you around.

Even more so when you move away from the trick catching and accuracy competitions. In the fast catch discipline, you have to make as many catches as possible in a minute. In this event, special faster boomerangs are used and can fly back to you at 70 miles per hour. The long distance challenge involves getting the boomerang to travel as far as possible. It only counts though if it comes back past you – in this one you don't have to catch it. Manuel Schutz is the undisputed king of distance boomerang throwing. The world record he set in 1999 was 238 metres with a full return. No one else has come close to this in years.

One of the most fascinating competitions involves getting the boomerang to stay in the air for as long as possible. Most of us would be happy with 20 or 30 seconds. At competitions its commonplace to be waiting a whole minute for it to land, but Britain's Adam McLaughlin remembers how he and a dog walker stood and watched in silent disbelief as the hovering and floating lasted for 2 minutes, 43 seconds.

What's more the boomerang landed only 30 metres from the launch point. It was as if some Aboriginal spirit had brought it to life, and it was making the most of its freedom.

The so-called 'Aussie Round' is regarded as the ultimate test of skills, because each thrower has five attempts to get their boomerang to fly out of a 50-metre circle and then come right back to the point where the player is standing in the centre. For a novice this is the hardest test and it will take a lot more training before I can lie on my back in the park, get out a paper and wait for my little boomerang to come home.

I went away from Stevenage with my eyes open to a whole new world. There are no boundaries. It doesn't matter how fit you are, how big or small, or how young or old you are. You can do it sitting down, and even practise from your bed. The only consideration needs to be other people who might not fancy having a haircut from a spinning boomerang, so please pick your throwing area considerately.

Two of the sport's big names, Manuel Schutz of Swizterland and American Chet Snouffer, were again among the winners at the 2012 world championships, held over 10 days in Brazil, while there are also now regular competitions and training sessions held across the UK. If you want to watch and learn from the expert throwers like Adam, and need to know the best boomerangs to start off with, visit the home of the British Boomerang Society, www.boomerangs.org.uk

ROPE SKIPPING

The sound of beating wings echoed around the sports hall. I imagined a frantic bat, flitting past on a daring insect raid in the dusky protection of a summer's evening. But the gentle noise was being chased by machine-gun tapping on the shiny floor. I widened my eyes, but still couldn't see what was making this sound. The rope was going so fast.

I am not easily shocked, but I had sat down in awe to appreciate the skipping skills of former world and European champion Beci Dale. Her feet were just flirting with the floor, and the invisible rope circled her so quickly she managed 95 skips in 30 seconds. This was just four off the world record at the time, in 2009, although this has now gone up to 102 in just half a minute.

Like throwing a boomerang, rope skipping is another sport that tests you in ways you'd never imagine and yet is based on the simplest and cheapest bit of equipment: a length of rope. There is evidence of rope skipping in some cave paintings, but it was in 1940s America that it really took off as a children's pastime, especially in towns and cities where there wasn't much space or money. Even now a starter rope won't cost you much more than £5.

But if you thought this was just something to do in the back yard or playground, then you don't know your 'double Dutch' from your 'toads', or your 'elephants' from your 'awesome annies'. It's no wonder boxers use skipping as a training exercise, and footballers as a way of building up strength after injury, because it is one of the most dynamic workouts I have experienced. It is regarded as one of the best ways to improve your all-round fitness. But it's no longer just a way to build up stamina for other activities. At an increasing number of clubs in the UK, it is now a sport in its own right.

I was warming up next to Beci and other members of the British team at the Studley club near Birmingham. I noticed what gymnasts they were. Lightweight, but remarkably strong. I was a heffalump in comparison. Yes I got into a rhythm and the rope was looping under my feet and over my head, but it was in slow motion, thudding heavily onto the floor, while Beci was levitating on a transparent cushion of air, so quick were her skips.

'It's my last 10 seconds that let me down. I start to fade and need to work on that to get the world record,' she explained. Such speed comes from over 16 years of practise, several hours a day, sometimes seven days a week – and if you think that might get boring, there are plenty of tricks to spice up training. In fact there are over 1,000 tricks in competitive rope skipping that you can try to impress the judges with.

'I love doing all the hard tricks, with the moving feet and flipping,' explained one nine-year-old lad. 'Doing the skills you have to use your hands as well as your feet,' he added, as his friend, slightly older, performed a 'toad'. This involved lifting up one leg and swooping the rope over, and then in a mesmerising figure of eight, sweeping it under the other leg. All the time the rope seamlessly cut through the air, like the trace of a sparkler on bonfire night.

This is only a basic move though. Most routines involve two ropes, hence you get 'double Dutch'. Beci was keen to demonstrate a more complicated routine. Two teammates, one on either end, were drumming the air furiously to get the ropes spinning. Once up to speed, they were impossible to see so using her instinct, Beci cartwheeled through the eye of a needle and into the middle without disturbing the flow. She bounced and danced before somersaulting in the vortex and spinning out the other side. Such teamwork is what's turned the British team into one of the best in the world, with gold medals in the double Dutch speed event at the 2012 world jump rope championships in Washington DC: competing against such countries as USA, France, Japan, Canada and Germany.

Their head coach is Sue Dale. 'It's so exciting. People don't realise the sort of things you can do. You've just seen the amazing acrobatics and speed, and people are always amazed,' she says.

And I was amazed that in my first lesson, they managed to teach my flat feet to get into the groove. Admittedly my rope was turning much more slowly and I could see the gap I needed to jump through. But keeping in time with the beat of each loop I leapt into the middle and then one bounce, two bounces, three and four before on cue I pounced down onto the floor. Like a poor frog which has just been run over, I flopped my hands and feet off the floor and into the air to clear the rope as it swung low each time. I was a lolloping lizard who risked being lassoed in a python's stranglehold if I was a split second out, but the cheers from the team fuelled my focus and I lasted a whole minute before springing to my feet and making a clean escape. It just shows what is possible with the right tuition!

To see for yourself, whether at school or your nearest club, contact the British Rope Skipping Association at www.brsa.org.uk or www.jumpruk.com. The next World Cup will be in 2014.

TABLE FOOTBALL

It's the one sport that made me nervous when around my grandma Olive. There was something about the metal bars and the plastic rotating players that changed her character completely. She had the meanest defence in the family and would live and breathe each headed clearance as if she had pulled the shirt on herself. Even in her seventies she would be like a cat on hot coals, with her wrist flicks and shrieks of passion.

For most of us, it's just an absorbing family tradition or a game in the pub, but there is now a flourishing British

'Foosball' team with a national BFA league planned for 2013. Indeed the British team went to Germany in January 2012, for the European championships and competed in front of 5000 people, in a packed sports hall in Bonn.

There are seven different stories about how table football began. One cites early children of servants spending time in backyards, using clothes pegs tied onto a pole. Another popular myth is that the game was started by a Tottenham Hotspur fan, Harry Searles Thornton, in the 1920s. Those who believe this version say he wanted to replicate the beautiful game at home. He had his lightbulb moment when fiddling with a box of matches. As he lay the matches across the box, the idea of bar football came to him. Some players dispute this tale – 'We won't ever agree on how it started,' said Ben Mason, coordinator of the British team.

There are now table football federations around the globe and a world ranking system, with Americans dominating most recently. The World Series is like the tennis tour, with five world championship events culminating in the end of season series finale, for the top 32 players in the world, in France, every January. Players and teams come from as far Kuwait, Argentina, Costa Rica, Iran, Malaysia and Japan. There is also a player to outshine even the likes of Federer, Sampras and Nadal. Belgian Frederic Collignon is the 19-time world champion.

HUMAN TABLE FOOTBALL

The other branch of this sport's development started as a joke. In their 1976 Christmas special, Morecambe and Wise gave us an insight, into what it must be like for the players being stuck on a pole and spun around. But it is no longer just a sketch, because table football has gone life size, and it is an increasingly popular team building exercise. Now we can all be those players my grandma used to spin and twist.

The pitch is enclosed by a giant inflatable frame, with metal bars like telegraph poles lying fixed across it. Human table football has been modified for health and safety reasons since it first started, soon after the Morecambe and Wise sketch, and so nowadays you are no longer harnessed to the bars. Instead there are two hand straps for each player. It's far less intimidating for beginners to know that they can slide their hands out if the bar moves too quickly or starts to spin. It's non-contact so different ages can play together, but don't let this fool you into thinking that it's not a physical workout.

I was on a team taking on one of the top table football sides in the country, from Oxford. We wanted to see how they would adapt to this giant version. I was on a bar in midfield, alongside the towering former Southampton player Brian Hague. Being at a bar together was actually nothing new, because he is landlord of the White Hart pub at Stoke in Hampshire, but now Brian and I had a different kind of bar work to do. As we were both attached to the metal bar everything he did, I had to match, and vice versa. He was twice my size, a gentle blond bear of a man, and so getting in sync with someone much smaller required some nifty footwork. If I went left for a ball, he had to watch and come with me, otherwise – as happened twice – one of us would be yanked over in a battle of opposing forces. So teamwork and communication are key, which is why it has become a hit at sports clubs and corporate events.

There are also similarities with the table-sized game. It is like being in a pinball machine, and is hard to keep up with the light inflatable ball as it pings around. In the middle of the pitch, a delicate touch is required, because if you kick it too hard, it lifts up, rebounds off the pole in front, and can smack you in the face. And of course I wasn't allowed to move my hands up to protect my now red nose.

The captain of the Oxford team was shocked. 'I thought this would just be a nice little kick around,' he sighed, 'but there are a lot of tactics involved. I have seen people playing off the walls to each other.' The Oxford striker was applying his usual table top strategy. 'One of the main things is look into the keepers' eyes, just like in normal table football. They don't know if it's coming down the middle, or at them off the side of the one of the walls.'

Our keeper, David Strauss, had indeed been bamboozled. 'You can't see it coming, as the ball flies at you so fast.'

It doesn't really hurt, even if I had been stretched in ways I hadn't imagined possible. A certain level of fitness might be useful though, because the striker on my team was stretchered off with a strained hamstring. It was almost as bad as when a friend of mine, David Gilmore, broke an arm playing Subbuteo in our secondary school days.

To get involved in human table football, then there are now several websites offering the experience. If it's the real deal, you're after and you want to see what got Grandma Olive so worked up then contact the British Table Football Association about joining a league or even working up towards the national team in time for the next World Cup. www.britfoos.com

GEOCACHING

'There are screams coming out of bushes right across the country,' beamed Sue Gough as she clutched her husband's hand. We were standing on a hill overlooking the Chilterns, and she was right. I had stumbled into another world, one in which country walks would never be the same, and one which has provided the world with one of its biggest family weekend activities.

It's one of the great problems for any parent. How do you tempt the kids out for a walk on a cold, wet January afternoon when they would much rather stay cosy in front of the television and on their computer games? Well, we all know a bit of bribery works, so just offer them some 'treasure' and the shoes and coats will be on quicker than you can say 'geocaching'.

It's a sport with a very short history. There are no records of ancient Egyptians doing this activity, although the basics of hiding and seeking do go back a long way. We can trace geocaching back to one day: the date when the much hailed 'great blue switch' in America was flicked to 'on'. It was 2 May 2000, and 24 satellites around the world were upgraded so that in an instant, the accuracy of GPS technology across the world was radically improved. A day later, a GPS enthusiast wanted to test the accuracy of the new system, so he hid a container in the woods and marked down the co-ordinates with a GPS unit. He thought he would see if someone else could find the exact spot, using their own GPS device. A note was left: 'take some stuff and leave some stuff.'

For the first few months, it was just experienced GPS users who played this form of hide and seek. It only became a worldwide phenomenon when a web designer from Seattle stumbled on the activity and created the first geocaching website. He started with the motto: 'if you hide it they will come'. And they did. Families, children, anyone who could download the geocache app to their mobile phones or tablets.

It sounds like you're a part of a secret society when you claim to be a geocacher. The 'geo' comes from the word geography, while the caching is simply the process of hiding a cache. Now, 13 years on, wherever you are it's more than likely there will be little boxes or containers hiding in the verges, trees and walls around you. Geocaching is an outside exploration activity which you join by getting a GPS device, or by downloading the app onto a mobile phone. You then register on the website, and get the rough locations of 'treasure' in your local area.

There was no stopping the children, teenagers and dogs in the group of 30 I joined at Longwick near Princes Risborough. We had split into groups of three and the race was on to find the first hidden boxes.

'There's nothing over there,' said the young girl on my team. 'We should try in the tunnel'. Before I could refer to my phone again, they were off, tramping through the muddy puddles under the railway tunnel, overtaking another huddle of excited explorers.

The information and clues that you collect from the website beforehand will only get you near to each secret stash – and that's if you have read the co-ordinates correctly. The rest is down to looking, rummaging, and sniffing out the target.

We were close to a find. Like a pack of hounds, the teams had converged on a footpath and were picking through the winter skeletons of blackberry bushes hoping to be the first to tick the cache off the list. It was getting increasingly frantic and noisy, when 'it's here!' and 'got it!' were the triumphant cries. We all poured over to a puddle where a tiny green canister, no bigger than a pepper pot, was just poking out of the mud. Its green lid was camouflaged like a tiddlywink counter, resting on the water.

Inside was a notebook, which we were invited to sign, along with pencils, rubbers and all sorts of small accessories. The value of the items didn't matter at all. This was all about the thrill of discovery. Finders are allowed to take something out as long as they replace it with something else, and so I rolled up an autographed picture of my lovely colleague Susannah Reid and popped it inside with an Olympic badge. I am not sure Susannah knows that her picture was placed into a bog in Buckinghamshire, but I am sure it has been taken and moved somewhere else by now.

'You see instead of just having a mindless walk with nothing to do we can go and look for treasure,' added rosy-cheeked Sue. She prodded her husband Mike: 'You are like a big kid on these hunts,' she joked. 'It's inexpensive and still a little bit geeky,' he chipped in. 'Although the children are off the computers for a day, they are still gadgeted up. It's another dimension and educational.'

It's a good idea to have a stick with you, to prize back the undergrowth. Suddenly we were running, as if the forest was alive with gold. News had come through that one of the first boxes to have been placed in the UK was nearby. We were at the top of a steep hill with the sweeping Chilterns draping away beyond the horizon line of grass. 'Down here, down here!' and we were charging, unable to stop, down the tufty bank, like a pack of wolves sensing a kill.

The teenager at the front led us to a small copse and the more agile among us climbed between the spider's web of branches to claim the prize. A green metal box, the size of an A4 folder, was dusted off and removed from its place in the cradle of a tree. Inside among the toys and the artefacts was a 10th birthday card. This had been signed by visitors in 2011, and it marked 10 years since the cache had been placed here, just after the birth of this sport. We had become part of the evolution linking the present to the past. For the kids, it was as if they had unearthed a Roman village, or Neolithic burial ground. Some of the secrets of our predecessors, albeit only from the last 10 years, were here for us all to pick over.

'I love going around, trading toys and getting others,' said one of the young explorers. 'It's really exciting and thrilling when you find something, and it's worth going in bushes and getting pricked for,' added another pioneer. 'I don't normally go out on a walk,' said another girl, 'I don't have a dog or anything but this makes it so different.'

We signed the card, added our own items, took a couple of souvenirs and the box was placed back to rest. From humble beginnings here, this game has exploded around the world in an almost unbelievable way. There are now 75 thousand caches in the UK with millions hidden worldwide.

'They are there on the International Space Station,' said Paul Burroughes, from the Geocaching Association of Great Britain, GAGB. 'There's one at the bottom of the Atlantic, and some in Antarctica.'

This is when you get into extreme caching, which is a more advanced version of this sport. It involves climbing trees, going underground, and using mountaineering skills to navigate rock-faces and diving beneath rivers and oceans.

For us on that January day in the Chilterns, the woods, the hedgerows and puddles were enough. I decided to slip away from the crowd. It was nice to get a moment of peace away from the chattering chase, but I now had my own cache to hide. Once you have registered you can plant your own box out there in the wilderness. It must be on public land or you must have got permission from the landowner.

I found a large hole underneath a tree and tenderly pushed my Tupperware box of treats inside. I marked the location down on my phone app, and when I got home, I put the clues to its whereabouts on the website. My cache was then 'live'.

I had also included what is known as a 'travel bug'. This is a little tag which has your own details on it. When someone finds one of these, they take it with them, on to the next geocache they find. They mark on the website where it's gone too and you can track your bug's journey. People often set goals for their travel bug. For example, to see how long it takes to get to every country in Europe, and how fast it takes to go from coast to coast. They note on the website where it has moved on to and it's a great adventure just tracking the voyage of your bug around the world. Within three days, mine had gone to Berkhamsted in Hertfordshire, and the last time I checked it was near Munich in Germany.

To join this world wide craze, please check out www.gagb.org.uk. This gives you more information about geocaching and has links to the main sites. It also tells you how to contact landowners about geocaching on their land.

Since I first came across this whole new world, I have been staggered by the number of people who go out searching through the bushes. The person next to you, right now, on the bus, or on the train, might be one of them, and when you're next on a walk and you hear shouts of excitement coming from the undergrowth, you know what it could mean.

3

BAGGY TROUSERS

New sports have been able to come into schools thanks to various schemes to get more children active. There was the Sports Unlimited programme run by Sport England, from 2008 to 2011, which offered grants to clubs and youth groups to target those not playing regular a sport. It gave nearly a million youngsters the freedom to choose a new sport and go along to a taster session, with the most popular being, climbing, free running, BMX, street dance and trampolining. More recently the government's School Sports Partnership has helped fund new activities in PE, which have helped bring children who used to be turned off by sport into the fold. Here's just a few of those brand new sports.

NEW SCHOOL SPORTS

Not one goal to aim at, but four. What's more, both teams can score in the same net. So one minute you are attacking and then a second later, it's time to defend. It may sound like a recipe for chaos, but it's the basics for one of the new school sports that have come in over the last decade.

I'm not talking about the unofficial school sports, the mischievous 'baggy trouser' moments. I was quite rightly sent off at school for getting into a clay boxing match, in which my pal David and I destroyed each other's clay model animals. It was proof of the inspiration that can come from adversity, though, because as a result of the lines I received, I went on to make a model of the Don Revie stand at Elland Road out of balsa wood (it was on display for months) and built a clay crocodile which is still standing in my parent's back garden in Yorkshire.

No, I am talking about the way that PE lessons have changed. There is no longer a hiding place. Were you one of the many kids left out on the wing, hardly getting a touch of the ball? Maybe you weren't as good as the others, or perhaps weren't part of the 'in crowd'. Or just perhaps, just maybe, you were just a little bit lazy, so you didn't mind opting out and keeping your head down.

Times have changed. Since I started my Saturday series, there has been an explosion in the number and variety of school sports, with the emphasis on getting everyone involved and giving more youngsters that 'back of the net' feeling.

CRAZY BALL

At John Hampden Grammar School in High Wycombe, where we filmed one of the new activities, there were eight sports offered to students in 2005. By 2010, there were 15 and one of the new activities was crazy ball.

International cricket teams around the world have long played a crazy catching game to sharpen up their fielding skills. The England rugby team played it during training camps in

2003 and South Africa did so in 2007. You throw a ball against a firm net, which is positioned on a frame at an angle. You then try to catch the rebound.

While this catching exercise is perfect for warm-ups and improving reactions, it doesn't exactly make a sport. So 'crazy ball' was born, thanks to a cricket fan who was coming to terms with his own PE nightmares. Richard Beghin, originally from New Zealand, but now living in the UK, remembers: 'I used to play at third man, and would get so bored and fed up. I wouldn't get anything down there and so never felt involved in the game. I wanted something that got everyone playing and all the time, so you can't just sit back and watch.'

You score in two ways: firstly by throwing the ball at one of the four nets and beating your opponents to catch the rebound, or secondly by intercepting the opposing team's throw. The switch between attack and defence is instant. You attack with your throw, but before you have had the chance to celebrate a point, you can be on the defence, trying to stop the other team making a catch.

The teams tend to move around the pitch in little groups. It's all about finding space and getting to one of the goals before your opponents can, so that you have a better chance of taking the rebound unopposed. It means you are constantly running around. My team had split into groups of three. We would lurk around one goal and then with a long throw, suddenly switch play to our teammates based near another net. At other times, we would move the ball across the pitch with short, sharp passes.

It does feel like absolute chaos when you are in the thick of a match. I didn't have a clue where I was or what was happening at first, with the game moving around so quickly. I would be picking myself up having dived at full stretch to palm the ball away from the expectant hands of an opponent, but no one was applauding because the game had moved to the far side of the pitch, where we had a scoring opportunity. I could see the need for speed of mind as well as feet, and also the need for team strategy.

To make the game even more interesting, the two sides of the net are different. There's the 'safe side', which produces a predictable rebound, and then there's the 'insane' side which produces an irregular bounce. Catch a rebound off the insane side, and it's a double score.

Some might worry that the introduction of all these alternative activities diverts focus and energy away from the mainstream sports, and dilutes the strength of the school football or rugby team. Well according to Dan Edwards of John Hampden, it's been quite the opposite.

'A lot of talented sportsmen and women have honed their core skills playing sports like crazy ball, and this has improvement has transferred back to mainstream sports. Plus it's drawn in the semi-sporting students we were hoping to target,' he explained.

Andrew, 12, said he never used to get the ball in football or rugby, but in crazy ball he has been one of the success stories. The teams need to rely on all of their players, as there are no set positions.

'I have so much more confidence, not just in school, but socially as well,' he said, nearly bursting with enthusiasm, 'and everyone has been praising me.'

Andrew and his classmates have learned this new sport together. It hasn't depended on who played more football at primary school and who the star players were.

For more information on crazy ball, please go to the website: www.crazyball.org

TCHOUKBALL

There is another new school sport which uses mini trampolines for goals. It's indoors rather than outdoors, but just like in crazy ball, both teams can score at either end. However there is one rule that makes tchoukball stand out from the crowd.

It was invented in a biology lab, by the Swiss scientist Dr Herman Brandt in the early 1970s. He was concerned by the amount of injuries in team sports and so he did a study on their physical effects. His conclusion was to draw up a new sport, which would minimise the risk of injury. Sadly he died before his new game started to catch on.

Hi legacy is tchoukball, which is now played all over the world, and is part of PE lessons for nearly 4,000 pupils in the UK. It has elements of handball, crazy ball and basketball, but there is no contact whatsoever. You are not even allowed to intercept your opponents' passes or obstruct them.

I went to Westbourne Sports College in Ipswich in 2009, where it was regularly played and where some of the British team were giving a lesson.

'It's very inclusive,' said one of GB players. 'There's no contact or interceptions and they are the biggest causes of injury, with all the banging into people and stuff'.

Scoring is different, too. I had to catch the ball from a teammate before taking a maximum of three steps. Then I jumped into the air and with my arm up above my head, threw the ball down onto the netted frame as hard as I could. It made a 'choo' noise as it thundered back off the net (hence the name tchoukball) and my shot was hard enough for the rebound to clear the semi-circle marked around the goal frame. My chances of scoring then depended on whether opposing defender Stuart could catch the ball before it hit the ground. Thankfully for me it was low and impossible to get and so the point was mine.

'As a defender you really must watch your opponents throw,' remarked Andrew St Ledger, one of the stars of the British team. 'You have to second guess where they are going to shoot and then position yourself ready. It's a battle of minds between attacker and defender.'

What's more if you do manage to defend a shot successfully, by catching the ball, you can then switch from defender to attacker immediately and shoot yourself. This is why team tactics are so crucial and in this sport once described as 'chess with a ball'.

There did seem to be a freedom about this game, because there was no danger of being tripped, shoulder barged or pushed off the ball. It meant that everyone, regardless of size, felt they could express themselves more. It's why it's completely mixed and why at this school, different year groups play together.

'The attraction is that it's non-contact, so I can have different ages playing together,' said the Head of PE at the time, Daniel Payne. 'There are not many other sports in which you can do that, and yet it's still great for fitness, because it's so fast. You only have three seconds on the ball, but have the freedom to think about the passes without the stress of being intercepted.'

There are now leagues across the country and it's hoped the strengthening of these foundations in schools will help the Great Britain team add the World title to the European crown they won in 2006, when the championship was held in Switzerland.

It's getting harder, though, with the Chinese team sweeping the board at the last world championship in 2011. Dr Brandt might not like the fact that the sport he invented is no longer dominated by Switzerland, but he would love the way it's taken sport to those who shied away in the past for fear of getting hurt.

Having said that, I did bend a finger back trying to catch a ball at full stretch, but that was my own failing rather than anything to do with the Swiss doctor!

To get involved, go to www.tchoukball.org.uk

HANDBALL

London 2012 has had the biggest impact on new school sports over the last 7 years. One of the cornerstones of the bid, was getting more people to try a sport, whether it be new ones, or established activities, that had been out of reach for most before, due to lack of funding and availability.

The sport of handball has been around since humans first learned to pick up a rock. There is evidence the Romans played a team version, while the Scandinavians created the modern game. It has been hugely popular across Europe for decades, but not in the UK, where there has been a tendency to put the ball down and kick it.

Now though, thanks to the Olympics legacy initiatives, the school door has opened for handball. It's estimated that over 50,000 school children have tried some form of the game, and figures from 2011 showed over 11,000 were then playing regularly in leagues and school clubs. That's three times more than the target set by Sport England.

Since the Olympics finished in August 2012 the sport has continued to boom. England Handball reports an increase of over 30 per cent in club memberships, along with a similar increase in interest from new clubs and schools. This could eventually give Team GB, which has struggled to make an impact on the international stage, far more home-based players to choose from, at grassroots level at least.

When I trained with the Ruislip Eagles, one of the most successful teams in the country, most of the players were from overseas. At the same time, the majority of the British teams were having to play their club handball in foreign leagues to raise their game. This could change now that the pool of British talent is expanding, but only if there is funding to build on the experience of playing at London 2012.

One of the main challenges has been bringing people to the sport in the first place, making more people aware that it's on their doorstep. Once people play it, it's easy to sell the appeal of this fast, furious, stress-busting team game. You can only take three steps before passing, so the ball is like a ticking time bomb. Teams have just five seconds to launch an attack. It's far more physical than I expected, too. While you can't hit or hold each other, there is plenty of body contact and I found myself spread-eagled on the floor on a number of occasions. To escape the fray, I foolishly volunteered to go in goal. Only then did I realise how fast the throws at goal are, and how alert you need to be to protect yourself.

While the future of the sport at grassroots level is looking very healthy, with more people joining clubs across the UK, Team GB's short-term future isn't so secure. Funding from UK Sport has been cut as they are not seen as a medal prospects for Rio 2016. It's been the same for other sports like indoor volleyball, and the concern among some is that without the elite level to aim for, what will the grassroots talent coming through have to grow into?

However the longer-term future is bright. The grassroots funding is healthy and supported by Sport England, and the game is largely now back the hands of the Home Nations associations. With regional and Home Nations representative teams beginning to make an impact on the international stage at youth level, the medal potential of handball may be realised one day in the future.

To get involved and find your nearest club in England and Wales it's www.englandhandball.com, In Scotland it's www.scottishhandball.com, **and in Northern Ireland contact the Irish** Olympic **Handball** Association, **www.olympichandball.org.**

ULTIMATE

Who ate all the pies? Who cares, quite frankly, but it's a good job they did, because it helped sow the seeds for one of the most popular school and university sports to have emerged over the past generation.

It all began in the 1920s, when truck drivers from the Frisbee pie company in the USA started throwing around the tin plates the pies had been cooked on. They would lob them to passers-by and it became a popular lunchtime activity which was then picked up on by soldiers in the Second World War. In 1948, a man called Fred Morrison developed a plastic version of the disc which he called the flying saucer, before this was taken over in 1955 and renamed the Frisbee.

Finally, 12 years later, American football fans Jared Kass and Joel Silver in New Jersey came up with a team game using the discs, which they called 'Ultimate Frisbee'. Like in American football the aim is to touch down the disc in the end zone, but there's no violent contact in the sport, even though at times you will collide with your opponents in the race to catch the Frisbee first. There is just one major element missing. If you do collide and there is a foul, you have to sort it out yourselves, because in ultimate there is no referee. Players have to be responsible for upholding the spirit of the game themselves, whether at the school ultimate session

I attended in Hampshire, or in a European final involving one of Britain's top teams, Iceni, based on Battersea Common in London.

'The principle of sportsmanship is so important,' Angela Wilkinson, one of Iceni's star players, told me. 'It's such an integral part of the game that even at the very top, you get used to playing honestly and it seems to work.' Just imagine a football match without a referee. Would it even get to half time before both teams were marched off by their managers?

Simon Hill of UK Ultimate added: 'It gets people talking to each other to resolve their problems, and it's this concept that schools taking on the sport seem so interested in.'

It's what got the pupils I joined in Hampshire hooked. 'We still play really competitively, but don't forget to do it fairly,' said one strapping 15-year-old, who claimed he had been put off football because it strayed too often into bad sportsmanship.

In the past these boys and girls alongside me, would have been playing football, hockey, rugby, or netball. But now they are weekly converts to ultimate.

'It's better for fitness. I run around and get involved a lot more,' said one lad. 'It's so fast and non-stop, it's point after point, and is exhausting because it never stops,' added his female teammate.

You can't run with the disc, so it's all about finding space and then receiving a pass. You must keep a foot anchored on the ground and you have nine seconds to outfox your opponents, who are trying to block and intercept your attempts to throw the Frisbee on to a teammate.

I found that running at speed and catching was a particular challenge. I tried slamming on the brakes for an emergency stop, but because I was looking at the incoming flying disc rather than my feet, I kept meeting the wall, or stumbling over my own shoes. If I did watch my step, I took my eye off the target and the disc would tickle my fingers before teasing me with a spin and change of direction.

During filming, cameraman Ian Da Costa wanted to give viewers a sense a sense of the speed of this game, which can leave you dizzy. So he attached a mini camera on top of a Frisbee with a load of tape. It's up there on the list of strange camera locations, along with the back of a pigeon, the wing of a plane, a polo stick and the mudguard of a motorbike.

Eventually I did get used to catching the disc in mid-air, but I still had to work on my spatial awareness. Twice I didn't see an opponent coming and we both ended up on the floor. This isn't a sport that usually hurts, though, especially when it's played outside on the grass and with such an emphasis on fair play.

To score a goal you need to catch the Frisbee in the end zone. You can be waiting there already or if you time it right, you can land there with a flying leap, taking the disc in mid-flight. If the momentum keeps you going and you run out of the end zone it still counts. Balance is a key skill.

This was one of the first sports I featured in my Saturday morning slot and since 2006, the number of schools and universities playing ultimate has more than doubled. A national school championship is planned for 2013 and millions now play worldwide. Its beauty is its simplicity. All you need is a Frisbee and a few mates in the park.

Higher up there are now national leagues. On the UK Ultimate website, there are 19 pages of teams, some with great names like the Air Badgers and Wink and the Gun. The British team has recently conquered Europe and is now trying to close in on the top teams in the world from the USA and Canada. They are getting closer. The WFDF World Ultimate & Guts

Championships 2012 were held in Japan in July. The British men's team won a silver medal in the Open division; Great Britain's best ever result at that level. For more contact UK Ultimate via www.ukultimate.com

STREET SNOOKER

'So, how did you get into snook...aaaaaargh!' I had to stop my question mid-sentence, as I recoiled in pain. The man I was interviewing, Marco Boi, didn't quite know where to look. It must have been uncomfortable seeing this reporter bent double and clutching his jaw. I thought I had acute toothache, but it turned out to be a jaw spasm, something to do with the nerves in my face, which without warning would stab with me blinding pain.

I didn't want to cancel the job, because Marco had arranged for me to visit the Watford school where the new sport of street snooker was being played. It goes down as one of the weirdest interviews I have ever done, though, as every now and then I would stop and hop around like a man possessed. Marco and cameraman Kevin Saddington were so patient, though, reining in their snorts of laughter. Eventually the painkillers kicked in and despite my facial acrobatics I was able to see the sport which has taken the reds and the blacks and the 147 breaks into schools.

I love some of the stories behind how a new sport starts. Some are by accident, some by chance, while others are more of a personal journey. Marco Boi was shy as a teenager. He had low self-esteem and says he lacked a father figure in his life to protect him from bullying at the hands of local boys who picked on him for being half Italian. When he was 14, sport saved him. His stepdad came along and introduced him to snooker. It was the mid-1980s and the sport was riding high on a tidal wave of popularity. Marco started practising on a 6ft table in the dining room and within six months was totally hooked.

'Finally I had found something that I could play on my own terms,' he said, 'in my own time and set my own personal goals such as trying to beat my highest break, rather than having to beat anyone else or have a team relying on me.'

He became pretty good and joined Watford Snooker Club with a few school mates. After winning junior competitions his self-confidence also started to improve. Snooker helped him with other key life skills such as maths, concentration, respecting others, team work, thinking strategically, social skills and achieving goals. He says he could well have been the next Steve Davis had it not been for girls. They tempted him away from the tables and so he went down another career path instead. He ended up in the music industry, as a singer-songwriter and then designing and selling playground equipment to councils.

But while Marco had been taken away from snooker, the sport couldn't be taken out of him and after eight years, he gave into his childhood calling and one afternoon in late May 2010 came up the idea of street snooker. He sat at the kitchen table and asked himself, 'What did I do as a kid that helped develop me as a person?' The answer was snooker. 'Well, snooker, pool and football,' Marco explained, 'and I thought if I can bring them together then it will help other children pick up some of the key life skills I learned.'

Now you might not think snooker is the best sport to introduce to PE lessons. It's perfect in the pub, or with the spotlights adding to the drama in snooker halls, but for youngsters trying to get more active, it doesn't seem like the most effective calorie burner. Street snooker is changing this, and it's also helping the sport meet its biggest challenge: how to get more young people involved.

You play on what looks like a giant snooker table, which is three metres by 4.5 and is turned upright, creating what is described as a 'multi-activity kick wall'. Then you leave the regular snooker balls and cues at the entrance to the school hall or playground, and instead you get a football or basketball. The rest is just like the table game. On the board you have the snooker balls painted on as they are at the start of a frame. From certain points on the floor you kick the ball and try to hit the various balls on the board. It's rather like the football games you find at village fetes, in which you have to kick a ball through holes in a wooden board.

This is a more involved, though. I lined up with students from St Michael's Catholic School in Watford, and the way we were limbering up in our shorts and bouncing on our toes, it was like we were getting ready for a five-a-side game, rather than going for the red and black.

One by one we'd step up and strike the ball from certain points on the floor. It took me three shots to hit my first red, from about five metres away. The first was too low, the second went over, but the third just clipped the top of the red circle on the board. That meant I could move on to a colour and my break was underway. At this point, a wheel was spun. This decided where I had to stand to take my next kick. There was a square symbol, a circle, a star, an oval, a cross and a 'snooker' symbol marked on the wheel of fortune, and they related to similar markings on the floor. I avoided the hardest spot, the 'snooker', but it would still be a challenge kicking from the square spot, which was further back and at an angle. Imagine taking a free kick from the edge of a football pitch out towards the halfway line.

I nominated my chosen colour, the blue, and my three attempts were agonisingly close. If there had been posts and a bar I would have hit them every time, but there was still a whisker of board between my shot and the target and so my turn was over with a break of just 1 on the snooker scoreboard.

The scoring is exactly the same as in snooker, and the game moves rather quickly so by the time I had worked out my next shot, I was stepping up to the plate once again.

'The aim is to get more kids understanding what the name snooker means,' said Marco, 'and what the game is and coming to terms with the basic rules, while still getting fit. Then hopefully in the future they can join a club and have a go at the real game, and get the benefits I did.'

The sports teacher at St Michael's, Steve Higson, certainly thinks it provides a very different PE lesson. 'It opened their eyes to a new activity, a sport they haven't tried before or normally don't have access to,' he explained.

It certainly seemed to change the students' perception of snooker.

'I thought snooker was boring, and was just the endless potting of balls. I didn't realise there is so much to it,' said one lad who usually just sticks to football.

'Snooker is quiet, but this isn't,' added a classmate who said she hadn't played the real game before either. 'I never knew about the rules, or scoring, and am now starting to enjoy this.'

There was more to it than I had first thought, especially when I became a physical barrier to get around in front of the board. A boy called Alex was trying to hit the blue from the back of the court. He couldn't see the blue, though, because one of his classmates was standing there trying to block the shot, and I was the second 'snooker', a second obstacle for Alex to bend the ball around.

Alex managed to get a wicked curve on his kick and it swirled past my right ear, but the angle was too much and it just missed, meaning my team took the frame.

It's not just the football team who have seen the benefits at St Michael's. The basketball players now play a frame in training to improve their accuracy and the school's top javelin thrower has found that by lobbing a ball at the target from distance he's added variety to his training and increased his range too.

Street snooker has come a long way in three years, with Canada, America, Italy and Holland now starting to play, while in the UK over 10,000 people have already got involved, either in schools or on housing estates where some local councils have painted street snooker boards on communal walls. In fact street snooker walls are now installed in 20 parks across the UK, and in 2013 the inaugural national league will start.

Crucially for its growth, the sport's governing body, World Snooker, now sees grassroots activities such as street snooker as a way of opening up the sport to a new generation, and it has featured at the Crucible Theatre during World Championship week.

Marco's biggest regret is that his mum passed away just as the sport was taking off, but she did know that Marco had become friends with his childhood hero, Steve Davis. The man he could have emulated had it not been for girls. Then again, without them, we may never have had street snooker.

For more information visit the website: www.playinnovation.co.uk

DODGING THE BALL

In most sports you are aiming at a goal, net or boundary, but there are two fast-growing school sports in which you are the target. Sports which are all about hitting your opponents with a ball.

'How cool is that?' said Tom Hildreth, who started playing rock-it-ball in 2007 and has since represented his country. 'In these days of health and safety, when you often can't play conkers, it's great to fire balls at your opponent.'

More on the start of rock-it-ball shortly, but first to the similar game of dodgeball, which first gave me a taste of being shot at.

'Look after yourself out there,' said the coach, as I prepared to join the England team at a training session at the Leon Academy School in Bletchley. I had already seen one teenage lad clutching his face after being struck in the eye by one of the football-sized balls with their much harder centres.

'It kind of hurts,' he winced, 'it hit me right in the eye. But it's OK now and really it's why I love it.'

Thankfully it is not as bad as when dodgeball started hundreds of years ago, reportedly in Africa and China, where it could be a deadly game played with rocks or even human skulls. One story suggests it was used as an intense training work-out for warring tribes, which also helped them establish tactics. It's reported that an American missionary was so impressed with the way the sport had developed an African tribe's athletic skills that he brought the idea back to the States and replaced the rocks with balls in the late 1800s.

Whatever the exact story is, what's not in doubt is that the physical demands are still as immense. It is two minutes of action-packed adrenalin. You are lined up against a wall with your teammates and up to three balls can be hurtling towards you at the same time. When I looked down to jump over one ball, which was trying to knock me off my feet, I was smacked on the top of the head by another which I hadn't seen coming.

You need excellent peripheral vision, lighting-quick reactions and the agility to jump, duck, dive and weave.

'You basically need to be a sprinter, a dodger and a thrower,' said Ryan Knight, the England captain at the time. 'It's putting all the athletic disciplines together.'

There was something extremely satisfying about surviving an attack. It means you stay in the round, because if you are hit, you have to drop out. The winning team is the one with the most players still in, at the end of the game.

There is an alternative to jumping out of the way like a scalded cat. You can stand up to the missile and try to catch it. If you manage this, you gain control of the ball and can call one of your expelled team members back into the round.

Most games end with one against one, the last two players standing, and they battle on until time is up or one gets hit. My problem was having small hands. I had dodged the ball easily enough to be the last one on my team, but my throws were bobbling balloons. I couldn't get my fingers around enough of the ball to give me the grip needed for a thunderbolt throw, and I was finally eliminated by a cunning strike to my feet.

I could see why the sport has become so popular in schools. It goes into the top five most intense sports I have tried. You never get a moment's rest to stop and think.

Beyond the school gates, there is now a thriving dodgeball league with eight teams in the premier division and nine in the lower national league. At international level, the England Lions, Scotland Highlanders, Northern Ireland Knights and Wales Dragons compete against the likes of Italy, Slovenia, Romania, France and Switzerland. In 2012, both the men's and women's titles were won by the English Lions.

To get playing dodgeball go to the website of the UK Dodgeball Association, www.ukdba.org

ROCK-IT-BALL

The other sport in which you have several balls in play at the same time, and in which you pelt opponents with them, is rock-it-ball. This is a little less daunting than dodgeball, as the weapons are long sticks with plastic scoops on either end and you use them to throw light tennis balls. They are the same size as tennis balls, but have had some air taken out to make them softer.

The sport was the result of three Yorkshiremen, Paul Law, Paul Hildreth and Bob Eldridge, working together on an idea to make school sport more inclusive. They wanted to come up with something similar to the games they had enjoyed as children. One from the 1940s had involved trying to hit mates with a tennis ball. 'Like war without casualties,' commented Paul Law.

Five years after it all started, the sport is now played by 10,000 school children across the UK, and has also taken off in universities, at military bases and in prisons. Overseas it has now been introduced in 23 countries. Key to its spread has been accessibility. It crosses gender and age gaps, being played by girls and boys together and by different ages on the same team. The balls don't hurt (most of the time) because you can only hit your opponents below head height.

The first time you play, it's pandemonium. I first came across the game in its infancy at a training session in Middlesbrough, but in 2012, when I returned to my old comprehensive school, now called Harrogate High, I realised how far the concept had come. In my day, school sport was football, rugby or hockey. Now they offer climbing, boxing, tchoukball and the rock-it-ball game I had first tasted five years earlier.

There were two teams of five lined up at each end of the sports hall. When the whistle went, we charged for the middle and for the five balls waiting to be scooped up. We then ran around frantically, trying to score points by hitting the opposing team's players with the balls.

There are no set ends like in dodgeball. Instead the whole arena is a free-for-all. If you hit someone they have to stop and put a hand up. The referee then marks down the point and your victim can try to move on. However, they can be targeted again, so have to rely on teammates coming to the rescue.

I didn't know where to look. I was haring around trying to scoop up a ball, but just as I thought I had got one, there was a thud against my back. The pain was no worse than a friendly slap, but I was left stranded in the corner working out how to turn defence into attack.

'Hunt in pairs, hunt in pairs!' England player Callum Watt screamed from the sidelines. His teammates were there to offer some top tips, as the school is just down the road from where the sport first started. Teamwork is key. If you are alone you can be picked off like the lame wildebeest at the back of a herd and the circling lions will feast on you in a scoring spree.

I was trapped in the corner by a 14-year-old lad who got me in the chest. He then called over to a teammate who came in for a repeat strike the moment the point against me had been noted. They took it in turns to shoot and score as I tried to protect myself with my stick, which you can use to block shots and swat the balls away. The other advantage of cornering someone is that you can score a double if you can catch the ball as it bounces off your opponent's body, but before my torso became a catching wall, the cavalry arrived and two girls came in wielding their sticks. With my attackers now victims themselves, I had time to dart away and scoop up a ball to strike with.

The launching action takes some getting used to. You pull

back the stick using both hands. The body of the weapon is plastic and no heavier than an umbrella, but using two hands gives you more control as you try to keep the lacrosse-like net upright and central as you jerk your arm forward. This is the theory, anyway. My shots were flying up, then down, wide to the left and to the right. The problem was I was also looking over my shoulder the whole time. I wasn't fully focused on the aim of my throw.

It's non-stop, and drains every ounce of energy. It's not just the running around, but the nervous tension that comes with being the hunted as well as the hunter. It's this that has made the sport so effective in drawing in less sporty children.

'Everywhere we have gone, the reaction has been the same,' said Paul Hildreth.

Helen MacKenzie is the head of sport at Ripon Grammar School and told me, 'I used to get pupils who shied away from sport. They would lose confidence playing more mainstream ones, because they wouldn't get the ball and would be left out.'

It's a common theme. Children alienated by a perceived lack of sporting talent, who in the past were frozen out, now lead a more active life thanks to these new alternative sports.

'This is different,' said Helen, 'I can't stop them. Even the less sporty children are playing non-stop, they are getting involved and love it. We are a grammar school, known for more traditional sports, but this has opened up so many new opportunities.'

It was such a frenzy that I couldn't tell who was scoring more points than who. If there were star players, and if the most talented kids were dominating, I couldn't tell, because the emphasis was on the team. Everyone was as important as everyone else. Because there are several balls in play, the focus isn't on the less sporty kid who drops a ball. They have as much chance as anyone of sneaking up on the class superstar footballer and scoring a point. This happened in a Durham school, when a boy who was small for his age and always picked last for the popular school sports was involved in his first rock-it-ball session. He found himself alone in a corner of the court with a ball scooped up, and struck the school sports champion on the back with the ball. It was his first real success in sport and he was over the moon.

It does seem to reach parts other sports can't reach. Paul Law recalls the time at a Teesside school when a girl arrived for an introductory rock-it-ball session dressed in high heels and her normal school uniform. When challenged she told Paul she hadn't done a PE lesson in four years and didn't like sport.

She sat out and watched, but after five minutes asked if she could join in. She was told she couldn't as she didn't have any PE kit, so she stormed out swearing. However she soon returned kitted out and played. She loved it so much that she became a regular, and after she'd left school she returned to run the afterschool rock-it-ball club.

It was also the one sport credited with taming a group of 52 students in West Yorkshire who had been withdrawn from schools for disruptive and anti-social behaviour. The team who came to introduce them to rock-it-ball had been warned the pupils would be difficult to handle, but they played for three hours without anyone getting into trouble.

The sport is now looking to spread beyond schools and universities. Getting access to a sports hall and finding 10 people to play can be limiting and expensive so there are now smaller formats. One of the new versions pits two against two and is played on a squash court. Because there's less space it's much more gladiatorial. Helmets are worn, as headshots are allowed and players clash together like rutting stags.

Then there is the version which pits one against one. I was up against the England junior player Amy, who was only 13. If you have ever seen a secretary bird dance around a cumbersome snake before stamping it to death, then you will have an idea of the knots I was being tied up in. There are three balls in play in this version of the sport, but every time I tried to get to one, a stinging shot seemed to whistle off my arm. It was cruel to watch for the baying crowd as Amy's agility, quick feet, speed of mind and spatial awareness snared me in a spider's web as I trudged slower and slower before in my final throes I scored a consolation point. We had played for three minutes and I believe the score was 24-6.

When you're in the thick of it, you don't realise how much you are working and how many calories you are burning off. The adrenalin of fear and suspense gives you extra speed and taps into hidden reserves of energy and stamina.

The first world cup competition, in 2007, was won by Scotland, but in recent years it's England who have dominated. The national finals in 2012 also involved teams from Northern Ireland and Wales. Rock-it-ball may have spread far and wide, but the basics are still as simple and primitive, just as when those Yorkshiremen first came up with the idea of throwing balls at each other.

WAVE BOARDING (ALSO KNOWN AS STREET SURFING, CASTOR BOARDING, OR RIB STICKING.)

There are so many new sports being introduced to schools that there are now several companies around the country that specialise in showing the teachers how to coach the new skills.

I was at the City of London Academy in Southwark where it wasn't just me and the students having a lesson in street surfing, or wave boarding, but the teachers as well. It was essential for us all to learn the 'wiggle dance' on the ground first. If you get this right then stepping on to the bendy board is not such a challenge.

I turned up in a wetsuit, not because I really thought street surfing was like its watery counterpart, but because I wanted a visually surprising opening for my report. I am fully aware that the good viewers of *Breakfast* are often busy with their morning routine and might not be able to give me their full attention. They might be dashing around getting the kids ready. They might be having a well-deserved lie in and I might just be a supporting role in their dreams. At the other extreme, I have been told by at least three women that they've had one eye on the Saturday slot while giving birth. I have to say that while it's an honour to be the first thing a baby sees when it enters the world, I hope no long-term psychological damage has been done.

It proves at least that I have to work to get people's attention, and so if I can do something that surprises them, they might just watch more closely. On this occasion then I stood in a playground on a street surfing board in a wetsuit. Initially, thanks to the camera angle, all you could see was my head and shoulders. I got the students to throw a bucket of water over me, which they seemed to love for some strange reason, and then I started my address to camera. It looked as if I was riding the high seas, but as I made the point that you don't have to go to the sea to ride the surf any more, the camera shot widened to reveal a sodden reporter boarding away at an urban school. I may have looked like a fish out of water, but it made for a more interesting start to my report!

This sport claims to be easier to pick up than skateboarding, because instead of pushing yourself with one foot while riding with the other, you have to wiggle your body and hips to get the board moving along. It has a gap in the middle, making it flexible. At the City of London Academy they said it was these boards that had finally broken down the barriers for two pupils who had never got involved with sport, and yet were here on this September day, still surfing the playground two hours later.

For more information visit one of the many websites by searching for street surfing boards, wave boards, rib sticks or castor boards in the UK.

4

INTO THE EXTREME

The most common question I get asked is: 'What sport has scared you the most? What has been the most terrifying white knuckle ride?' This chapter is dedicated to fear, and also to pain. Mr Mouse, the creator of the Tough Guy challenge, reckons 'it's fear and pain that draws us together'. Indeed, the sport that has hurt the most is another frequent enquiry, whether I'm at the supermarket checkout or on the train. So hold onto your seats, have a cushion handy and get ready to wince as we go extreme.

UP UP AND AWAY - A WING AND A PRAYER

It was just another day at the office for Danielle and Stella. They clocked in and changed into their uniforms before grabbing a coffee and stealing time for a chat. The same old routine and the same old faces. The day started with a meeting, before a bit of brainstorming and then the usual flying around by the seat of their pants, trying to fit everything in.

Sound familiar? Only for Danielle and Stella, this isn't just a saying. 'Flying around by the seat of their pants' is exactly what they do. Wind up the windows, everyone – in terms of fear, this is like going into the lion enclosure at the safari park, as we take a look at some magnificent moments in flying machines.

I am proud that despite some of the painful and terrifying situations I have been faced with over the last seven years, my reactions have never had to be bleeped to hide a swear word. In an earlier life I did swear on the hallowed airwaves of Radio 4, but it was during my days in the National Youth Theatre and I was playing the part of Fleggie, a nasty piece of work, in the Peter Terson play *Good Lads at Heart*. Actually there comes a point when you can't actually speak; when you freeze. This is what happened when the incredible Felix Baumgartner did his record-breaking skydive from the edge of space. I am not just talking about the man himself – the same thing happened to the people watching, open mouthed, their hearts racing as the tiny dot on the screen hurtled to earth, reaching 834 miles per hour and breaking the sound barrier. He was the first person to do so without the help of any vehicle, and it redefined our understanding of the extremes the human body can be pushed to.

It's relative to what we are used to of course. Whereas Felix somehow managed to stay conscious despite the pressure he felt overwhelming his brain, I have felt close to passing out while flying at tortoise pace in comparison.

IN THE AIR

RED BULL AIR RACE WORLD CHAMPIONSHIP

Air racing has to be one of the most daring and potentially dangerous sports in the world. It's designed to stretch the ability of the world's fastest and most skilled pilots, and it is a race against the clock. It's not just about speed, but also precision and skill. It's edge-of-the-seat stuff for the spectators, because at certain points the planes come within 20 metres of the ground to slalom through giant inflatable pylons known as air gates.

Ahead of the UK Red Bull Air Race in 2008, which was staged over the water in the Docklands area of London, I was invited for a test flight to the east of the capital with one of the emerging talents, the German Matthias Dolderer. I got into my flying suit and strode towards the plane, feeling nauseous having already seen my pilot loop-the-loop and then drop like a stone before pulling up at the last minute to almost shave the tops of the trees.

Getting up to the starting height was stomach-churning enough, but nothing prepared me for the whirlwind of senses that was about to be unleashed. Matthias told me I must keep looking at the horizon so I was less likely to pass out. 'Ready for looping?' he then asked. Suddenly it was as if we were in the hands of a child playing with a toy as we were thrown one way and then flicked upside down. These weren't graceful loops, they were violent swirls. Before I had a chance to adjust my eyes, the sky was there – and now here – and wait, was that the ground? Or just the clouds? Where's the horizon gone? Ah it's back round here...no, it's gone again...!

I had no idea which way up we were, as it changed every split second.

My head was in my stomach, my ears around my shoes. What's more the G forces were such (I am told around 4–5) that it felt as if a large Mod from Brighton beach in the 1960s had put his boot through the back of my head and was crushing my brain against my eyeballs. 'Ah my head, my brain! Oww...this is madness...!' was all I could shout.

Lovely Matthias couldn't see any of this because he was behind me in the lead driver's cockpit, although he could hear the muffled groans and strained screams. He simply turned to the right and in the calmest of voices said: 'Ah, Michael, are you enjoying the scenery? Isn't it a great view of London? If you look over there to your right, you will see Canary Wharf.' *See Canary Wharf?* We weren't on an open-top tour bus, we were upside down, heading for an appointment with Armageddon!

By now I was drifting into a dream-like state and I made the sign to indicate the sick bag might be needed, and that was all it took for Matthias to make a hasty descent, landing perfectly safely of course. These pilots are the masters of the skies, the Formula One drivers of the air, and for Matthias it was just a warm-up.

I was fascinated to find out how the pilots can train the human body to cope with such pressures. Matthias explained that they have to build up resistance to the G forces gradually at first. They fly as a passenger with a more experienced pilot and go through the same suffering I went through: the nausea and the head and eye pain, and sometimes they even pass out. However, slowly, over weeks and months, their minds and bodies adapt and learn to cope with such forces, until eventually they are able to operate with razor-sharp judgement, while being hit with G force 10.

Despite its popularity, the Red Bull Air Race World

Championship hasn't run since 2010, due to the enormous expense. The organisers are considering potential changes, to make it 'a stable and economically viable sport' and are looking at a potential return in 2014.

When we do once again hear the 'smoke on' call from the loudspeakers, the defending champion will be the British pilot Paul Bonhomme. He was Britain's first World Series champion in 2009 and retained the title a year later. He's the most successful pilot in the history of the championship. He grew up next to an airfield and started by piloting 747 passenger planes, but don't worry if you spot him in the cockpit – he will save his stunts for the air race.

'Normally when I fly over this part of London, I am on the way into or out of Heathrow in a 747' he explained. 'This is rather different, though.' Talk about understatements.

HELICOPTER AGILITY

There is another flying sport in which the aim is to race through a series of gates, but thankfully when I had a go at helicopter agility we were only 30 metres from the ground. This gives you a false sense of security, though, because if you make any mistakes in this slalom event it's still going to be very messy.

It was my job to hang out of the door and call instructions to pilot John Jackson. I was strapped in, of course, but my arms were at full stretch hanging on to a length of rope which was connected to a bucket at the bottom. I had to guide the bucket through a course of obstacles, and it all depended on how accurate my calls were, and how well John could steady the helicopter before then turning on a sixpence. There was a 20-second penalty if we missed any of the gates, and the final challenge was to plant the bucket on a target.

I was helping the British team train for their latest event at the Cholmondeley Pageant of Power. John and squadron leader Craig Finch, from the Defence Helicopter Flying School, had become the UK champions and were getting ready to take on the talented Russians and Austrians at the world championships. There is a purpose to this sport, because it helps hone the skills needed on low-level flying missions into jungles or remote areas, to rescue people or drop off supplies. The control John had over the huge flying machine was staggering. Such restrained power at his fingertips.

WING WALKING

Helicopter agility is something we can all admire at shows, where pilots demonstrate their slalom skills, but it's not an activity most of us can get up off the sofa to try. It is possible, however – if you have the stomach for heights – to join Danielle and Stella and the rest of the British team who spend their time on top of planes.

The way it has worked with all the ideas that have come in over the years is that after my shift in the studio (previously at Television Centre and now in Salford) I would sit down with a cup of tea and sift through emails, texts and in the early days, that old-fashioned medium of the letter. I would then compile a list of the best ones and take them in to the producers on *Breakfast*, Katie and Julia, while also consulting with my colleagues in the sports department.

There was one idea that I kept putting in the file marked 'tomorrow'. Not consciously, perhaps, but there was always a reason. It was the suggestion titled 'wing walking'. This was going to involve a lot of health and safety considerations , but finally in the Summer of 2009, there was no way to avoid it anymore, and I am glad because it will go down as one of my top five sporting activities.

Wing walking, which is the sport of performing gymnastic-type moves on the wings of a moving aeroplane, started in the 1920s, soon after the First World War. Once the fighting was over, there were hundreds of planes that were no longer needed, and which could be bought cheaply by those who had caught the flying bug.

Most were content to perform daring stunts in their planes at the growing number of Flying Circus shows, but one man stole all the headlines. He was an American army pilot called Ormer Locklear. During the war, he was said to have climbed out onto the lower wings of his plane during pilot training, and then became an expert at fixing mechanical problems in mid-flight. He was able to climb from one plane to another, and as other daredevils saw the fame he was getting by thrilling the crowds, they started to follow suit. It's quite fitting that the first female wing walker was called Ethal Dare. She performed the first mid-air transfer from one plane to another, and unlike today, the early wing walkers did their stunts without any kind of safety harness.

Many paid a high price. Ormer himself perished while performing a stunt for a film. Ethal, known as the flying witch, wasn't immortal either and fell to her death during an air show in Michigan. In these early days, one slip was usually fatal, and so during the 1930s American authorities made parachutes compulsory and wing walking was eventually banned.

In the decades that followed the Second World War, flying changed beyond all recognition. It became accessible to all, and people soon took it for granted. The novelty had worn off. But the show days of the 1920s and 30s weren't completely forgotten. A few wing walking teams started up in America in the 1970s, and then a decade later an Essex man, who'd flown on his dad's knee as a boy, was convinced that he could popularise wing walking again. Vic Norman had got his pilot's licence and started mucking about with planes because they were cheaper than racing cars.

Then in 1986, he realised his ambition and founded the AeroSuperBatics team. Later that year, having proved that they could maintain safety standards both on and in the planes, he was granted permission for performers to climb out of the cockpit again. They became the first wing walking display team in Europe.

AeroSuperBatics now operate a fleet of Boeing Stearmans, which are 1940s two-seater bi-planes, and from their headquarters in the Cotswolds they go off to demonstrate their skills all over the UK and across the world, from China to Dubai and from Nice to Nantwich. Wherever they go, the professional performers – who all happen to be young women – are treated like film stars. They are watched by hundreds of millions of fans each year on television, and are still the only formation wing walking team in the world. In other words, they are the only team that will fly more than one wing walking aircraft in the same display

Unlike in the days of poor Ethal, safety is now the priority. Walkers are attached to the planes at all times, either strapped to the rig or tied to the cockpit with a safety wire and carabiners. The athletes communicate with the pilots using hand signals and they always keep their routine within the restrictions of the weather.

The weather was something I didn't have to worry about as I made my way through the sun-baked Gloucestershire countryside to meet cameraman Ian Da Costa. The team were in their office, a converted hangar, sipping coffee in their bright overalls. I was nervous, but at the time I was going through a difficult patch in my personal life and this was a distraction.

The fear made every other feeling redundant for the day. I had postponed this day long enough, but finally I was shaking hands with Sarah and Rhiannon, who I'd spoken to so often on the phone.

What struck me immediately about the girls was how physically fit they were. You have to be strong, athletic and agile enough to climb around an aircraft while battling against wind pressure of 150 miles per hour. What's more, as Sarah Tanner told me, throw in a bit of rain and it feels like you are being stabbed in the face by thousands of tiny knives, while trying to maintain a smile. It all takes jumbo amounts of stamina too, which is why they spend so much time out running and in the gym every day to keep up their fitness.

I felt at home with the team, being short. They are inundated with applicants every time there is a new place available on the team, but the ideal candidate is under 5'4" tall, and eight stone. You have to be small, to cut down on the air resistance that battles against your every move.

Danielle, with long brown hair and huge reassuring eyes, had been part of the team for three years, and had been dreaming of being a wing lady since the age of six, when her parents had taken her to an air show. By the age of 14 she was a national taekwondo champion and might have competed at the London 2012 Olympics had it not been for the calling of the skies.

Stella, the new girl on the team, had blonde hair and also wore a laid-back, calming smile. She came from a gymnastics background, but had always harboured a love for high-adrenalin activities. As we limbered up, stretching and rolling and bending, the girls discussed their favourite moves. Danielle favoured the arabesque, where she stands on the rear cockpit and waves back to the crowd. Stella likes being upside down in the rig, performing a handstand as the pilots loop-the-loop. Mind-boggling – in fact everything was boggling now.

I was on top of the bi-plane, standing legs apart in the take-off position. I was able to lean back and perch on a padded support behind me, but it was important for the routine that my legs and arms were free to move. There was a harness around my waist and a strap between my legs, and one over each shoulder, and I kept checking that I was most definitely attached to the plane.

The most important thing in these situations is to trust the experts – in this case the pilots – for whom this was just another day, just another flight in near perfect conditions. I was on one plane, Danielle on the other, and thanks to my stature the team thought there was a chance of using me in one of their most daring routines.

First things first, though, and we started off with a basic display. We had gone through the first sequence on the ground with the pilots. Having talked it through, we then walked it, with Martyn Carrington, at the controls of my plane, strolling boldly in a figure of eight while swinging his arms to illustrate the movement we would be doing as we looped-the-loop. I must admit I was sort of lost after the first sweep past, but for me just staying on the plane was going to be an achievement and I was sure all would become clear once we were several thousand feet up in the blue.

Engines purred and propellers stirred, whirred and then roared as we bobbled along the grass runway. We came closer to the trees and then on to the edge of a hedge, which seemed to jump out of the way as we veered upwards away from the sloping field below,

When faced with such forces, you feel so small, so insignificant – like plankton floating in the Pacific or the seed of a dandelion, stripped of all power, thoughts and emotion. Reality had disappeared, life's reset button had been pressed and I had almost ceased to exist. Nothing else mattered now, and given my new supernatural state, it was time to just sit back and enjoy the ride.

Within minutes I had got used to the ferocious roar of the wind that was pinning my ears back flat against my head. I looked across at Danielle and managed a wave. The world below was like the backdrop of a 1950s B-movie. If I had been able to jump off, I would surely have dropped straight through the canvas.

If you are reasonably fit, it is possible to move your arms and legs when the plane is upright and you are cruising at 3,000 feet. There are G forces and it's like moving in slow motion, but I could see how it was possible to move gracefully and elegantly, which is what makes their routines look so slick.

I had been warned about what was coming next. The thumbs-up from Martin in the cockpit signalled that we were ready to go into a steep descent, to pick up enough speed to perform a loop. And so it began, tilting and hurtling towards the end of the world, the earth racing towards me so fast that in 3, 2, 1 seconds I would surely be inside one of the cows grazing obliviously in the field below. I was pressing back with all my might to stop myself falling out of the harness, which of course was never really going to happen. I was shaking, rattling, the bones in my body jiggling. My eyes bulged against the Biggles-style flying goggles, and then in the blink of an eye the green grass turned to blue sky.

The pressures of the universe were cranked into reverse, and now my shoulders and pelvis were straining at the leash like a dog who's seen a rabbit. I was hanging upside down, surely about to drop headfirst to my doom. In contrast Danielle was dangling from the other plane with hardly a hair out of place. Like a ballet dancer, she raised one arm and then the other, and then pirouetting effortlessly she stretched her toes out across the carpet of air.

I had practised the arm and leg routine on the ground, but upside down I was paralysed. I had once moved a piano up a flight of stairs, and just the week before I had towed a lorry under the guidance of former Olympic shot putter Geoff Capes – but here I was unable to move my arms even just an inch from the handles of the perch they seemed to be cemented to. It wasn't the fear, it was the incredible G force. Eventually, with the right technique and concentration, I did get my arms in out in line with my waist, but it was like lifting King Kong and they soon flopped back to the handles in defeat.

Back on the ground the verdict wasn't what I was expecting. Had they been watching someone else? They apparently thought I had handled the forces up there commendably, and so I was deemed ready to take part in the mirror exercise.

Martin talked through the plan and remarked that it was pretty unique for someone to attempt the mirror on a second flight. The plan was for my plane to turn upside down, and then in this position move down towards Danielle's aircraft, which would be flying the right way up. The planes would inch closer and closer until, when the wind was right, I could dangle down and actually touch Danielle's outstretched hands.

Her face is now etched in my memory. If I close my eyes, I can see her right now, so clearly, and although Danielle doesn't realise it, she will always be there in my head. It's not a bad image because she is very pretty. Regardless of that, though, when you are hanging upside down from the wing of a plane, and when all the weight of the world is pushing through your body from your toes to your eyebrows, you are not going to forget this moment in time. It was a partially eclipsed image, though. As my safety straps stretched, my goggles clung to my face and fell over one eye. Yet through the storm I could see the serene, smiling face of Danielle. She was just a few metres away, beckoning me closer, as if we were long-lost friends meeting on a station platform. She was an oasis of tranquillity, using all her superhuman powers to reassure and comfort me. The moment seemed to last for hours rather than the 10 seconds in which I was supposed to drop my arms down to hers.

Alas the wind was too much for us to actually touch, and after coming so close, life slowly trickled back into my fragile frame as we soared back down.

At my partner Emma's house several days later, when the report aired, it was the first time her children Roly and Lara had seen their mum's new boyfriend. They stumbled into the lounge bleary-eyed at 8.45 on a Saturday morning, just as I was hanging upside down from the plane. I hadn't met them yet and Emma thought she had better explain who was dangling like some giant bat with goggles across his face.

'Oh right, is that what he does then?' was Lara's reply. 'What time is *Tracey Beaker* on?'

Back to the action and after the failed mirror attempt, we ground to a halt. The propellers went to sleep and I ran my hands though my hair, feeling on top of the world. It had been a life-changing experience and to this day I believe it has made me stronger and calmer when blasted with life's challenges. When you have dealt with some of the strongest forces the universe can batter you with, what else is there left to worry about?

I must point out that despite what I felt, they have a 100 per cent safety record at AeroSuperBatics and you couldn't be in better hands. Plenty of others have come away feeling the same as me, including the Olympic medallist Beth Tweddle, who as a gymnast was a natural up on the wing when she went to unwind there after retiring from her sport in the late summer of 2012. In contrast I am told by the team that Robbie Coltrane was only allowed to sit in the cockpit because he was too big for the wing.

This is an activity which is limited by size, but if you are six foot or under and below 14 stone, you will be allowed to walk out into the land of dreams. It is at the more expensive end of the spectrum, but it is worth saving up for. It's a once-in-a-lifetime activity, unless of course you make the team like the professionals Danielle and Stella, for whom it is just another day at the office.

For more information on wing walking go to www.aerosuperbatics.com

AEROBATIC GLIDING

Seeing the world upside down was becoming a recurring theme. It happened again when I was introduced to the world of aerobatic gliding by Booker Gliding Club at Wycombe Air Park, High Wycombe. At least you are inside the plane and not on the wing, but there is one big difference: there's no engine, which makes looping-the-loop even more surreal. You are totally dependent on nature and on reading the air for thermals, down drafts and wind. This goes beyond the bounds of sport. It's a science.

The pilot takes to the skies and in competition flies a programme of manoeuvres such as a loop, a roll, a spin and a combination of all of those pretty much at the same time. Each routine has a difficulty factor and points are also scored for joining the figures harmoniously and keeping the whole routine within a specified part of the sky, the aerobatic 'box'.

It was an awesome sight watching my pilot in full flow, reacting to the atmosphere around him like a bird of prey. Then, once your plane is released from the towing aircraft, it's just you and the sky. Far from being thin air, though, there is a myriad of forces at play, all deciding whether you rollercoaster over the thermals or climb in hot spots before making your descent. In the right conditions, you can travel hundreds of miles and it's a powerful feeling being able to conquer the forces of nature.

You have to get used to the eerie silence and lack of reassuring engine noise, but once you convince your inner demons, the whooshing of air over the canopy becomes just another of the data inputs used by the pilot in maintaining efficient flight. Looping-the-loop felt gentler than in the air race or wing walking and this time there was a chance to enjoy the scenery.

But gliding isn't only about aerobatics – you can race cross-country too, and Great Britain is rather good at it. This involves flying as quickly as possible over courses that typically range from 200km to 1,000km. In sky gliding, Team GB got silver in the Team Cup and there was an individual bronze for Mike Young at the World Championships in Texas. There is also a Grand Prix series now and the UK's Andy Davis won the African Sailplane Grand Prix in November 2012.

I could see how so much of it was down to thinking clearly and keeping calm. Coming in to land over the M40 at 60 miles per hour the angles were critical, but former British champion Graham Saw, my experienced pilot and the club's Aerobatics instructor, could have landed on a sixpence, and don't think this sort of judgement only comes with age. Down on the ground preparing for their gliding lesson were two 16-year-old pilots.

What's more, another big development in October 2012 was the law changing to permit 14-year-olds to fly solo in a glider in the UK, once they have received sufficient training. It means it's now the same as in Europe and the US.

I had witnessed two of the UK's most talented 16-year-olds, Will Hilton and Siena Whiteside, training at Booker and the skies are no longer the limit for others even younger than them now.. In May 2012, history was made at the Buckminster Club. 13-year-old Robbie Rizk was the youngest person in the world to take part in a national aerobatics contest. He did have to fly with a safety pilot, because of his age, but wasn't just there to make up the numbers. He scored 83% in an aerobatics competition, winning the beginners section. He also gained the highest score in the competition for his positioning, finesse and accuracy.

To get involved in cross-country or aerobatic gliding visit the website of the British Gliding Association at www.gliding.co.uk to find your nearest club.

AEROTOW HANG GLIDING

There is a way to get even closer to the birds. In gliding you've ditched the engine, and now it's time to ditch the plane as well. In hang gliding or paragliding, you just have a canopy with a thin metal frame dangling beneath to hold on to. It may seem to be a sport out of reach to most people, one which you'd never consider. This is because until recently, you had to launch yourself off a hill or mountainside. In hang gliding, you have a frame and sail, whereas in paragliding, you have a canopy and often have an instructor strapped to your back.

Whichever way you do it, when you step off the edge of the world it's a heart-in-the-mouth moment, and one that had my common sense screaming, 'No!' years before while on holiday in the Alps. It's too late to turn around when you have a 6'3",

15-stone Terminator of a man on your back and he's just pushed you down the slope of no return.

I had paid 30 Francs for a parapenting experience. I would never normally give a ski instructor a piggy back, but it's a reassuring cuddle when you have just left the earth behind with skis dangling from your feet.

His stubble sandpapered my ears as he adjusted our flight path on his ninth descent of the day. The mountain had become a whiteout behind us as we soared over the valley. It wasn't the view it should have been, because a thick mist was clinging to the foothills. We had no choice but float down through it and with our judgement clouded we only narrowly avoided a cable car line which appeared out of nowhere. The startled Frenchman tugged frantically at the canopy handles and with a large bunny hop, he averted the danger and we touched down into the snow.

I could see from this that learning the skills for this kind of activity could be a slow and frustrating process, especially at the start with its run and leap of faith off the top. This alone has put some people off, and for those in a wheelchair it used to be impossible. However, something has changed that has opened up the skies to everyone, old and young, and people of all abilities can now get involved.

It was George Ransome who emailed me with this idea. He'd always wanted to fly, but in the past hadn't been able to get to the launch points in his wheelchair. Now, though, it couldn't be simpler. In aerotow hang gliding, you start from a flat field. You are put in a harness, which is just like a sleeping bag, and suspended from the frame. You are hanging on with your tummy just a few inches off the ground, holding on to the bar as a microlight tows your hang glider up to 3,000 feet. It feels incredibly fast at first as the ground rushes past at 25 miles per hour, but it's an incredible sensation as the earth falls away into a patchwork tapestry of greens and browns, and as the cows become toys and people turn to ants.

If it's your first time, then you want the best instructor alongside you, and I was flying over Derbyshire with the world record holder, a former world champion hang glider, Judy Leden MBE, who now runs the aerotow school.

'The best thing of all' Judy told me, 'is to see empty wheelchairs as the likes of George go up into the wide blue yonder. People who can't walk, that can fly, it's just fantastic.'

George from Bournemouth has now started to fly solo.

'There was no hill to climb, I don't need any extras, I am as able bodied as anyone...there is no difference between us all in the air.'

The BBC's Disability Sports editor, Tony Garrett, wasn't going to miss this opportunity to soar into the sky either. I had worked with Tony on pieces focusing on Paralympic skiing, wheelchair rugby and tennis, but this was new ground.

'These opportunities really give you the chance to open up to new sports. It takes you into the sky, and takes you away from the wheelchair...it's a quantum leap. Gone are the days of just doing safe sports, like a bit of table tennis or wheelchair basketball,' Tony said.

At 3,000 feet you unhook the line from the microlight, and then it's all down to your birdlike instincts. Judy uses every sense to interact with the changing atmosphere around her. The wind noise helps you judge speed and position. With just the slightest of squeezes with her hand on the bar she can tilt up and down, or turn and soar on the breeze. If there's an instructor alongside, you can take your hands off the bar, and this is the closest you can ever get to flying.

'It's the most sensational feeling,' said Tony, 'as you mingle with the clouds, it's just the peace and tranquillity below, the cows and the animals…just an unreal experience.'

It's open to teenagers too. 13-year-old Cameron Dawes is learning to fly. 'Just brushing your hands through the clouds, and just being up there, and watching the birds circling below you. It's incredible,' he says.

For more information about all kinds of hang gliding, visit the website of the British hang gliding and paragliding association, www.bhpa.co.uk, or contact Judy Leden via www.airways-airsports.com.

It's about time the extreme sports opened up themselves more people, regardless of ability and I was delighted to see that the Body Flight centre at Bedford is now offering indoor skydiving experiences for people who are visually impaired or blind. There are also sessions for deaf activity groups and some of the army amputees from the Battle Back scheme have also started to fly there.

ALTERNATIVE WAYS OF REACHING NEW HEIGHTS

There are ways to experience great heights without having to take off, or book a flying lesson. Mountain climbing is an incredibly demanding sport, but so rewarding. Starting off on a climbing wall, it will give you upper body strength to die for: powerful and yet flexible, lean and muscular arms. It's also about immense reserves of inner calm and mental strength, which is how some of the most daring athletes on the planet manage to scale rock faces hundreds of feet high, sometimes without a safety rope.

That's one sporting experience most of us will never get close to sampling, and we would perish if we tried – however there are ways of reaching those new heights which get you fit and are demanding, but which are also very accessible.

TOWER RUNNING

Yes, folks – you may not know it, but there is a global race series which is all about running up the stairs: hundreds and hundreds of them.

In 2014 tower running will come to the UK for a sixth year, after being introduced by the housing charity Shelter. This explains why I found myself limbering up in my running vest and shorts on a cold, brisk morning on a London pavement, with my race number pinned on as we inched towards the start line. All around us, taxis were jostling with buses and frightened cyclists for space in the London morning rush hour. The roads around were a frantic fog of metal, with no space to squeeze through to cross any road.

That didn't matter a jot though, because the finish line in this race was 600 feet up, where silver skyscraper nuzzled blue sky. It was Tower 42 in the City of London, one of the tallest buildings in the area. The 700 starters from all over the world went off in waves ten at a time, all trying to get up the 920 stairs without stopping to walk or crawl. 15, 16, 17 – the early pace was sapping, as the next wave of practised runners pounced past me, leaping several stairs at a time. 28, 29, 30: keeping a steady pace was crucial, I thought, as I focused on the next twist of the narrow stairwell. 45, 46, 47: and for goodness' sake, I told myself, stop counting or you will go insane.

'You are into seriously anaerobic exercise here', the defending women's world champion from New Zealand told me. 'Your legs will burn, your heart is going, everything is pumping flat out. You really have to train hard for this, if you want to be in with the elite runners.'

Pictures on the wall of Big Ben and other London landmarks help mark your endless journey. It is like being in a time warp because all you can see is the stairs, the white walls and the polka-dot blur of people's bottoms bobbing past you.

Even Bob the Builder (a fireman in fancy dress) passed me at one point. It's a popular event with the emergency services, especially the firemen who are used to running up stairs. There is the individual race and also the team event, and the record for all 920 stairs here, is 4 minutes and 22 seconds.

43 storeys later, and I could hear the voices of the officials at the top. All around me there were yelps of relief. 'Nothing can prepare you for that,' said one lady in her thirties, sweating and resting her arms on her knees.

'It was a constant pounding on these knees, but wow – the view and the feeling at the top blows you away,' she added.

My time was nine minutes. There was no shame in that, and I now always try to take the stairs. However, after an energy drink and cup of tea at the top, we all crowded into the lift to go back down!

It's now the annual London race on the Vertical World tower running circuit and the Vertical Rush, which has become Shelter's flagship event, involves 1,500 people racing up the stairs, knowing that their pain will also raise hundreds of thousands of pounds for the charity. You are likely to rub shoulders with some celebrity entrants on the way, and training couldn't be simpler, unless you live in a bungalow. Ah, so that's where I went wrong...

Find out more via the website:
england.shelter.org.uk/.../vertical_rush

TREE CLIMBING

It's one of the best parts about being a kid. Worrying your parents to death by clawing your way up a towering tree when out for a family walk.

As adults, as sense and fear enter into the reasoning part of our brains, we don't see it as such a good idea – unless you are one of a growing number who take up tree climbing as a hobby or even do it as a competitive sport.

I went back to the Isle of Wight in 2009, soon after the British woman Josephine Hedger had won four titles at the world championships in America. The International Tree Climbing Championship was initiated in 1975 as a way of preserving the skills of tree surgeons and climbers who were saving lives during aerial rescues using just a rope. The first competitive climb was held a year later and the sport has revolutionised tree climbing techniques and the equipment that is now available.

There are now many competitions around the world, which promote safe ways of working while introducing new people from all walks of life to the skills that arborists use. It's now become an edge-of-your-seat sporting activity for hundreds of people across the UK.

You wear a 'sit' harness, and by sliding either a knot or mechanical ascender up one rope, you gradually hoist yourself up through the branches. There is also a loop around your left foot which you use for grip, moving this out and higher up to give you the next foothold. It's a little routine you learn on the ground first and while it takes a bit of getting used to, it becomes automatic after a few minutes.

'It's great because there are so many components to it,' New Zealander Paul McCathie, of Goodleaf Tree climbing, told me as we swung in mid-air with our knees brushing a huge branch.

'You have to think it through, trust the equipment, work out how you do everything, and it improves your fitness as well.'

I found it requires mental strength to keep calm, not look down, and concentrate, while also developing those arm and leg muscles as you haul your body weight up, knot by knot. Above me the green canopy was speckled with light, and every so often the hanging bottom of a climber would swoop over, blocking the light like a giant fruit bat. If you are a beginner you take your time, and I felt any stress lifting as I hung there amid the leaves. It was quiet, too, with everyone concentrating on staying safe.

It's very different at the top level, with Josephine was swinging up and ringing a bell at remarkable speed. When she won the world championship in 2008, she set the world record for women in the footlock competition, climbing 40 feet in just 15.88 seconds.

'It doesn't matter how many times you have climbed, there's always something different, and you always learn something when you compete, it's a great way to educate yourself,' she said.

Although Britain has a decent record in this sport, New Zealand normally dominate, as over 50 climbers from 18 nations try to become king and queen of the swingers.

For most of us though, it's about getting to the top safely, and without banging your head or arms into too many branches. As you lift higher and higher you do start to swing and I had a few interesting physical encounters with some of the other beginners. 'It's sort of terrifying in a way, but you really get into it,' said one teenage lad. 'It wasn't as safe as this climbing trees when I was a lad,' added his father.

He was right. As long as you follow the instructions, you will get to the top and can view the world from 50 feet up. The best bit was still to come, though, as you can then swivel into an upside down position. It's one of the oddest pieces to camera I have ever done, as the blood rushed to my head.

There are several companies operating tree climbing sessions, so shop around. There are also an increasing number of treetop assault courses, on which you spend several hours, negotiating a man-made course up in the branches.

In some, you are in charge of yourself and your children, once you have had the full safety briefing on the ground. Again as long as you follow the instructions, which involve hooking and unhooking two safety clips onto wires and safety lines while wearing a harness and helmet, you will be safe, and can enjoy heart-stopping rides through the air into nets and between the branches of giant trees.

'Compared to so many things in this health and safety culture, where it seems people are wrapped in duvets, the whole thing about keeping some adventure, is an element of risk,' said Will Blair, of the Go Ape adventure company. 'It's considered risk, though, but it's there and that's what makes it so exciting.'

It was eerie at times, hearing screams as zip wire lines sizzled with people riding through the forest like Tarzan, and it takes all of your courage to leap off a platform into a net several trees away. Especially as you have to trust your own safety checks. 'Your stomach just leaves your body,' said Alice, clinging onto the net so hard it rocked. 'My heart is beating so fast...it felt terrifying at first, but I loved it, such an adrenalin rush.'

The various challenges are graded like ski runs, with the rings, dangling in mid-air and my only way of getting to the next platform, definitely a black run. Go Ape started the craze and have sites across the UK, and there are now tree top adventure courses, offered by several different companies for all ages including primary school children. Supervision is given all the way around at some, and the best advice is browse the web and shop around. It is great for getting the heart going and for all round fitness.

POLE CLIMBING

For some that want their climbing even more extreme, and without branches getting in their way, there is another sport which brings athletes from all over the world to demonstrate their vertical speed. For most of us, climbing trees is a slow, complex journey, as you pick your way through the branches, but at the world pole climbing championships, it's a sprint up a smooth pole into the sky.

It's for those who like running vertically, rather than horizontally, and the sport was started by lumberjacks in Canada. Pole climbing came to the UK in 1996 and now attracts a crowd of 25 thousand. It's a sight to behold watching the professionals scamper up using just spiked boots and what is known as a strop. This is like a lasso that goes around the pole, and if you get the angle right it will support your weight as you lift it up and up. When they reach the top of the 100 foot high Douglas fir poles, weighing over six tonnes each, the athletes have to strike an electronic timing button to register a time.

I was getting into a strop quite literally when I had a go, as I found out the hard way that this sport requires incredible upper body strength, fitness and technique. It suits experienced climbers and gets easier once you are into a rhythm. The world record for sprinting up a 25-metre pole is 9.07 seconds, and so the top pole athletes were already up and down by the time I had managed just half the distance.

My aching arms seized and cramp brought me back down to a ripple of polite applause from the sympathetic crowd. I had missed out on the £3,000 prize money and chainsaw to take home. I can't blame my age, though. Of the 45 pole climbers taking part at Cannock Chase, the oldest was 77. Ah well, I thought, there are other events to focus on here next year, like sawing and axe throwing...

For more information on pole climbing, visit www.poleclimb.com

5
EXTREME SPEED

I've tackled some of the most terrifying, gravity defying aerial challenges I have faced, but for sheer terror it's back down to earth to experience the fastest glimpses of the grim reaper, when the difference between life and death can a split second decision or just a few millimetres. Speed, like great heights, is all about adrenalin, pain and fear.

HOLD ON TIGHT...

RALLYING

Baboons and giraffes were the main worry as the helicopter rose over the trees half a mile away. As if in panic women picked up their children and sprinted from their village homes, as if their houses were on fire. Men were shouting and screaming as the roar was getting louder. It was coming. The stream of people became a river, as i stood on a mound, alone with a camera near the equator in Kenya. Suddenly I was surrounded.

Younger members of the running crowd had paused to join me, attracted by this stranger with a movie camera. Feeling needlessly threatened I backed away, but they just advanced nearer. I could feel the hot breath on my face of five, ten, now a dozen children, some teenagers, some younger. The moment was seconds away. The metal mirage from another world would be here for this once-a-year encounter. A cooking pot of cultures that I needed to capture on film, and yet suddenly I was dropping. The ground beneath my feet fell away, and I felt a clawing on my shin.

I looked up from the open hole I had fallen into, which had a metal grate on its floor. The camera, up on the tripod, was still on pause. The children's faces broke into smiles, which would have turned to laughter, but their attention was snatched by the blue flash whizzing past. One older boy responded to my cries and offered me his hand. The hole was only six foot deep and I clambered out just in time to see the Subaru car of British rally driver Richard Burns disappearing beyond the ocean of cheering heads.

It was one of the most powerful sporting moments I have ever witnessed. Any preconceptions I had that this was a sporting wilderness had been blown away in the cloud of dust kicked up by the car's back wheel. Burns was a hero here, and the cars normally only seen on television had been within touching distance. It was one of the remote stages of the Safari Rally, which back in 2001 was part of the World Rally Championship. I was following Richard Burns, who went on to take the title that year, for a series of reports for BBC South. To cut down the cost of the trip, I was travelling alone with Subaru team, reporting and doing the camera work. Being what is known as a video journalist can be especially effective in assignments like this, because as a solo operator you are less disruptive to your subjects and can get closer to the team. I was also able to get some footage from BBC Sport, who were covering the event at the time.

The Safari Rally was different from the rest. It was regarded as the world's toughest, going along untamed tracks through the Great Rift Valley past isolated villages, and along routes that couldn't possibly be closed off for race day. They were the roads used by the locals, crossed by animals, and so the helicopter would go on ahead to scare creatures off the path and let residents know the cars were coming.

Many told me it was one of the highlights of their sporting year. A Masai Mara tribe leader told me people would travel for miles to get just a fleeting glimpse of the cars. 'We all know Richard Burns, we follow his career, and to us the drivers are heroes,' he explained.

They would have been saddened, then, when after the 2002 rally it was struck off the championship calendar. The sport's governing body felt the necessary safety conditions had not been met by the Kenyan organisers, while the teams were becoming increasingly unhappy about the expense of taking part. However, at the time of writing, the Kenyan Motor Sports Federation have made many reforms, including working with police to close roads and to ensure the safety of fans and competitors. In 2013 the event will be in the running to rejoin the rally fold.

My week with Richard Burns, who was a real team player, one of the gang, someone who tried to make everyone feel important, was to have a special place in my memory because at the age of just 34, one of the nicest blokes I have met in sport died of a brain tumour, just four years after winning the world championship. It was a tragic time for British rallying because two years later the other household name, Colin McRae (who had once thrashed me in a slot car race) was killed in a helicopter crash in Scotland. They have been impossible to replace, and the sport has not enjoyed the same spotlight in the UK ever since. Matthew Wilson is trying to raise the profile again as the country's only regular WRC driver, and he managed eighth place in the Wales Rally GB back in September 2012.

I have been lucky enough to experience at first hand the driving skills of the top drivers. They often reach speeds of 120 miles per hour on the narrowest of dirt forest tracks. They use their frightening speed to launch into the air on bumps before landing and then turning and sliding on a sixpence to avoid the onrushing wall of trees. Throw in rain, snow and other unpredictables and you have the most resilient set of drivers. They rely on their co-drivers to warn them of what's coming up, read from a booklet of so-called pace notes. It's another language made up of letters and symbols and read out at speed to map out the twists and turns ahead.

At the Goodwood Festival of Speed, it was my job to co-pilot World Champion Petter Solberg through a stage of Sussex countryside. Strapped low down in the passenger seat I could hardly see over the dashboard (I should have brought a cushion, Petter said) and yet I was supposed to relate each tree, bump and turn that was rushing past in a blur to the notes in the book in front of me.

I had walked the course, trekking through the woods beforehand while reading out loud my pace notes. 'Four right plus, opens 50, three right long tightens, long left minus...'

To be a co-driver you must be mad,' said Petter, 'or from Wales like my co-driver' (Phil Mills at the time). 'You have to be special, and I couldn't do it.'

That was reassuring as the forest scenery was a blur as we hurtled through the trees at 90 miles per hour, often sliding sideways, bumping and taking off over the tiny humps on the fast straights. The best co-drivers, like Mills, hardly ever look up. They have their heads down reading the notes 99 per cent of the time, and can tell where the car is just by feeling the speed, the turns and the bumps by instinct. It's a mistake to look up as it really disorientates you. My head was bobbing up and down, and I have never been able to read on journeys at the best of times without feeling car sick.

My instructions to the champion beside me got quieter as I swallowed harder and harder, trying to keep my lunch to myself. Not that he needed my instructions, really, on this occasion. He read the forest tracks instinctively and wasn't always looking at the road as he glanced over to chuckle at my sorry state. He said I would get used to it if I was his regular co-driver, but there was no chance of that happening as I rushed from the car to the nearest bush as soon as we stopped.

We went twice round the stage at incredible speeds, sliding up and banking over on one wheel and then drifting back the other way. Trees became a flicker, like a hand-drawn cartoon, and it was all over in less than two minutes. I hadn't noticed anything different about the second run, but Petter said we had suffered a puncture after 100 metres. Incredibly a flat tyre didn't affect him at all. He made the necessary mental and steering adjustments the rest of the way round, and completed the stage only a second slower than when he was on four inflated tyres. I rest my case on the skills of the rally driver, and also their co-drivers. For more information: www.walesrallygb.com and www.wrc.com

FORMULA ONE AND KARTING

I've sat in a Formula One car, but it says it all about these super human drivers that it would be far too dangerous to put someone like me behind the wheel in one of these cars and send me around the track. I couldn't deal with the forces and speed that assaulted my body. My stomach couldn't handle reaching 60 miles per hour in less than two seconds and my arms couldn't keep control of those touch sensitive machines, nudging towards the 200 mph mark. Apart from the fact I couldn't reach the pedals, my neck wouldn't be strong enough.

That's what F1 driver Adrian Suttil was working on when I joined him for a training day. He was in a boxing gym, swivelling his neck like an owl, pushing it one way then the other with his coach. Then it was on with the boxing gloves for some sparring, and that was only the warm up for the run and bike exercises. They have to be the leanest machines themselves to cope with these road rockets.

Mark Webber is typical of these all-round athletes. I joined him in the woods of Buckinghamshire for a mountain bike ride and run. He'd cycled 10 miles just to get there and was training for an adventure race he was organising in Tasmania, which also involved abseiling down a 300 foot high cliff.

He toyed with me in a running race through the woods, allowing me to keep up before opening the throttle 10 yards from our agreed finishing line. He's so easy to talk to: no ego, no airs and graces. He just likes a bit of banter and was interested in a lot of the stuff I had tried on Saturday mornings.

I also felt some of the forces these drivers are subjected to when I took on the Red Bull boss Christian Horner in the simulator they use to train drivers like Mark before flying them out to new circuits. I was tossed around like a ragdoll, and despite not crashing was a full minute off Horner's qualifying time. In contrast he showed he's lost none of his own racing skills. He always came across as so relaxed and there wasn't a hair out of place. He said he'd give me a call if they were ever short, but for some reason I am still waiting!

Former Formula One driver David Coulthard has experienced at first hand my erratic handling. I took him for a spin quite literally in a van: the sort a decorator would use to store paint in. I followed the line well enough, but my cornering was pedestrian and I am sure DC was tempted to get out and walk. It was ahead of the latest in the van race series, and the chisel-jawed Scot had a few more grey hairs after we'd finished. To be fair he was a very calm passenger and only crossed his heart and screamed twice. Imagine his face then when two years later, it was my turn to be his chauffeur again – this time around the *Top Gear* track. It's why I have to be over-cautious and careful behind the wheel.

I realised early on then that I was never likely to follow the path of Lewis Hamilton and get into Formula One through karting. In the past, though, even young kart drivers with cutting-edge talent were unable to get out of first gear unless they'd had a pot of gold in the glove compartment. The cost of karting, with engines and parts, sometimes runs up to £50,000 a year and that has taken many potential stars off the track. Times are changing now, though, thanks to the new Elite Karting League. It started in 2012, and enables young drivers to be picked by their local track to race for their local club. In the same way speedway does, this pits city against city, town against town, with the clubs picking up most of the cost. There were two all-girl teams in the inaugural season too. For more information on this league go to the website www.kartingleague.co.uk

DRAG RACING

There is a motorsport that leaves even Formula One in the slow lane. You need a parachute, because the start has been compared to the take-off in the space shuttle from Cape Canaveral.

The fastest drag car speed was achieved by Tony Schumacher (no relation to Michael) in the USA, when he clocked 337 miles per hour – that's nearly 100 miles an hour faster than the quickest track speed of an F1 car, driven by Antonio Pizzonia in 2004 at Monza.

What's more, in drag racing Britain can boast the undisputed king of Europe over the last 25 years. Andy Carter is that man, winning the championship four times. He has now retired but will go down as one of the all-time greats. Even he admits to the brutality of this kind of motorsport:

'It's a really intense pushing on your chest at the start. It's a very violent launch in these cars. If you think they go from 0 to 100 miles per hour in less than a second, 0.8 of a second to be precise, that's why it's such a physical experience.'

Imagine that – reaching 100 miles per hour in less than the time it takes to say '100 miles per hour' out loud. The top drivers reach over 300 miles per hour over the course of the race which is just one quarter of a mile.

I wasn't exactly reassured then by talk of the violence as I put on my racing overalls ahead of a warm up session for the British leg of the FIA 2010 European Drag Racing Championship. Hundreds of drag racing teams were gathering at Santa Pod Raceway in Northamptonshire, and my nerves weren't any calmer when I noticed the fireballs shooting out of the back of the cars as they edged towards the start line.

As a beginner I wasn't going to be risked in one of the top cars, but I would still be catapulted to 100 miles per hour in less than two seconds, so that's still the same as in a Formula One car. I would need to brace every bone in my body. I'd raced giant trucks before, and that was a real shake-up, but in the drag cars you are so low down and close to the track that it seems even faster.

The deafening revving as we jerked towards the start intensified the beads of sweat trickling from my forehead. I watched for the lights to change and then my skeleton flew forward, leaving my organs behind. It was like being fired out of a cannon, a furious frenzy of motion as I was flung into another dimension. But then, just like that, we were slowing down again, the parachute dragging us to a standstill, and after just eight seconds on the track my run was over.

I will never reach such speeds on the ground again – and remember I only went half as fast as the drag king himself, Andy Carter.

Santa Pod Raceway is the home of European drag racing and hosts over 50 events during the year from January to November. Visit www.santapod.com for more.

SOAPBOX

While drag racing is jaw-dropping and ear-splitting to watch, most of us can never think about taking part, and there's only so much watching of motorsport you can do before the crazy beast inside breaks free and makes you want to get involved.

Soapbox racing starts with a simple trip to the dump and local recycling depot, because there you will find the old prams, the wheels, and all the odds and ends you will need to enter a machine. In 1933, a newspaper photographer spotted some kids on his street racing in what were no more than crates on pram wheels. Myron Scott was so taken with their creativity that he spread the word and bought the rights to the national soap box series.

Most soapbox races held these days in the UK and abroad still stick to the same rules: no engines, the car must have three or four wheels, they must have some kind of brakes, helmets must be worn, and the competitors are allowed a push start at the top. After that it's all about gravity and how well your design harnesses the natural power. The top cars can reach speeds of almost 70 miles per hour.

That's on the longest, fastest and most testing course in Britain, the Cairngorm Extreme. The total drop is 195 metres and it says in bold letters on their website: 'This course is not suitable for novelty carties. This is not a sedate trundle down your local village high street. It is a full-on race down a mountain. If you make a mistake, there is a risk of serious injury or death.'

OK, well maybe I will build up to that one, I thought, as I opted for the high street of Whitehill in Hampshire for my first taste of this sport. Hundreds of people were lining the hill, protected by hay bales from the inevitable carnage that would at some point unfold.

The paddock in a car park at the top of the hill was like a scene from the Wacky Races: there were contraptions of all shapes and sizes, some with three wheels, some with four; some with high sides for extra weight and clout, while some were lower and lighter. One driver was in a pirate ship, claiming skulduggery would knock the others out of the running. In contrast a replica Ferrari Formula One car was on the ramp in scrutineering. 'It's made of three kitchen bins, a bookshelf, a Ford Transit roof-rack, lots of plywood, and lots of tea,' said the head designer in his red overalls. All around drivers and their team mechanics, often members of the same family, were checking and testing and looking over their shoulders to see if they had the most aerodynamic design.

'In a straight line, having more weight can make you go faster,' said Ian Round, of the UK Gravity Sports Association. 'As soon as you put in corners and have to break to get around those, it doesn't always work out like that.'

It certainly doesn't and as if to illustrate his point, a driver dressed as the Crazy Frog in a low kart with a side car, got the wobbles on the first bend and lost control, rolling over and over as the sides broke off his kart. Gravity can hurt and sometimes the months of hard work end in bits and pieces and tears scattered over the track. There wasn't much left of a brown, high-sided taxi-shaped four-wheeler, either – it wasn't able to turn after the chicane, and the driver was helped off by paramedics.

A 16-year-old girl in the car next to me at the start summed up the pre-race jitters you get having seen the wipeouts from the competitors before you. 'You are going pretty fast. 50 miles per hour, in something you made yourself. That's quite worrying.'

Ian Round says the fact that all ages compete and help build the car is what makes it such a valuable exercise.

'Lots of people are into motorsport, but it's an expensive pastime, and so this is accessible – to families, to schools, to groups of friends – cheaply and it's great fun.'

Fun had taken a back seat for me as I focused on the tarmac ahead while getting my push to the start line. I hadn't built the soapbox I was in, but was handed a ride, for one descent only, in a low, slick green machine with a rounded nose cone. There was less risk of crashing, but being closer to the ground made it seem much faster and I felt every bump.

I have been lawnmower racing and even warmed up for the annual 12-hour mower endurance race held in West Sussex, but those grass cutters were like a Rolls Royce compared to this bone rattler of a soapbox kart. I was beaten to the chicane by an old-fashioned post van which had the extra weight, but which might just topple. No such luck, though, and I lost further time when a drain cover sent a jolt through my back and into my rib cage. I felt every grain, every tiny pebble, and managed second place...in a two-car heat. But to get down in one piece was a relief and I had seen a new, much more accessible form of motorsport: a raw kind of racing.

To find out more about gravity soapbox racing, visit the UK Gravity Sports Association website at www.ukgsa.org

STREET LUGE AND PEDAL CAR RACING

This is even more basic and potentially even more extreme than soapbox. The street luge is a cross between a skateboard and a more traditional ice luge. You lie down on it and steer and brake with your feet. I tried this on a road near Beachy Head and reached such speeds that I ended up mowing a grass verge with my bottom and had to bail out to avoid being a Bushell in a bush.

If you don't fancy the extreme descents, but like the raw racing and home building challenge of the soapbox derby, then pedal car racing could be for you. These are light racing karts, but this time instead of an engine it's pedal power that gets you around . The legs will burn the first time you try, but it's superb for fitness and it's as much about stamina as speed. For more visit www.pedalcars.info – the British Championship runs through the summer.

ON YOUR BIKE

In terms of fear and pain, four wheels can't compete with two, and looking back it's the motorbike that has come out on top when it comes to ageing me quickest of all.

I didn't come into the sport with a great history. For example, I didn't go down the teenage route of owning a bike:

football and running were my games, and I had managed to crash every time I had got on a motorbike.

My first experience came at the opposite end of the spectrum to the superbikes, when I was on holiday in Greece on a hired moped. Luckily their top speed wasn't much over 30 miles per hour, as I came around a corner in Naxos town to find a line of German tourists all holding hands in the road. I tried to stop but skidded onto my side and bobbled along the tarmac past their bewildered glances as they stepped out of the way.

I needed cleaning up in hospital and had a couple of shiners for the rest of the holiday. The very next day, though, more was to come. I was going around a corner in a mountain village when a mule's bottom suddenly appeared in the road. I put on my brakes but my destiny lay with the animal's behind – at least it cushioned my flight over the handlebars. The mule hardly noticed but the owner did and chased me down the road with a stick, teaching me some colourful Greek language.

The saddest motorbike incident, though, came a year later as I rode down a hillside on the island of Thassos. Dusk was falling and as I glanced out across to the azure sea beyond, my world went black. I was being slapped in the face by a dark force. It was a bat that had somehow flown into me and got its wing wedged between my sunglasses and my face. Its furious flapping in a bid for freedom took us both down as I lost control and careered into the hedge. With my wheel still spinning, I pulled myself onto my haunches and realised the flapping had stopped. The bat had torn itself loose but had perished. One wing still formed an eye patch under my glasses, but the rest of the poor creature was flittering away on the other side of the road, in its final throes of life.

I have never fully recovered and these holiday experiences meant I came into my biking assignments with a bit of baggage.

SIDECAR RACING

In terms of white knuckle rides, they don't come any greater than being on the back of a world champion's bike – or in my first instance, on the side of their bike.

In sidecar cross and sidecar racing, there is no comfortable passenger seat to settle down in like in the *Wallace and Gromit* films. Oh no, you're on a tea tray, clinging on to a pole, leaning one way then the next, at speeds on the track approaching 170 miles per hour. In the motocross version, on a dry muddy track near Winchester, I was thrown from side to side, cowering from a shower of mud and gravel.

On the track at Brands Hatch the speeds were greater, and rather than being able to shift my weight right and left to help the four-time World Sidecar champion, Britain's Tim Reeves, take the corners, I was paralysed by fear.

Sidecars were once a cheap and maybe even romantic way for couples to get around, but not when it comes to racing.

'Mention side cars to most people and they have images of George and Mildred or Wallace and Gromit, but this couldn't be more different,' Tim explained. 'You are kneeling on the tray and holding on. You are low down on wider tyres and can do 0 to 60 mph in three seconds, with 200 brake horse power nearly.'

Tim won the title most recently with passenger Ashley Hawes and I can vouch that Ashley, and previous passenger Stuart Graham, deserve every part of that title.

'You are literally only just holding on,' said Stuart. 'If you grip too tightly your arm will pump up and you will get tired so quickly, so you have to be relaxed.'

Relaxed? That wasn't the feeling that came most naturally to me as Tim carried me around Brands Hatch as he prepared for the British leg of the world championship.

At every corner I thought I was off to Southend, as the tea tray seemed to snake and wriggle beneath me like a cobra's tail. It felt even faster because i was just millimetres from the track. I was supposed to be Mr Flexible, shifting my weight around to help Tim increase the aerodynamics of the bike and speed. But all I did was hold on so tight that they almost had to peel me off with pliers at the end.

MOTO GP

Despite all this, there was still a ride which topped the sidecar experience. A most terrifying adrenalin-pumping trip to hell and back with Britain's Moto GP rider Cal Crutchlow. This even beat going down the Olympic-size bob sleigh run near Riga in Latvia, where for extra speed they have built a seven-storey building at the top of the slope, and where I couldn't lift my head to look beyond the Latvian skipper who was taking us down.

What the Moto GP and World Superbike riders do week in week out is just beyond my comprehension. They have bones of steel and must be bionic, the way they crash and bounce like rag dolls across the gravel before thankfully, on the whole, walking away seconds later.

Crutchlow himself broke his left ankle before the 2011 Silverstone Grand Prix, but still lined up on the grid on the Sunday and managed to come sixth. It reminds me of the black knight in *Monty Python's Holy Grail*, when he refuses to give in after losing several limbs, commenting ''Tis but a scratch!' The riders must also have degrees in geometry, because how else can you explain the way they judge angles by the millimetre as they lean over on a knife-edge around the corners, touching their knees on the ground?

I never imagined I would be doing exactly that on a pillion ride with Cal around the Snetterton circuit in Norfolk. He's such a down-to-earth, calm, normal-seeming guy, and so as we got ready it was as if we were going off for a game of golf. His main advice was to hold him around the waist as he accelerated up the straights, and then push myself back against the fuel tank as he braked into the corners, just to stop myself flying off over the front.

I hadn't expected such a lift off at the start, as he wheelied down the first straight. I held on with all my might as I tilted backwards until I was almost horizontal, and then a jerk – oh yes, the brakes were on – and in a frantic changeover it was hands off Cal and a push against the fuel tank...whoa, I was off the seat, bottom in the air, and I was almost on top of Cal's back. My head was straining to pull the rest of me over and off onto the grass, but slowly I flopped back in relief into the seat cushion before the rollercoaster ride then threw us to the side. I could feel my leather knee pad scraping the tarmac, and was imagining the friction burn you'd get at 80 miles per hour. Thank goodness for such quality leathers. Then we were upright again and it was time to brace for another wheelie and the routine started all over again. I hugged Cal and shook his hand so hard at the end.

'I have done some scary things in my time Cal, but there they don't come near to that. That is it; that is crazy, the whole time balancing on a tightrope of life and possible injury or death!' I panted. He looked chuffed that he had scared me more than anyone else. But it was true. The margins in this sport are so thin, and the judgements they make with instinct on the throttle to maintain the balance at such blasting speeds so critical, they are the biggest risk takers I have come across. Steve Parrish, BBC Moto GP commentator, said: 'You need your head looking at going on the back of the Honey Monster! I wouldn't have done it!'

I stopped in my tracks – froze on the spot – just a couple of weeks after my ride with Cal, when I heard that his fellow Moto GP rider, Marco Simoncelli, had died following a crash at the Sepang Circuit in Malaysia. A shadow hung over the sport, a reminder of how dangerous it can be. Simoncelli will never be forgotten and the Misano World circuit near to his home will be renamed in his honour.

PERSONAL WATERCRAFT

Whereas the Moto GP stars are on the BBC and the likes of Valentino Rossi and Casey Stoner are household names, the same can't be said about their water-based equivalents. James Bushell made history in 2012 by becoming the first man in history to win back to back world titles. What a year it was for the Bushell clan, with Mickey sprinting his way to gold at the London 2012 Paralympic Games in the 100 metres T53 and James winning the British, European and World titles…and then there was…er…me. Well two out of three isn't bad, and there are probably more brilliant Bushells out there for me to report on.

Anyway I am not just mentioning James because he is a Bushell: he gets in here on achievement alone. He is the undisputed fastest man on the planet on a personal watercraft (more commonly known as a Jet Ski, Seadoo or Waverunner, though these are actually brand names). Bushell is the world record holder and the first person to win the World Pro–Open GP titles in successive seasons. I knew, sitting on the back of Bushell's craft as he took off across the water, it wasn't going to be as fast as Cal Crutchlow's bike. The GP personal watercraft does 0–60 in 1.4 seconds, but their maximum speed is about 90 miles per hour, much slower than the bikes. However, I have to say that the launch on the water felt much quicker. There were no wheels to spin and so in an instant my stomach was wrenched from my ribcage, and it was up in my mouth before I could yell out in horror. With two flicks of James' finger on the throttle, we had been fired to the other side of the lake. In a race, James is taking off with 19 other competitors alongside him all trying to get to the first buoy first. 'You see them go off so close to each other at 80 miles per hour and me and his mum close our eyes, we can't watch,' said Steve Bushell, James's father, who's also chairman of the sport's governing body, the JSRA.

I can only compare taking the controls of one of these watercraft, with their 520 brake horse power, to what it must be like trying to ride a giant mutant wasp. Not that I have actually done that, but the way the thing buzzed angrily through the water trying to sting me with every twist, as I jerked and wrestled its weight, made me respect its power in the way I would a giant mutant wasp. The throttle and brake were so sensitive that as a beginner I had to be super aware of the craft's explosive speed. Having said that, this is now a much safer sport than in the past. Accidents now are rare and it's a very accessible form of motorsport. The racing machine I was on would have cost me over £15,000, so it's far cheaper to join your local club and use theirs. This activity may have once had a bed reputation, but now it's governed by the Royal Yachting Association and is tightly regulated.

In my first lesson I am proud to say that I did get up to 45 miles per hour, on the Tattershall Lake near Lincoln – once I had realised that it was much easier to ride the waves and turn with a bit of speed. The controls were easy to master, and it's more about how much nerve you have. James Bushell of the 158 Performance Team has that in abundance and so did the two girls who I was surprised to see coming down the jetty for their lesson. Chloe was 12, while Reana was 10, and Chloe had come along after first seeing the sport while on holiday. Now they have joined the junior racing circuit. 'It's the speed and adrenalin,' said Chloe. James said it had been the same for him, and his only disappointment is that his landmark achievement hasn't been recognised in the UK. He may be a star name in other parts of the world where the championship is big news, such as the USA, Thailand, and Dubai, but at home he could be anyone just out for a play on their personal watercraft. Well James, all I can say is like Mickey you have done the name proud.

For more information about taking up the sport of James Bushell, go to www.jsra.co.uk

6

OUCH

I 've dealt with fear, now it's time to remember the pain, and consider the times I have winced the most while reporting on Saturday mornings. It's not just about taking it, but I have dished it out as well, especially the time i flattened a lady interviewee from the National Trust, when i tripped over in a bird hide. So plasters at the ready, as we go through some of the sports which have most potential to inflict the pain.

MISHAPS

I have taken it on the chin – quite literally. By a tramp outside Reading Crown Court, while recording a piece to camera. I had refused to sip his can of lager. In contrast the deliberate slap on the cheek I got from Enzo Calzaghe (father of Joe) in a boxing gym in Wales was a mere tickle.

Pain can also come from humiliation, like at Margate football ground. I was practising my filming technique for a preview of their FA cup tie against Tottenham. The ball was kicked out of play, over my head on the touchline. However, as I turned and started walking towards the ball, which was several yards away, I left headphones on, and plugged in. I felt the yank of the wires around my ears before I swivelled around in slow motion to see the camera smash onto the floor. I was left twisted in a coil of cable as the sniggers from the crowd became an avalanche of laughter. At least there were only a few hundred people there that time. Millions witnessed the moment the former England prop Jeff Probyn jumped off his stool and wrapped his arm around my neck with a tight boa-constrictor squeeze.

Jeff had come onto the *Breakfast* show to look ahead to the six nations. Being a presenter who likes to push the boundaries and take the interview beyond just a static chat, I asked him to demonstrate what England needed to do in the scrum. As ever with Jeff, he was so enthusiastic getting his point across that for a few seconds my speech was replaced by the squeal of a deflating balloon.

One of the things I love most about working on *Breakfast* is the way we interact with the guests on the programme. On Saturday mornings, when the programme has that weekend feel, the *Football Focus* presenter, Dan Walker, helps with this. Dan is the same wonderfully genuine, warm and friendly guy that you see on the TV, and his involvement has become one of the highlights of my week, and judging by people's comments to me in the street, it is the same for many viewers too.

He's more than just a football presenter and has enhanced the programme with the way he's got involved, whether it's throwing a match ball at me, or engaging in a sword fight with pens after an item on fencing. (Actually, that reminds me – there is now a sport called finger jousting which has an organising body and world competitions. If you don't believe me, look it up...)

The time it almost got out of hand, though, was in the build-up to the world heavyweight title fight between Nikolay Valuev and David Haye. Even though Haye is over six feet tall, he is short in comparison to the man they call The Beast, and Dan and I had worked out that our size difference was pretty similar. So to give us and everyone watching an idea of what it would be like, we stood up like prize fighters and as we jostled, Dan placed his hand on my forehead while I took a few shadow swings at the air. I couldn't get near the big man, but luckily David Haye found far more effective ways of downing his giant opponent. I maybe should have challenged Dan to a shin-kicking contest instead. More of that later!

The award though for taking most pain in the line of duty when working with Bushell, has to go to cameraman Simon Monk. His determination to get the best possible shots has brought us much closer, literally.

MOUNTAINBOARDING

I gave Simon a big cuddle when we were filming a mountain board feature in Herefordshire. Well, the only way I could stop my out-of-control descent down the grassy hillside was by grabbing him, and then enveloping him in a bear hug embrace. We have been close ever since.

Mountainboarding is like skateboarding, but on boards suited to grass, and it is a great way of getting down a hillside. Many come into the sport from snowboarding or surfing, wanting a way to ride more than just once a year on holiday. It's said to have started on Cleeve Hill near Cheltenham, and there are now nearly 20 centres around the UK where you can learn to ride safely. Then the countryside and hills all over the country will be your playground.

The experienced riders passing me at the Out to Grass Centre near Hereford were showing off their full repertoire of skills: jumps, turns, and even front and back flips. Most were teenagers, but this can be a sport for all ages and abilities and for me it was a case of getting down in one piece, and learning how to steer.

British mountainboarders are the best in the world at the moment, with Matt Brind, from Essex, being the World Freestyle Champion, and Jonathan Charles from Derbyshire the World Downhill Champion. As a result, the mountainboarding community in the UK is thriving, tempting those who enjoy a gentle cruise down a grass slope, as well as the ones, who like to go extreme down woodland tracks.

It's definitely worth a go one weekend – and maybe Simon will be available to cushion your fall. www.mountainboarding.uk.com

HOVERCRAFTING

Not far from Herefordshire, across the border in Shropshire, Simon stepped out onto the grassy track as I emerged from a large puddle in the hovercraft I was learning to control. I am not talking about the huge passenger ones, of course, but the single-seaters which are no higher than a go-kart.

I can highly recommend a hovercraft experience day. They are fantastic fun to ride, as you go from land into water, through the spray, and out the other side again. Trying to steer these craft is a bit like rallying on ice with flat tyres. Having very little friction, the ability to turn quickly is severely compromised.

There are clubs up and down the country and there are numerous places to try it. The first round of the national championships takes place in May, with around 60 hovercraft in various categories. Just type 'hovercraft experience' into a search engine, or if you are more serious about it and want to enter races in the national championship, then first find a club via the Hovercraft Club of Great Britain, www.hovercraft.org.uk. It's a brilliant spectator sport too.

Anyway, a top tip when hovercrafting: tell your friends and any cameramen called Simon to stay off the track, because at first these things are hard to steer.

I had filled in the health and safety forms and was going by rules, but to be fair to him, Simon thought I was coming to a stop, and that I could turn, so he stepped out to get my reaction on camera. Maybe he just fancied a ride, because the next thing I knew he was lying down beside me, camera in the air, cursing a pinched hand.

It made a tremendous final shot, and wasn't the only time I finished a report by saying in the studio afterwards, 'No Simons were hurt in the making of that feature…!'

Simon is one of the most creative cameramen I have ever worked with and certainly likes to get stuck in there.

KITE BUGGY

It was a windy day on Pembrey sands in South Wales and we were filming the dramatic and stunning skills of UK and European kite buggy champion, Craig Sparkes. This is similar to kite surfing, but on land and instead of a board, you have a buggy on wheels which is powered by the kite. You can reach speeds of 60 miles per hour along the sand, and Craig was also able to show the freestyle side, taking off and spinning like a ballerina using just the power of the wind.

'When you are out there and it's just you, the kite, the buggy, and the wind, it's an incredible buzz, a pure adrenalin kick,'

Craig enthused. 'It's fantastic for blowing the cobwebs away and relieving stress'.

He promised it's not a difficult sport to learn, but it can take an age to master. To begin with, it's all about controlling the power of the kite before you get into the buggy – and this was rather different from the sort of kite flying I had been used to on the beach. You have to keep your hands close together, to tame the kite, before then learning to loop-the-loop by tugging down with one hand and then digging your feet in. You can really feel the force, which is enough to pull lighter people into the air, and it had me scampering across the sand before I showed the kite who was boss. I did manage to get into the buggy after a couple of hours and was off on the three wheels, steering with my feet, albeit at a running speed.

Craig though was able to take off like a giant albatross, gliding several feet off the ground, and despite trying to keep cameraman Simon back, he strayed across the sand. As the wind picked up, Craig drifted through the air, and in slow motion came down on poor Simon, as he tried to roll clear. Again his hair was ruffled, but no damage was done, and once again the shot was the perfect finale to the piece.

Kite-buggying is not at all restricted to the coasts. I once filmed with a club that rides and flies through the air on a hill near landlocked Sheffield. For more information check out the website of the British PowerKite sports Association, www.bpka.co.uk

STOCK CAR RACING
It's the dirty end of motorsport – quite literally. There's plenty of mudslinging, sliding and argy-bargy on the corners, and what's more some of it is legal. There are rules, but even so

smashes and bumps are common, and you won't necessarily be relegated to the back of the grid.

Formula One stock car racing, which is far more controlled than banger racing, can be traced back to the birth of oval track racing, and the first race was held in London in 1954. Since then over 5,000 meetings have been staged at 94 venues. The current championship involves nearly 50 races in a season culminating in the November World of Shale final, and every one of these meets is a gruelling physical and mental challenge. You are trying to get around a 400-metre mud and gravel track in the fastest possible time, while jostling for space with up to 30 other cars. It's not speed, aggression or strategy, but a combination of all three that determines the real winners.

The first time I saw it, I was left speechless by the noise, the drama, the non-stop action. I didn't know where to look. From behind the thick fence at the Coventry track, it was like watching a cartoon, as the colourful collection of cars, all with their different characters, chased each other like a swarm of bees around the circuit, at speeds of 50 miles per hour, sometimes more. It didn't seem to matter if they took a big hit, because they were indestructible, and the drivers would also emerge seemingly unscathed. They were protected by metal cages, and by their own bravery.

'It takes a lot of steel and nerves just to get out there,' said one of the top Formula One stock car racers, ' and there will be 60 out there tonight, all calling on strength and courage.'

Over 3,000 excited fans applauded, and maybe laughed, as the name Bushell appeared on the grid scoreboard. Nothing can really prepare you for the sheer amount of power. From the off I was harried by the fleet of world and European champions. I was the wildebeest for their pride of lions and one by one they hunted me down.

I first took a hit at the back on my right, and as I rocked in my metal tomb, I turned to see who it was but got a spray tan from the shower of wet mud, flying up from the track. It would be too dangerous to have glass windows. They wouldn't last the first bend and so beyond the frame of my cage was nothing but the night air. I had two choices: put the visor down on my helmet, which meant I couldn't see through the steam cloaking my face, or leave it up and have my eyes, nose and mouth covered with the muddy face pack that was slapped on with every spin of my front wheels.

Either way I was struggling to make out anything beyond the steering wheel...the wing mirrors had been lost to the sea of silt right at the start and so I had no time to brace myself for the big one. After five laps, the slam of the World Champion's car into my back bumper left me winded. I was protected by the padded seats and the protective cage, but unless you are toughened and strengthened by months of training, you are going to feel rocked to your core. I was fine after a few seconds, but I was off the track and therefore got to enjoy the rest of the race with a cup of tea, as the animated annihilation continued.

Although like in all motor sports, the build of the car is important, it does not make huge differences to performance, in stock car racing. Getting around is more about the drivers' individual skill behind the wheel; their ability to balance aggression and patience with their own car and an almost psychic ability to read the track ahead, spotting the gaps in traffic before they appear, and avoiding spinning cars before the crashes even happen. The driver that showed such talent to win the world title in 2012 was Lee Fairhurst, from Lancashire.

There is some order to the chaos. You can spin the car in front of you either off the track or towards the barriers, but you can't deliberately fence off an opponent by turning into them. The stewards at the meeting can impose various penalties including docking places, disqualification, and even suspension.

I recommend that if you fancy a bit of downright, dirty motorsport, either as a driver or as a spectator, oohing and aahing at the bumps and bangs, then visit the website: www.brisca.com

SHINTY

Thankfully life has become a lot less brutal than it was in the bloody days of Braveheart. That is unless you play shinty. It's a fast and furious contact sport, and if you play any kind of stick and ball game, this is probably how it started.

You can thank the marauding warriors who came across the Irish Sea, bringing with them their game, which they played to show how tough they were. It's said that shinty is older than the recorded history of Scotland, and some think it even goes back to the days before Christianity. Its roots are similar to the Irish game of hurling, but it has developed different rules, while in Wales it became known as bando, and could involve teams of up to 30 players on each side. Bando is thought to have been one of the first mass spectator sports in South Wales, attracting thousands of people before it eventually gave way to other sports.

I was given a taste of how little shinty has changed over the centuries by the Bute club on the west coast of Scotland. After warming up, I was just about to get my stick onto the ball for the first time when I was flattened by a body charge that sent me nose-diving into the wet turf. I had wrongly assumed it would be like hockey, the game I had loved at school, but I was told not to mention that word again.

'We are harder, faster – it's more in the air, and not quite as soft as field hockey,' said the deep bass voice of the captain, Hector, with a tongue-in-cheek smile.

Anyone who has played field hockey will know that it's far from soft – it's just that shinty takes the physical side to another level. For a start, unlike in hockey, the rock-hard ball (about the same size as a baseball) is allowed to ping around at head height. Plus, you can use both sides of your stick on the ball, and you can even use your stick and shoulders to block, tackle and knock your opponent out of their stride.

The Bute coach used to play rugby in Scotland. 'I came from rugby and thought "what have I done, coming into this sport?" All of a sudden you have a stick flying straight at you.' There are variations to the rules in the children's game, called 'first shinty', where such aggression is not allowed, and they play with plastic sticks and soft balls.

In the men's game there are 12 players in each team, one of whom is always the goalkeeper. Each player has a curved stick, and being the only Englishman in a Scottish team, I was invited to go in goal (called a hail) just so I could admire the speed with which they can strike the ball (often at 100 miles per hour). Imagine getting in the way of that – and these sporting gladiators don't wear helmets out on the field. In the rules it says that a player may stop the ball with his stick, chest, or feet. The goalkeeper can use his hands to palm the ball away but cannot catch the ball.

Shinty was once played competitively on a widespread basis in England, and other areas in the world, as it migrated with travelling Scots. In those areas it has been crowded out by other 'softer' team sports, but it remains stronger than ever in its homeland.

Shinty could also boast the most successful club team in world sport after Kingussie won 20 league titles on the trot.

However in more recent seasons they haven't been able to dominate in the same way. For the last three years it's been Newtonmore who have been crowned champions, while Kyles Athletic are the most recent winners of the Camanachd cup.

In terms of raw contact, this certainly goes into my top five of pain league. Not that you notice it in the thick of the action and I did manage to smash in a goal. And don't let my impression put you off. The Chief Executive of the sport's governing body, Torquil Macleod, told me:

'The perception is that it's fairly violent and brutal, but part of the skill is being able to defend yourself in that environment and statistically there are no more injuries in shinty than in other field team sports.'

The harder the ball and the greater the falls, the better it feels – and anyone who thinks they are tough enough to play or just watch this action-packed field game should get more information from www.shinty.com

HOCKEY

Despite not quite having the same brutality that ties shinty to its traditional past, its great-grandchild, hockey, is still fast and intense. Anyone who has suffered an injury from a ball or stick will have the scars to prove it.

It is a fantastic team game which we can now play almost anytime, anywhere thanks to a new initiative started ahead of the London 2012 Olympics. Hockey now has its own five-a-side version which makes it more accessible. Rush Hockey is designed to get more people into the sport, with both men and women playing together. You can play indoors or outdoors, depending on the weather, and on much smaller pitches. The sticks and goals are also scaled down, and the balls are lighter, so you don't need shin pads or mouth guards and you can play in your lunch hour and be confident of going back to work without any bruises as souvenirs.

It's easier to organise, too. You don't have to join a club to play hockey anymore – just get a few mates together and play. Because it's so accessible, it also gives players of all abilities more of a chance and more confidence. To use that sporting cliché, it's a real leveller. I took part in a match with the GB men's hockey captain Barry Middleton and with everything scaled down from the size of the sticks to the pitch, he found it harder to impose his international class and I was able to tackle him and score. For more information: www.rushhockey.co.uk

ICE HOCKEY

Another direct descendant of shinty, which those original warring tribes would surely be proud of, is ice hockey. I have been stuck in goal many times by the teams I have gone to train with, and never was it more painful or intimidating than when I was padded up to the eyeballs to face the best that the Coventry Blaize ice hockey team could throw at me.

Ice hockey is a direct descendent of shinty, and started after Scottish settlers in Nova Scotia first played a game on ice. Unlike other ball-and-stick games, it has kept true to its clan warrior tradition. The little black puck, which is used instead of a ball, is like a bullet as it rears and lashes up like a cobra. As a beginner in the net, all I could do was throw my padded bulk across its path and hope that when I picked myself up, the puck wasn't nestling in the net and there wasn't a stinging sensation spreading across a part of my body that wasn't so well protected. What I found most awe-inspiring was the controlled power the players could pack behind a shot, while still travelling at such speed across the ice.

It's what makes it such a great spectator sport. For a night out, it's hard to beat the intense noise and raw atmosphere, and one reason people go is to see the brawls that break out on the rink. The Coventry Blaize team were keen to demonstrate what it's like in the thick of the action and so when I was learning the moves of the outfield players, I was singled out for an attack. Like an injured wildebeest struggling to keep up with the herd I was picked off by three predators and sandwiched in their train crash. The impact sent me spinning into the wall of the rink and I was face down on the ice, with bodies now raining down on top of me. At least with the protective body guard under my vest, the impact was cushioned – it felt the same as when I was taken out in mid-air by an opponent during a feature on the growth of American football in the UK. Certainly no damage had been done. I was merely slightly winded, dazed and rather confused, as I stared at the boots now skating away on the frozen floor. Often in sport, impact is also cushioned by adrenalin, and you don't feel the knocks until you are in that hot bath later.

Brawls have been part of ice hockey since it first became popular in Canada – the early rules passed on from the ancestors in shinty encouraged physical intimidation and control. Today it's an established tradition, and while it may be a reason for criticism and concern, the highly charged atmosphere the conflicts create is one of the reasons people love the sport.

Each team has so-called enforcers who do most of the fighting and who try to impose themselves on the other team. The brawls are governed by a complex system of unwritten rules, often referred to as 'the code', but while officials will tolerate a certain level of aggression, a variety of penalties are now imposed on players who cross the line. In the UK elite league, this usually means five minutes out of the rink, in a 'sin bin', to cool down. During this time, the offending team has to carry on one player short, making the game even more open.

The British ice hockey team had a major breakthrough in the autumn of 2012. They moved a step closer to making the 2014 Winter Olympics after beating hosts Japan in a pre-Games qualifying tournament. Britain were Olympic champions in 1936 and bronze medallists in 1924, but last competed at the Games in 1948. Unfortunately they didn't make it through the final qualifying tournament in February 2013, but it does perhaps show that the sport is on the up.

An ice hockey match is a unique sporting experience, a cauldron of colliding chaos combined with the serenity and elegance of ice dancing. Put it on your list of sports to see, and find your nearest club by going to the website www.britishicehockey.co.uk or www.icehockeyuk.co.uk

FLOORBALL

Floorball and the outdoor game of street or ball hockey are bringing the skills of ice hockey to the masses and into the sports hall. Floorball was developed in Scandanavia in the 1970s and is now so established in the UK that it's played at over 100 schools. It's designed to give players all the speed and excitement of ice hockey, but without the punch-ups, the risk of getting hurt or the need to book an ice rink.

It is played in a school gym or sports hall with light plastic balls. These travel extremely quickly, and the game is non-stop. During my session with a school in the Cotswolds I found that the ball is such a livewire that the biggest challenge was bringing it under control.

For some reason I was again put in goal. Thankfully the padding, helmet and face cage did their job. For more information go to the website of the Great Britain Floorball and Uni-hockey association, www.gbfua.com

ICE DANCING

What we often forget in the collisions and calamity of ice hockey is what accomplished skaters the players are. They have to have the grace, poise and ability to move around like ice dancers.

I am your average once every six months with the kids kind of ice skater. I can now get around the rink and build up a head of steam, but it usually comes with a pandemonium of arms and legs like a bison in ballet shoes.

However, refining our style might be easier than you think. Within an hour in the company of British ice dancing pair Penny Coomes and Nick Buckland, I was moving around without drawing attention to myself, and had even learned a few moves. I could spin on the spot, albeit with arms flailing, and I could skate along low in a crouching position, even if it looked as though I needed the toilet. It was a start though, and by my next Christmas trip to an outdoor rink, I hope to be able to leave my daughters speechless with my execution of the 'death spiral'.

Ice dancing in a pair, though, is another world entirely. For beginners, it's hard enough getting around on your own, so trying to keep in time with someone else, invites double the trouble.

My trip onto the ice in Dumfries in Southern Scotland, however, wasn't about just learning to skate in sync with one partner. Oh no, in synchronised ice dancing it's about learning the moves with 15, 16 even 19 other people. The tidal wave of movement you can create is immense; you are all cogs in the wheel, and all under pressure not to put a foot wrong. If you do make a mistake, the whole pack of cards can collapse around you, and if you are at the end of the fast-moving group, the force and momentum can catapult you out of the rink and into row Z, and most likely A&E too.

It reminded me of the time many years earlier when I had joined Olympic hopefuls in the British synchronised swimming team. I have heard people question whether this counts as a sport. Well don't for a moment dare to think this is lightweight. The graceful movements we see on top of the water are a Dr Jekyll to the Mr Hyde at work underneath.

Below the surface is a horror show of physical pain. I was sinking under the weight of what I was meant to do. I was gasping for air, and credibility, and ran out of both. Even putting up with the pinch of the nose clip for hours on end was bad enough. Don't let that put you off though – it is an incredible team sport, and it gets you supremely fit. If you are a good swimmer and like gymnastics, you could one day be an Olympian. www.swimming.org is a good place to start.

Back on the ice, learning a synchronised skating routine, I could at least see what we were doing without the sea of bubbles and froth of the pool. Not that it made the actual moves any easier. Synchronised skating started in North America, but in recent years has grown rapidly in the UK. I joined the Solway Stars team in Dumfries, who had just narrowly lost to Nottingham, who've dominated the national championships over the last decade.

I watched the skaters link arms, then twist, turn, spin, break up, rejoin, go down on one knee, glide and rise in one flowing liquid move, and in perfect harmony with the music.

'When you do this together, there's so much more speed, more force and more strength,' said coach Louise Nairn. 'They rely on each other and they learn to rely on other people.'

I had plenty of new words to learn. Moves include the twizzler and the counter, or you can try a rocker, some Mohawks or Choctaws. My repertoire was limited to my own moves: 'the windmill' (flap your arms randomly) and 'the pheasant' (crouch down and hope for the best).

For safety reasons I was placed in the middle of the 19-strong formation known as a wheel. It turned like a giant watermill, faster and faster. My arms were entwined so that when I did lose my balance there was plenty of support, and as my confidence grew, I was able to glide down and under a team mate's arms. It felt like a barn dance on ice – until I was put on the end of another sweeping move. This time I was clinging on for dear life. I could feel the force and speed of 18 other skaters pulsing down my arms. The rink spun by in a blur and all I could think about was not letting go.

The sense of speed, though, was something this beginner hadn't ever felt on ice before and so for that reason alone it is worth finding your nearest synchronised skating club. Visit www.synchronisedskating.co.uk

SPEED SKATING

If it's pure speed you are after, and if you are looking for a sport that's really on the up, then look no further than speed skating. In recent years the British speed skating team has been gaining momentum.

Its funding has trebled thanks to 21 medals won at major competitions, success at junior level, and top-six finishes at the last Winter Olympics. So the race is on for the podium at Sochi in 2014. It is an awesome sight watching the team shoot past like a speeding train in a streak of colour, thanks to the Team GB kit that the new funding has provided. There's now a talent-spotting squad too, to ensure that the recent success is only the beginning. I joined the British team to see that it is a very different learning curve from figure skating. 'It's faster, better and bolder,' said one 14-year-old recruit.

I noticed straight away that the blades are longer and narrower, so there's not as much surface to balance on. Plus, there aren't toe picks at the front. To get any movement, you have to use your legs to create pressure and push out to the side. This will get you going, but the first major hurdle after that is the crossover. To really ramp up the speed, you have to put one foot in front of the other, and get a scissor-like motion going. When done properly it looks so effortless, but I was a tangle of tentacles and on my before the first bend.

My legs and feet were already cramping up. The bent, squatting position you need to adopt over your skates is hard to hold, and creates more lactic acid than in most other sports. It's this that makes it one of the most painful sports around – although you do learn to cope, I am told.

It would have helped if I'd started aged six, like Britain's medal hope for Sochi in 2014. Just over a decade later Jack Whelbourne was part of the relay team that broke the world record, and he also became the 1,000 metres Junior World Champion. He's now set his sights on an Olympic medal in the short track speed skating event and thanks to recent investment has a much better chance. 'We can get more venues to train on now,' he said. 'Plus we can go out looking like a team in our kit, and we didn't have that before.'

The top speed skaters can reach speeds of over 30 miles per hour, and just to prove how fast you can go if you get those crossovers right, Jack challenged me to a race. Could he do four laps of the rink before I could do one? We put it to the test. I stayed on my feet, got up a head of steam on the back straight and came around the final bend still in the lead, and then with the line within touching distance, there was a swish, a splash of colour and a shower of ice as Jack put the handbrake on to stop right in front of me. He seemed to relish the fact that he had timed his run perfectly so he could pip me on the line. To find out how to follow in Jack's wake, go to www.iceskating.org.uk/category/short-track

RED BULL CRASHED ICE WORLD CHAMPIONSHIP

The newest winter extreme sporting event to test the resolve of speed skaters is the Crashed Ice World Championship. This is for those who want to skate downhill on a near vertical sheet of ice. They valiantly try to stay on their feet, but with four athletes hurtling down the track at the same time, wipe outs are part of the spectacle.

It tends to favour downhill skiers or speed skaters, while for me it was just a case of getting down in one piece on the temporary slope built at Valkenburg in the Netherlands in January 2012. The flatter descents were manageable but it was onto my bottom to negotiate the steepest parts, and this is within the rules. There is talk of the series coming to the UK at some point, as the man-made course can be transported anywhere in the world. Canadians dominated the 2012 series, but they were pushed all the way by the Finnish skaters. For more info go to www.redbullcrashedice.com

ROLLER SKATE SPORTS

We're down to the top few most painful experiences I have had. While the speed skaters suffer from all that lactic acid in their muscles, I didn't do it for long enough to get the full effect. The Crashed Ice course could have been my downfall, had I stayed on my feet. While the ice hockey terminators are equally indestructible, they couldn't unleash their full force on a TV reporter, and under the protective padding, the blows were one step removed.

So to really make me wince, we have to swap ice skates for roller skates.

Before we get to the real pain, when I am at the mercy of torturers who go by the names of 'Debbie does Malice and 'Correctional Felicity', let me first tip my hat to inline and roller hockey.

INLINE ROLLER HOCKEY

When playing inline roller hockey, you have a body protector under your shirt, and a helmet, because you can expect shoulder barges or flying sticks to make regular contact.

I was in a match involving, my old buddy, the former French Olympic ice hockey player P-Y Gerbeau. Yes, the man who transformed the Millennium Dome. After crushing me into the wall and whipping my stick away with a brilliant bit of Gallic flair, he told me that we had something in common. We'd both been nicknamed 'Gerbil'. He was affectionately called that by the press while I earned the rodent name tag in my King Alfred's College days at Winchester.

All these years later, as I teetered around on my inline skates, brandishing my stick, I just wished I had the same skating skills as my fellow gerbil, who was rolling away to fire the puck high into the net. We are roughly the same height but I was no match for the brawn of P-Y and his years of ice hockey experience. So perhaps I would be more suited to a non-contact version of the sport.

RINK HOCKEY

This is played on the conventional roller skates, and is for those looking to avoid the big hits. It's non-contact for a start.

According to the history books, a Belgian man called Joseph Merlin conjured up the first roller skate in 1760. It's said he wore his new invention to a party to impress his friends and crashed into a mirror. Others then invented roller boots with wheels in a line, to make them more like ice skates. Further modifications were made, until by the late 1800s roller skating was a popular hobby. It was then only a matter of time before people started spicing up their skating by introducing a stick and a ball, and it's claimed that roller hockey was invented in England in 1896. It's since spread around the world, and although it's an English creation, it is now most popular in countries like Argentina, Spain and Portugal, where it's played professionally.

That's not the case as yet in the UK, although there are now eight teams in the elite premier league and seven more in the national division one. Despite being non-contact, it's fast, you need to be fit, and if you are in goal, you need guts and protection. The tactics are similar to basketball in the way you screen and block your opponents as you pass the ball around.

To find your nearest club go to www.englandrollerhockey.com or rollerhockeyuk.com

To find out more about inline hockey try http://www.bipha.co.uk/ and www.inlinehockeyuk.co.uk

ROLLER DERBY: LET'S GET JAMMING
I should have heeded the warning when I walked into the sports hall. There were around 50 people, mainly women, wearing pink and blue shirts with names like 'Fox Sake', Debbie Does Malice', 'Correctional Felicity' and 'Duncan Disorderly' printed on their backs. They were all wearing helmets, some had mouth guards, and they were all pumped up and ready for battle.

'You constantly expect to get knocked down,' said a smiling pig-tailed woman who went by the name of Ninjette, 'especially the jammers, everyone is targeting the jammers.'

The jammers, I thought? Music was playing, but I knew that's not what she meant. I had entered the crazy world of roller derby, one of the greatest and yet most bruising sports I have sampled to date. It's like rugby crossed with British bulldog on roller skates, played out on a tiny narrow track around a sports hall.

I will first try to explain the idea behind the mayhem. It's a contact sport, played by two teams of five skaters. Both teams skate clockwise around the track marked out by cones. You have to keep inside the track. In each session, both teams designate a jammer, who tries to score points. To do this, they have to skate through the pack, then go around another full lap before trying to muscle their way through the other skaters for a second time. This time, their own team will try to help them through, while at the same time aiming to knock the opposing team's jammer off course. It is a recipe for chaos. Just picture it: two skaters trying to get through, with eight others, known as blockers, all jostling for position.

The blockers are trying to look after their own jammer, while hindering the other team's chosen one. So you are attacking and defending at the same time. The jammer scores points for every opposing team member she or he passes.

Roller derby grew out of the roller skating marathons held in the US in the 1930s. Professional roller derbies then developed so quickly that in 1940 more than five million fans watched bouts held in dozens of American cities. But then it became a victim of its own popularity and was seen more as entertainment, with theatrical showmanship overshadowing the athletic ability. There's no doubting today, though, the participants' fitness and strength. Its revival as a sport within the last two decades has seen it take off in the UK.

From just 25 teams across the country three years ago, there are now over 100 leagues in the UK. In November 2011 the first Roller Derby World Cup was contested, and the UK came third, behind Canada and the winners from Team USA. The cup also featured teams from Ireland and Scotland as well as countries across Europe, Brazil, Argentina and Australia. It's no surprise that it's now recognised as the fastest growing women's sport in the world!

'Ladies are better physically suited to it,' I was told by one of the few men in the hall in London, Duncan Disorderly. 'They tend to have that lower centre of gravity and move around more gracefully than the guys.'

Graceful wasn't the first word that came to mind as a battering ram of a shoulder barge knocked me sideways towards the wall. I had come for a training session with the inaugural British champions the London Rollergirl Allstars, and one of their star blockers, 'Bette Noir' – who had a distinct American accent – was leading me around by the hand on my first lap.

'You can use your shoulders', she showed me with a bang and a whack, 'and you can get stuck in there with your hip.' Yep, I see that, I thought, because I had spun around and was facing the wrong way. She was taller than me and had developed a powerful technique.

It is a full-contact race but while the aim is to block with force and knock your opponents flying to the ground, it's not just about brute strength. It's about tactics; about how you position your blockers ready for the arrival of the two jammers. It's also about knowing when to make your move. The first jammer through the pack on the first lap becomes the lead jammer and can call the shots, deciding when to make the break through the pack the second time around.

There is some mercy. Elbows are not allowed and you can't just push someone off course with your hands. This is a foul and could mean time out, in the 'penalty box'.

'It's a physical release from our everyday lives,' Felicity explained, 'but we're on wheels so you get the buzz of speed. It takes agility and is really hard work too.'

Teams normally pass around the honour of being jammer during a contest and, despite my lack of roller skating experience, I got to have a go. The girls couldn't wait for me to come around having done my first lap. I wasn't lead jammer, so I had to bide my time, waiting for the opposing team's point scorer to dart for the pack. It was just prolonging my appointment with doom. I have been rolled and scythed down by members of the England women's rugby team before, but that was on grass and I knew how to fall. Here, on a hard floor, on roller skates, it seemed a far more gruesome way to go. Suddenly the lead jammer broke for a gap down the left-hand side, and with two of her team's blockers engaged, I made for the centre right, where a tiny space had appeared. I got up some speed and bunny-hopped on one skate. Past the first and then beyond a second blocker – but I was out of control, and all it took was a shoulder shove from a third blocker to send me on my way.

I sailed off the track and past the bags of kit and the wide-eyed coaches, and then I was saying goodbye to the sports hall. I had enough momentum to get me out of the open door and before I could regain control, the wet grass outside stopped me in my tracks and I was flat on my back gazing up at the stars. At least that had been a soft landing, unlike the second time when I tried to score points as a jammer.

This time my team's blockers got close, and I was shielded in a sandwich before a stray roller skate snagged my left foot. My whole leg bent back and I twisted and writhed and yelped in pain. I folded in two on the floor: a leg sticking out one way, an arm the other, taking several skaters down with me. It had been a spectacular wipe out. But what fun. It was only later I that I realised how high this must rank in the list of painful sports I have tried.

Don't let this put you off, though. Falls are part and parcel of roller derby but you are wearing helmets and knee and elbow pads, and if you are a better skater than me, you will have no such problems. It's a top team sport, with everything, tactics, action, and lots of laughter. We all have a Debbie Does Malice in us somewhere...For more information and to find your nearest club to join or watch visit: ukrda.org.uk/

FREE RUNNING/PARKOUR

I was standing there, minding my own business, about to try a forward roll on the South bank in London when someone jumped feet first onto my back. I was pushed forward and turned around to see this man somersaulting off me into the air before landing on his feet with a huge grin.

It's more interesting than shaking hands, I suppose, and this man just happened to be a former world champion in the sport of parkour or free running.

It's another sport which looks ridiculously physical and painful, but which is actually more about what goes on in your mind. Normally when we go for a run or walk, and something gets in the way, we go around it, but not in parkour, which is all about overcoming obstacles and moving from A to B in the fastest and most effective way.

'Parkour is not a physical thing,' enthused Ryan Doyle,

who's been free running all over the world and who had just vaulted me. 'It's more about getting over obstacles mentally. You can then apply it to life. If you have a position to get to, a job to go for, you will have obstacles in your way. If you have a death in your family or money issues, you now think, well yes I can overcome these problems, because I am in the habit of overcoming obstacles.'

All around me were experienced free runners, running, climbing, swinging, vaulting, leaping, and rolling around the concrete structures of the South Bank. I had come to a taster day and have to admit I was the oldest there. It was a chance to get the parkour feeling but in a safe environment. We weren't up on a building, but surrounded by mats, padding and various bits of gym equipment. Of course when you become experienced enough, you get rid of the equipment as this is meant to be 'free' running.

Now given the free spirit at the heart of this movement, its history is hard to pin down. In fact working out how it started is near impossible. For a start what is it? Is it a sport, an art, a philosophy or simply a discipline?

There is no general consensus and in his article on its history on the website www.parkourgenerations.com Dan Edwardes writes: 'You can't just go and ask the founding father, because this great movement is pretty damn far from being a nuclear family, 2.4 kids and all the rest. This child has had a whole host of surrogate step-parents influencing its development down through the years, the centuries, and indeed even through the millennia. It has drawn on many sources and supped on inspiration from all over.'

He adds that somewhere along the timeline a little area of France should be given a special mention. During the 1980s, in the suburban towns of Evry, Sarcelles and Lisses, to the south of Paris, a group of young men formed a group called L'Art du Deplacement. At the core of the group were Yann Hinautra and David Belle. One of their main reasons for wanting to explore their urban environment in entirely new ways came from David's father Raymond. He had introduced his son to the military training methods of a man called George Herbert, who'd had a major influence on the development of physical education in France. Herbert created the *parcours du combatant* – the obstacle course.

Herbert himself had been inspired when he was travelling with the French military, and had been struck by the natural, physical conditioning of indigenous people in Africa. He wanted a training programme that freed one's natural instincts, and stripped away conditioning to get a more innate, effortless way of moving around. A movement that used the entire body rather than consciously employing isolate muscle groups. This is still at the heart of parkour.

It's important to note that Belle was only one of a number of individuals who nurtured this art, along with the likes of Sebastin Foucan who trained with David Belle and is seen as another leading figure in spreading the word.

Over the years that followed the children who had played to alleviate their boredom grew into teenagers with a goal in mind, and by the age of 15 they were attempting some of the big jumps we now associate with free runners. They had taught themselves to be athletes, moving through their environment in a way never seen before in such an urban setting. They may initially have been reviled by the French authorities and seen as wild men by the public, but their reputation had spread. The media became interested and more around the world started to embrace their ideals.

Its spread to the masses is partly thanks to films such as

Breaking and Entering and *Casino Royale*, which popularised the techniques and vaulted it, into the public consensus. In the UK it's been one of the sporting success stories of the last decade, and 15,000 people do it every week. It's also now taught in some schools.

That's why I found myself crawling along a wall on the banks of the Thames in 2007, before squeezing myself through some railings and jumping off a wall. It's why I watched in disbelief as one of the country's top free runners leapt like a leopard across a huge gap from wall to wall, soaring over people below who didn't even notice him.

It is so important to learn the techniques properly and it's why clubs up and down the country teach it safely. In this sport, you always have to give 100 per cent. It's not like football, rugby or cricket, in which you might just miss a goal, try or run if you are one per cent out. If you put a toe wrong in parkour, it could mean serious injury or worse.

There was no such danger for me and the other beginners on the mats at the South Bank where we were getting a feel for the freedom. I may have stood out like a stick insect in a field of grass hoppers, with my moves lacking the fluidity, but I completed the course and despite winding myself on the final landing, stood to soak up the polite ripple of applause from the 100-strong crowd.

'My heart's buzzing, I am racing. I've never done anything like this before,' exclaimed one fellow first timer. 'That was awesome. It helps to be a gymnast,' gloated another.

'Our ancestors the great apes spent their time up there, swinging through the trees, and it's still in us,' reasoned Anthony Doyle, 'But in today's society we are told not to. We're in queues, and are socially oppressed within barriers the whole time. But this sport teaches us to view the world, without boundaries.'

My boundaries were my body's flexibility, but ever since I have been known to roll over the settee in the living room now and then, and after introducing my report live on air, I was challenged by presenter Charlie Stayt to demonstrate what I had learned. I couldn't let him down and so climbed off my chair, jumped off the small ledge on which we sit, and dived straight into a forward roll across the studio floor.

It was seamless. I even rolled back onto my feet and walked out of the studio, before turning to nod at co-presenter Louise Minchin...and knocking into a camera.

I need to work on that bit, but surely if I can perform such a move in my mid-forties, that free running spirit must be alive and kicking in us all. To find out more, and to learn how to participate safely in this potentially dangerous activity, I recommend www.parkouruk.org. For official coaching qualifications in the sport it's www.adaptqualifications.com

7

FIGHT NIGHT

As we continue our journey through the field of pain, in search of the sport that has inflicted the most suffering on me over the last seven years, we have come to the chapter that pulls no punches. I have come across some of the strongest, the biggest, the most fierce some fighters during my journey and some will stop at nothing to land the knockout blow.

ON THE ROPES

WRESTLING

The billowing pink buttocks advanced. Casting a shadow before eclipsing all light and smothering my face. It was if I had been swallowed by Mr Blobby, but these were the cheeks of British wrestler QT McFluff. His bottom was imprisoned in a fluorescent pink leotard as he performed his 'cheeky' party piece; his most lethal weapon. There was one last final blubbery squeeze and I could breathe again, released from the cellulite sandwich.

I was near the Dartford Tunnel at a wrestling school called Drop Kixx to report on the re-emergence of this sport from the glorious shadows of the past, when the greats like Big Daddy and Giant Haystacks were live on television every Saturday afternoon.

I had made the mistake of suggesting that wrestling was just a stage show, a rehearsed performance, and that it didn't really hurt. So a few minutes later, after being shown a few moves on the mat by wrestling legend Frank 'Mr Knuckles' Rimmer, I was spinning like a weathervane on top of Mc Fluff's shoulders, as he proved my ignorance before launching me into the corner padding to await what promised to be a total eclipse of the fart.

QT Mc Fluff had given me a glimpse of the punishment that wrestlers take, but in the years that followed I wondered how I could feel the full force of a fighter in the ring. Thanks to the body zorbs, in 2012 that question was answered.

The man behind body zorb football, Angus Lancaster, is a huge wrestling fan and a follower of the WWE Slam Down spectacular that has helped make the sport a hit again. Angus himself fought briefly on the amateur circuit.

In the same way that the body zorbs helped smaller kids stay injury free in football, this inflatable body armour would now enable a mere mortal like myself to take on one of the giants of the ring. So in Didcot in Oxfordshire, I found myself in the red corner, while opposite me in the blue was one of the most feared professionals on the Welsh circuit, The Bison, Adam Humphries.

Hoofing his feet back across the canvas and snorting at my earlier suggestion that this wasn't real sport and that the pain was fake, he made his charge. The walls of the body zorb are transparent so I could see 340 pounds of bearded brawn speeding towards me before the bellowing thud hit. Like the aftershock of a nuclear explosion, there was a split second before I rocked back onto the floor. However the pain never followed.

The Bison kicked and punched with all his might, and having downed me again, jumped with surprising agility onto the top of the ring frame and then, beating his chest like King Kong, launched himself in a skydive. Armageddon approached as he landed on top of me. But again the rhino skin of the tough ball cushioned his impact. Although The Bison plus gravity was almost enough to force the two layers of see-through plastic to touch, I was unscathed.

It was like an explosion underwater, but gingerly I got to my feet just in time to duck and dive. I even caught him with a rebound, using The Bison's own force to reverse back on itself. However there's nothing more dangerous than a wounded animal and he summoned his strength up enough to lift the ball with me inside it, and in one final attempt to shake me from my rubbery nest, he slam-dunked the sphere onto its side, sending a shudder through the canvas that rattled the china tea cups in the café outside. I had faced, seen and captured on mini camera, the force of a pro-wrestler at first hand. No wonder they get so angry at suggestions this doesn't hurt.

'As a rugby player in the past, I got a few bumps and bruises,' said the soft Valleys voice of Welshman Humphries, whose Bison bravado was back in the box to reveal a gentle giant of a man, 'but I can honestly say from the bottom of my heart that whenever I wrestle, the bumps you take are extremely painful. That's why when people question the authenticity of what we do – it puts people's noses out of joint.'

How The Bison didn't rearrange the nose of fellow pro James Mason as they fought the next bout I will never know. There were flying scissor kicks to the face, huge throws, slams and blows with locked fists. The room shook with each kerpow (it does feel as if you have stepped into a superhero comic strip) but unlike a cartoon, this wasn't scripted. Yes, there was showmanship, and in the same way that magicians don't reveal the secrets of the magic circle, some tricks of the trade might remain beneath the brightly coloured shorts. But I believed them when they genuinely insisted that it wasn't staged.

'You have got an idea of who you are on with,' said the friendly Mason, 'so you might know certain things about what moves they will do, but we never say "I will do this, and you will do that". We just go out and do it. I am lucky that I can feed off the crowd, and tell if the crowd want the fight to go in this direction or that direction.'

Their aim is to get the sport back into the big time, and sell it as all-round family entertainment. Thanks to the success and worldwide exposure of the American WWE series, the British wrestlers are now in action five to six nights a week on the Grand Slam and Welsh wrestling circuits, while an increasing number of new recruits are learning their sport safely at one of the UK's professional wrestling schools.

'You're gonna get battered,' said one trainee at the All Star school in Birkenhead, Sean Morales. 'You can't choreograph pain.' I had just witnessed Sean and fellow young teenage wrestler Jack Walker grimace and clutch their wrists as they threw each other through the air and onto the deck.

'The pain in there is real. You can't drop kick off the top and land on your back and not expect it to hurt,' Sean added.

'It's just 100 per cent dedication. I mean it's travelling to shows across the country, and getting up for training early, to put the ring up. But you do it, because when you want something, you just want to go out and do it.'

All these years on from Giant Haystacks and co, the passion is still as strong as ever in this sport, and with new talent being nurtured it has a solid foundation for the future. Never let anyone tell you it doesn't hurt, or you might just get McFluffed, and that doesn't include fries.

If you think the ring is calling you, then find out more about how to get started visit www.dropkixx.com, www.wrestleschool.com, www.bigtimewrestlinguk.com or www.welshwrestling.com

SUMO

I was standing in a circle in a small gym in the backstreets of Derby, wearing what resembled a giant nappy and slapping my naked thighs, while shouting something in Japanese. You might not expect to find Sumo wrestling, the ancient sport of Japan, alive and kicking in the East Midlands, but Derby is home to the UK's king of Sumo Steve Pateman's gym, which has produced wrestlers who have gone onto beat the best in the world. Steve himself defeated the world champion only four years ago and is now inspiring a whole new generation to take up this sport.

Steve is stocky, as you might expect, a completely bald hulk of a man, and when I am greeted by his generous smile, he's sitting there in just his mawashi – the traditional cloth that ties around the waist and then folds under your nether regions. While Steve's belly and moobs hang out proudly, forming the weapons in his armoury and a protective shield for his organs, I notice how strong and lean his legs are. There is a lot that will surprise you in this sport, and despite Steve's appearance, it's not necessarily about size. It's more about technique.

'Some of the best sumo wrestlers in the world are not that heavy, believe it or not,' beamed Steve. 'You have to be quite sneaky,' he added, 'you have to be so determined, just try to hang on in there and if you get hold of your opponent's mawashi, just lock in, mill around and don't give up.'

He also suggested lower body strength was key, and that suited me to the ground. Ever since doing the six marathons in six days when I was 15, and in subsequent years playing football, I have had strong, resilient legs. They might be holding up the wrong upper body, but they were the anchors for my truck pulling achievement, when Geoff Capes got me to move that lorry using mind over matter.

It was the same here in Derby. Nevertheless, having stripped down to the bare essentials in the changing rooms and having put on the mawashi, I still turned red with embarrassment as I stepped out into the circle to join a group of trainees. There was no time for blushes, though, as we went straight into a series of thigh-slapping exercises. Then it was a waddle across the floor, to further strengthen those thighs, so essential when it came to the first contest.

My opponent was Anthony, a lean, firm, athletic-looking man in his early 20s who was slightly taller than me. We stepped up to the dohyo, the mat used for sumo wrestling, observed the traditions that teach you to respect your opponent from the start, and then after a bow and a chant in Japanese from Steve, we advanced, and like rutting deer locked horns.

I dug in at an angle, feet slopping back into the mat while my head and shoulders nuzzled into Anthony's chest. My arms didn't quite know where to go, to stop Ant getting a hold, and to allow me to force him to move. The objective is simple to understand. Just push your opponent out of the circle or onto the floor. Neither of us was budging, though, as we nudged and grunted and slow-danced in a circle.

'Keep your elbows in!' bellowed Steve from the side. 'Use strength from your legs, from your quadriceps, and not your biceps.' It really was more about getting the power from your lower body and legs to drive like in rugby, up through and out via your shoulders.

I drew on my memory of the hypnotic roaring from Geoff Capes when he got me to tug that lorry along with just a harness and a rope, and with a swerve of a shoulder caught Anthony off guard.

It was as if I had unblocked a sink, and suddenly we both surged towards the edge of the mat and he was off and out. This 5'5" novice had won a sumo wrestling match. It was like a Shetland pony winning the Grand National.

Anthony wasn't too perturbed, and he confirmed it is more about technique than brute strength. 'It's hard,' he said, 'but you get into it pretty fast, and you learn that it's mostly in the head.'

Next up was the only female wrestler in class that evening. 'It's a bit scary being the only girl, but it doesn't bother me that much, especially if I win,' she said – and she did win, against a boy who was taller but several years her junior. His pride wasn't dented either. 'It makes you big and proud of yourself, being here, because you can be the champion if you keep working,' he said.

Before I had any such delusions I was put into my place by the Derbyshire junior champion, Ryan, who was the thinnest and leanest competitor there. With pure technique he sent me flying from the ring and into the buffer mats around the edge. Ryan offered a hand to pull me up. 'For me it's a lot more than about just pushing people about, most of the time. It is a contact sport though and that's what I like about it.'

The contact hadn't hurt, though. I have noticed that in all the martial arts, there is an emphasis on respect and the ancient traditions which are still at the heart of the sport. The discipline this gives young people is a tower of strength in whatever they go on to do.

CHESS BOXING

'Take his Queen, his Queen – you can get it!' screamed the delirious crowd. The two men either side of the board sat sweating and breathless in their shorts, unable to hear the chants above the heavy rock music blaring into their ears through giant black headphones.

One man advanced a bishop to remove the white queen, and beer sprayed up from the jubilant mob, dancing on the spot in celebration.

Surely it couldn't be long now. Surely this was it. But then things turned violent. A man wearing a dinner suit and black bow tie entered the fray and removed the table and chairs. The two men in their shorts were now up on their feet and the man whose queen had just gone, landed a right hook then a left, with a frenzy of blows raining down. The noise from the crowd built to another crescendo.

I was at a working men's club in East London in 2009, to witness one of the most exciting sports to have emerged in the last decade. One that combines the toughest mental challenge with one of the most physical. I was getting my first taste of chess boxing – yes, a mix of chess and boxing – and this Friday night fight was as much about rooks as Rocky. While it may sound crazy, they are in fact natural bed fellows.

The fans around me, men and women of all backgrounds and ages, were loving it. 'It's putting the brawn with the brains and the sweat,' said one man, who normally goes to rugby matches, while the lady next to him added, 'Yes, it's amazing how similar the chess and the boxing are.'

Similar? Really? Well, they both require tactics, strategy and quick thinking to outwit your opponent, and both involve thinking ahead to your next move. And you have to bide your time before knowing when to strike.

As chess commentator Malcolm Pein pointed out: 'A lot of very good boxers are also chess players. Lennox Lewis is a pretty decent chess player and the Klitchko brothers are also serious players, and are friendly with the former world chess champion Vladimir Kramnich.'

I was able to see how good Vladimir Klitchko was three years later, when we met in East London. He didn't knock me out in the ring. To be fair to him he was in a suit, while I had put on a vest and shorts in a boyish bid to get some top tips. He offered me some sparring advice about ducking and weaving before flooring me within 10 moves on the chess board. He was delighted that I too had been involved in chess boxing.

So it goes to show that the sports do complement each other, even if it does sound like something out of a comic book. Actually, that's where chess boxing is said to have come from. This hybrid sport was envisaged by the German cartoonist Eriki Bilal when it featured in his novel *Froid Equaleur* in 1992. But there are other references before that. The 1979 movie *Ninja Checkmate* is otherwise known as *The Mystery of Chess Boxing*, but it was a more of a move than a sport in this kung fu-based film. Out of this came the song in 1993 by Wu Tang Clan, also titled 'The Mystery of Chess Boxing'. It's also claimed that in London there was a boxing contest that involved some chess at the Samuel Montagu Boys club in 1978.

Whatever its true beginning, it was the Dutch artist Lepe Rubingh who took the baton and ran with it, helping to establish the first world championship in Amsterdam in 2003, which he won. In more recent years Nikolay Sazhin and Andy 'The Rock' Costello have become two of the biggest draws.

Lepe Rubingh's background was chess, but he had put in the hours in the ring too. He is now president of the world chess boxing organisation and on that night in 2009, he looked teary-eyed with emotion that hundreds of people had queued around the block to get a ringside seat. He told me the aim was to train people in the number one thinking sport and the number one fighting sport. 'Fighting is done in the ring and wars are waged on the board', he explained.

His concept has taken off around the world, from Los Angeles to Tokyo, Russia, Iceland and India. London and Berlin have seen the biggest growth, and in 2011 the Scala Club in Kings Cross held the first women's chess boxing match.

The capital has also secured funding to develop community chess boxing in inner cities and to drive it into other cities around the UK. The British chess boxing organisation now has a youth section. It offers chess coaching with a safe, non-contact fitness programme, and claims the sport, can improve classroom behaviour, mathematical skills, self-confidence, social awareness and performance.

The man who helped bring chess boxing to London, Tim Woolgar, almost burst with excitement when he told me, 'When I had my first taste of chess boxing, I grew as a person. I know it sounds crazy, but I came out feeling ten inches taller.'

I was about to find out, as I entered the ring to face the experienced Swede Conrad Rickardson. I played chess for Hertfordshire when I was at primary school, and although I had never recovered from a shock defeat to Robin Chapman, I could hold my own on the board.

It works like this. You have 11 rounds: six of chess, which are four minutes long, and five of boxing, which last three minutes. It always starts with chess and then alternates, until either there's a knockout or the referee stops the boxing round for safety reasons, or there's a check mate on the board or one of the players runs out of time to make their chess moves. They play what's known as fast chess, in which you only get 12 minutes in total to make all of your moves, and players are timed by the chess clock. To stop better boxers from stalling during the chess rounds, each player must also make a legal move during the four minutes, or they face a warning and possible disqualification.

The concept seems straightforward and the early exchanges on the chess board were simple enough. 'Rook to E4', shouted the referee. I couldn't really hear him with the headphones on, which block out the commentator and the crowd, but his lips, seemed to move in that way .

Then, when the bell goes, it's a tap on the shoulder and you have less than a minute to get rid of the board, and the headphones, and to flex those muscles, pull both gloves on, and take your stance. I hadn't had much boxing training and so Conrad was careful not to connect properly, but it was an intense three minutes of bouncing on my toes and letting the odd paw come through my guard. I shied away from learning too much about trading punches, and got Conrad talking instead:

'There's a lot of adrenalin pumping through your veins after the boxing and coming back to the chess game, and having to concentrate, that's not easy,' he explained.

He wasn't joking; the pieces seem blurred as we returned to the board. You are bulging with testosterone and yet you must wipe away the sweat and think calmly and rationally, with the headphones back on.

I got through another round of chess, but with the boxing promising to become more intense I lay down my king and let the experts show the crowd how it's really done.

Now while world-class chess boxers must be experienced

fighters, and at least Class A strength in chess, this isn't the case if you want to get involved in the sport as a beginner.

Don't be put off by the idea that they are all experts. The British organisation caters for all levels of ability in both disciplines. It will be a challenge, there's no doubt about that, but whether it's just for fun, or at a competitive level, all the people I met were sure of one thing. The rewards are worth all the effort, and it prepares you to deal with anything life can throw at you. I went to the gym that night with issues hanging heavy on my heart, but I came out energized. The atmosphere plugs you in to a heady mix of sporting thrills, glamour and intense concentration.

As for which comes out on top, well, all the bouts I saw that night were won on the chess board. For more information and to attend an event or get involved visit www.londonchessboxing.com or the world organisation at www.office@wcbo.org

8

WALK ON WATER

We've been thrown around in the air, pummelled by shinty sticks and flattened in the ring, but for the next adrenalin rush and potential for pain, we step onto the water. It's not a case of paddling about on the river like ratty and mole in Wind in the Willows, when you meet it at speed, water can be like a wall of concrete, On this island, there's water, water everywhere, and not surprisingly as a nation, its where we are most at home, whether we are sailing on it, riding on it, rowing on it, or finding new ways to enter or get across it.

GETTING WET

THE TOUGH GUY EXPERIENCE

'Jump, jump, jump', the school party bayed. It wasn't just the distance, about three metres down from the wooden plank, that I was worried about. It was January, and the murky water would be close to freezing. In the distance a couple of bull mastiff dogs took their seats for the humiliation, while the ringleader, a distinguished gentleman called Mr Mouse, tapped his cane and twitched his white crossbow of a moustache.

Was this punishment for my watery crime when I was 10 years old? Was I being made to walk the plank above this lake, on a farm near Wolverhampton, because I had pushed my close friend Peter Haynes into the Ashwell village springs?

A drop of water from the damp air skied down my nose and took the plunge, reminding me of my precarious position. The school kids on the steps of the wooden tower were almost shaking with excitement. So I closed my eyes and let myself fall through the crisp air, holding my breath and waiting for the chilly wet embrace. If the water didn't shiver me timbers, there were plenty of other hurdles to break my resolve: the electric shock treatment, the rat-infested barn, the barbed wire and the fire.

I was getting a taste of one of the UK's most popular winter sporting events. Yes, people actually pay for this experience in their leisure time. There is also a 'Tough Guy' event in June, but I reckon the ice and the snow add that extra bit of fun.

The Tough Guy endurance race was the concept of an ex-army barber who has renamed himself Mr Mouse. 28 years ago he set off on a mission to give people in these 'molly-coddled days' an idea of what it was like in the First World War trenches.

'People come here and they say "it's changed my life",' he mused. 'They say it's made them a man, or a woman, as we say nowadays. When you are really down there and on the front line, on the wall or wherever, what have you got? You have got your mates, your companionship, and it's fear and pain that joins us together.'

Whatever it is, it's working. 5,000 people take part from all over the world. I went along at the start of 2012, when the youth event was launched for children over 10. Now they don't have to go through the burning straw, and they have to be 14 to jump off the plank into the chilly pool. They also don't have to go through the barn with live electric wires dangling above them. To be fair it's only like touching an electric fence, but when you're wet, that still nips.

The kids who had joined me on this eight-mile course with its 100 obstacles, from huge climbing towers and rope challenges to tightrope walks over water and muddy crawls under barbed wire, loved every minute.

'It's good exercise, and fun, and I loved getting muddy,' said one. 'I wanted to fall off and jump into the nettles,' added another. 'It's real, whereas when you go to a theme park, you know you are strapped into the ride and it's safe whereas if you look at these obstacles, they're big and hard to overcome and they push you to your limits.'

One girl had been less sure. 'I was shaking because I was scared, in case I fell through, but I overcame that and now I feel good and proud.'

Imagine being the head teacher of the school, taking your students along and having kittens in these days of health and safety.

'Well, yes, if I had seen it before hand I might have done,' said the glowing head as he emerged from a tunnel of mud, 'but look at them, they have done fantastic, and am so proud of them...and there's no braver head teacher in the country than this.'

For more information on the Tough Guy event, visit www.toughguy.co.uk

WATERSKIING AND WAKEBOARDING

There's surely no better feeling than walking on the water, especially when you can master it before you leave primary school. That's what Jack and Joe Battleday could boast when I met them at the JB Waterski centre in Surrey. Jack was the under-11 National Wakeboarding champion, while his brother Joe was still only eight. Their blonde locks bounced through the sunshine as they skipped across the water, skimming over jumps and performing twists and somersaults on their way around the lake. All around them, much older enthusiasts were crashing head first into the water as they tried to follow the young brothers' lead. It helps that their father, John was a former European waterski champion. He'd made the switch to wakeboarding when it became popular, at the same time as snowboarding was tempting skiers to try something new.

It's no surprise, given the young talent I saw in 2008, that in 2012 Team GB won the overall gold medal at the European Championships in Kiev after picking up three individual golds and two silvers.

It was my first go at wakeboarding, but I was up on my feet behind a boat and bobbling over the wake within the first half an hour. I had once had success barefoot waterskiing, when you just use your feet as your skis, but having a board strapped on gave me much more flexibility and movement. After your first lesson behind a boat, you can graduate onto a cable tow. Once I had got used to the initial jerk off the jetty, it was turning into a pleasant and even smooth ride around the lake – until that is I realised that at some point I would either have to turn, to continue around the circular route, or eat the grass on the bank. The turning cable out-foxed me every time and rather than ending up head first in some moorhen's nest, I let go of the bar and slowly sank into the water. It was then a swim back to the start again.

I had the same problem turning when I filmed a waterskiing feature at the Hazelwood Waterski Centre in Lincolnshire. There I would meet the Extreme waterski jumper June Fladborg. She held the world record with an incredible jump of 57.1 metres, and was world number one at the time. That record has since been broken by the Italian Natalia Berdnikava.

For more information on waterskiing and wakeboarding go to the website: www.britishwaterski.org.uk.

Don't let the cold, dark winter nights put you off either, because help is at hand.

INDOOR SURFING

No, I am not talking about the internet here, or about my small nephews Ben, Sam or Dominic using a cushion to surf down my sister's new sofa.

I am talking about the reason I was standing half-naked on a pelican crossing in Bedford on a cold wet November night. There are so many new ways to cross the water these days, whether it's standing up on a paddleboard (one of the more accessible water sports for beginners) or rekindling old traditions by going out on the ocean waves, surf-boat rowing, or gig rowing. And for those who like their speed, and have great balance, surf ski will test that to the limit.

Before we get back to Bedford, I must tip my hat to one of the hardest sports I have tried, and therefore one of the most humiliating sporting experiences I have had (and there have been a few). Kite surfing looks spectacular from the shore, given the air that boarders can get, but it does take some working on. I was told I needed several weeks learning how to master the power of the wind on the shore first. It can lift you off your feet, and you need to know how to harness the power so it's on your side and not trying to remove the arms from your shoulders. But I had just a couple of hours to practise on Watergate Bay in Cornwall, which is why I subsequently spent the afternoon hurtling horizontally through the surf, with arms clinging on to the line before spearing the water, like a harpoon.

Take it from me, that's not a good idea and kite surfing needs to be treated with the respect it deserves. Allow plenty of time – as I am planning to do in 2013 – to lay this particular ghost to rest.

You might think that surfing is just a summer activity, which gets more difficult once the nights start drawing in, making it difficult to do after school or work. Well not any more, which is why cars were flashing their headlights at me as I crossed that pelican crossing in Bedford. It was perfectly normal in fact for us all to be dressed in wetsuits and nothing else as we sauntered across the road, boards tucked under our arms, that damp November evening. After all, 'surf's up', we had been told.

At over 100 centres around the world, they have brought the sea to the people and so now in landlocked Bedford you can ride the waves in the warmth of a large hanger-type building. You step with your board onto a huge springy trampoline, which is bigger than a tennis court and slopes down from a wall to a level area at the bottom.

Over this flows 100,000 litres of water, which is recycled every minute. It's four inches deep, which may not sound much, but when it's travelling at 30 miles per hour it will knock you flying back into the deeper trough at the top, unless you can really master its flow. There's no waiting for the big one here – there's no let up at all as the surf just keeps coming.

Even experienced surfers start off on their bellies, and then it's up onto their knees as they launch themselves down the slope and into the onrushing white froth. It's a case of how long you can stay there. If you quickly tuck your knees up onto the board, it's possible to stand, but the slightest of slips causes you to catch an edge of the tickling tide, which will flick the front of the board and send you tumbling up into the white wash at the top where you can get out. It doesn't hurt, but will tumble dry your senses as you are engulfed for a second or two in this washing machine of water. After just a few goes, you do find your feet and the great thing is that children as young as four can take part, without anyone worrying about them being swept out to sea.

Elliot Eames thought it was the funniest sight ever when his dad, Mark, lost his balance first and disappeared in a tunnel of turbulence.

'I've had a one-hour session and you can go over and over again. Down in Newquay, or wherever, you can be out getting cold for three hours, and maybe get only four waves,' said Mark as he shook the water out of his ears.

Obviously the view isn't quite the same as the stunning coastline of Cornwall, but it has helped British surfers improve their standings. Having triumphed at the European flow riding championships, Europe's finest took on the world in the world championships in Singapore and came a close second to the USA.

There is now a flow boarding League Of the World, and watching the top riders jump several feet through the air, before landing in the surf and then gliding up and down the ramp with board flips and jumps thrown in as well, you realise why they want to stay on the waves all day. You never reach the shore, and so never face that long walk and paddle out again.

There are now two indoor surfing locations at Bedford and Castleford. Visit www.flowhouse.co.uk

BRUSHBOARDING

There is also now an alternative for those who don't even want to get wet. What's more it's a form of indoor surfing that would push those expert flow riders to the limit. It's called Brush-Boarding and involves a quarter-pipe skateboarding ramp that has thousands of specially designed rotating brushes. They turn at variable speeds so fast they create a carpet of air on which snowboarders and surfers can hone their skills.

You wear a helmet and knee and elbow pads, but again if you fall, it doesn't hurt and it really works your core, thighs and knees, as you try to push against the tide of moving brushes and air to stay on your feet. It's like standing on a giant electric toothbrush.

Again there were primary school children lapping up the experience when I went along to have a go. 'It's fun, I absolutely loved it,' said Amy. 'If you can't swim, this is a great alternative to surfing,' said an older lad who had come to try it with his school.

The head of the Exeter School Sports Partnership added: 'Not everyone gets turned on by mainstream sports, so I am very passionate about offering a wide and varied extra curriculum programme, and BrushBoarding is an excellent way to do that.'

The Australian who brought the idea to the UK in 2009, Kyle Dent, admitted it will never fully replace surfing or snowboarding, but said: 'Work-life integration means most people don't have the time to get to the pistes or the ocean, but having practiced on the Brush Ramp, they will be more physically ready to enjoy the thrills nature delivers.'

Above: Heads down and arms in! The G forces were so intense hurtling down the Riga bobsleigh track I couldn't even lift my head up to admire the scenery.

Below: Zorbing football – Mr Blobby meets *Match of the Day*. It may not be the beautiful game but it's fun, and has proved effective at getting non-sporty pupils into sport.

Above: The river is wild… in Cardiff. You don't have to go to the Rockie‹ for some rapid action anymore with these man made wild water courses now being built in Cardiff and at the Olympic London 2012 venue.

Below: Ice cricket is all about slipping and sliding – and it's the one crick‹ trophy that the Australians have never won.

Above: This is the closest you can get to being Superman. Fly boarding can be great fun, but kink that hose and it's a very fast sinking feeling.

Below: Snookered by the tree! A common hazard in Crolf.

Above: There are so many ways to surf now: on waves, huge carpets of brush, or in inner cities.

Below left: Wife carrying is a steeplechase for couples. Originally Finnish intimate competition is making its way in Britain.

Below right: Steph and I made wife carrying history by reversing the role Despite my fidgeting we finished, and Steph is still speaking to me!

BMXing is now an Olympic sport, with popular riders like Shanaze Reade at the fore. They normally start young, at 3 or 4. I was slightly older.

Worm charming can be incredibly competitive, with thousands flocking to the annual championships in Cheshire. And don't worry, no worms are hurt in the process.

op tips from Luke Donald. He went on to have a nightmare at the
Ventworth PGA and blamed me.

Above: *Strictly Come Dancing* winner Louis Smith put me through my paces on the pommel horse and I ended up flat on my face.

Below: One of the iconic moments of 2012 was Richard 'The Monster' Whitehead storming around the bend to take 200m Paralympics gold. Incredibly, he is also a marathon record holder.

It certainly helps you keep going through the winter without getting wet, cold or lost and the mobile Brush Ramp is taking snowboarding and surfing into the inner cities. It's bringing the mountains and shore to thousands of youngsters and adults who rarely get the chance to develop such skills.

There is now a BrushBoarding international championship too, and for anyone who thinks they have mastered this sport, the speed of the brushes can be ramped up or down according to ability and until it's almost impossible to stay on the board. The top riders are judged on their tricks and jumps as well as how long they can stay up.

For more information on BrushBoarding visit: www. info@extremesportszone.co.uk

FLYBOARDING /JET PACKING

At least in indoor surfing you will never have to face any of the dangers that lie in open water. If it's possible to sweat while under water, I lost buckets when hanging out at the bottom of a shark-infested tank at an aquarium near Chester for a Children in Need challenge. I didn't fancy being the 12 foot long sand tiger shark's lunch, so it was essential I went in after they had been fed, and the advice was to keep still on the bottom of the tank, and don't make any sudden movements. Naturally I didn't flinch.

But the adrenalin rush I got at the bottom of that shark tank was nothing compared to the 'Bad Girls' in their cougar powerboats. If you are looking to be slapped in the face by jowl-stretching speed, then join Shelley Jory and Libby Keir, the fastest girls on the water.

I joined Shelley as her co-pilot, but to my horror there were no seat belts or straps to keep you in – apparently because you need to get away from the boat quickly if it crashes. 'You won't even have time to think about it,' Shelley reassured me, 'you will be spat out like a cork'. She broke into a wicked laugh as we jumped the bow wave from an Isle of Wight Ferry.

Leaping out of the water in the boat is an incredible feeling, and there's now a sport in the UK that spits you out at the rate of 60 litres a second. And you don't have to worry about being crashing at speed.

In a quiet marina on the west coast of England, they have spotted a new sea creature gliding between the swans and the boats. Is it a bird? No. Is it a plane? No. But flying like Superman is involved.

I was on my stomach waiting in the calm waters of Portishead Marina, waiting for it to strike. There was a gurgle and a gushing of bubbles, which grew louder as the sea snake got nearer, and then before I could turn around, it grabbed me by the feet and pushed me into the air...

It was a rushing sensation I had never experienced before, and I was powerless to stop it. I felt like a tiny toy in a giant kid's hand and expected to see two huge eyes peering through the cloudy sky. I was looking down, though, because as I glanced to my left I was level with the people who had stopped to wonder on the harbour wall. I was nine metres above the water, tottering on a tower of froth.

My feet didn't know what to do with themselves. They were wobbling to and fro, just to stabilise my fear, and to further steady myself I titled to the right. Now I was turning, spinning to the right, too fast, and out of control. I was tossed aside like a stone, and fell with a smack on to the water. I let out the cry of a shot pheasant, but realising I was only stunned by the anticipation of pain, I soon wanted another go.

I had joined a group of beginners aged 17 and above for my first taste of flyboarding, or water jet- packing, as it has also been called. It has caught on in other parts of the world, but only really took off in the UK within the last year. There are now centres in Chepstow, Peterborough and Dumfries that offer this experience. Further centres are planned for 2013 at Farnborough, London Docklands, and Loch Lomond.

You put on special jet boots which have two giant holes in the bottom underneath your feet. You are connected via a giant red hose to a jet ski, on which sits your driver. They can control your power and height with their throttle, but it's up to the rider, like a water skier, to control speed, movement and direction. The power comes from a jet of water that surges up the hose pipe and into your boots. It then thrusts at enormous speed out of those boots, propelling you into the air. In theory you can rise as high as the hose, to 10 metres, but once I had got to nine, it felt enough distance to fall – if and when I did lose my balance.

The first time you will pop in and out of the water like a bird learning to fly, rising just a metre or two before flopping back in. Then as you find your feet, and start riding like a snowboarder, you can get up higher, and stay there for longer, and the nose dives become less frequent. My mistake had been to turn too tightly and too quickly. Just as when you get a kink in the hose in the garden, it immediately shuts off the water, so my power was cut and I was poleaxed. Once I had learned to avoid this, I was staying in the air for 20 minutes at a time, and could start to learn some tricks.

Communication with your jet ski driver is key. It was 'thumbs up' to increase the power and height and 'thumbs down' to slow down and drop gently to the surface. The rest is up to your feet. I followed the lead of a tattooed man who'd gone before me without a wetsuit on, and his cries of pain when he slapped the water convinced me I had done the right thing by wearing one. I noticed he was flicking his toes back and forth like a rudder. You tilt them forward to move and rock back onto your heels to slow. Then lean the top half of your body to turn. Once you have relaxed, the turning happens more naturally and you can start slaloming, swerving through an imaginary course of obstacles. Then with the help of you driver, you can rollercoaster like a dolphin, dropping on a steep curve forward through the water, face and hands first, before rising straight out of the wash again and up for another go.

When it was done at speed, by expert Angus Lancaster, (the same man who had introduced those water walking giant balls), it looked so majestic. 'It's just like being a superhero,' he said, 'like the movies, and you've seen yourself it's not that hard.'

The other beginners nodded. 'Weird', 'Amazing to get levitating like that', 'I screamed a lot but wow, rising out of the water like that, just unreal' were the general reactions.

When you are ready you can go solo. This means you have hand controls known as hand jets, up with you that let you remotely work the controls of the jet ski. In this case you are in control of your height and power. It does give you more to think about as you become more experienced and it's the way competitors raced in the last world flyboard championships in Doha, won by Stephane Prayas of France.

The first UK championship is due to be held in 2013.

As a beginner, though, I was only too glad to have the jet ski instructor 10 metres away below me, even if he couldn't prevent me plummeting onto my back those couple of times. Also if I'd had handles to control, I wouldn't have been able to flap my arms like a bird, and this seemed rather important to maximise the sense of freedom.

Water jet packing and fly boarding are still so new in the UK that they are expensive to run, and so an initial session won't leave you much change from £50, or £100 if you want enough time to really master the basics. This will restrict its spread initially, but with the UK championship in the pipeline and more people doing it, the hope is that it will become more common, and that the price will fall and surfers and boarders will see this as the new wave to conquer.

It certainly makes for a spectacular spectator sport, and by the end of my session a large group of school kids on their way home were clapping admiringly on the harbour wall: a contrast, I thought, to the teenagers calling goading me to jump into that freezing lake on the Tough Guy course.

For information about flyboarding and water jet packing, please go to www.wetjets.co.uk, www.flyboarding.co.uk or www.waterwalkerz.com

RAFT RACING

It was a cold, damp autumn night and I was climbing through a weeping willow tree to see what was stirring on the water. An owl hooted and there was a cry of 'hut' coming from the dark void below. To my right a web of smoke danced its way elegantly through a pool of light which beamed from a houseboat moored on the Grand Union Canal in Hertfordshire.

I stumbled down the wet bank towards the canal, and suddenly out of nowhere it appeared: a big black hairy dog, ran around the bend. Its ears pricked as droplets of water bounced off its beard onto the path and into the pools of moonlight. The hound didn't stop at me though; it was anxious to keep up with what was lurking in the canal.

It may have been pitch black, but there on the canal were three large rafts with four people paddling away on each. They had a couple of head torches which lit up the end of their boat, but apart from that they were training in the dark.

'It's because we are nutters,' said Tom Fryer, captain of the men's team. 'Us rafters have a reputation for being nuts and we love training right through the winter in the dark.' Indeed they keep going even when the canal is thick with sheets of ice and they have to pick their way through the solid blocks.

'It's beautiful at night,' Tom added; 'we have bats swooping down and looking for insects in the tiny shafts of light from our torches. We seem to go faster when it's dark too. It heightens our senses because we have lost our sense of sight, and so our others make up for it, and we are much more focused on our technique. It does improve our strokes.'

So much so that when they train during the day or in the summer, they close their eyes for part of the three-mile run up the canal.

The captain of the women's team, Cherry Fryer, also reckons it develops a greater team spirit. 'It could be scary out there in the dark on your own, but because there are four or sometimes 10 in a team, there is a feeling of togetherness in the blackness,' she explained.

The team are one of about 20 raft clubs now left in the UK, who race at weekends. There used to be over 90. The teams build their own rafts for about £500, and they usually involve two long fibreglass bows with aluminium poles joining them together. The little plastic seats are your perch and are no wider than your bottom. Despite this, I found the raft to be incredibly sturdy as I joined the women's and men's teams for a paddle into the darkness. I had my legs out in front of me and started paddling to my left. At night it is a magical feeling, with just my head torch lighting up my outstretched trainers as I sat precariously on my leg of the raft.

I couldn't see the water. It was just a black carpet on which we were sliding and I was only reminded it was there by the regular splashes thrown up by my paddle. On the cry of 'hut' from my team member Isla Mae on the other aluminium pole from me, I had to count one stroke, before paddling on my right. The black hole ahead was drawing us in. The shaft of visibility from the canal boat was fading behind us, and it was now down to the teams' natural instincts.

The club has members from 16 to 65 years old and stressed that this sport is accessible. 'If you have 10 people on a hockey team,' Cherry told me, 'you might have one weak link and it will show, you might concede a goal. But in this sport, if you have one weaker person on the raft, they aren't going to slow you down much.'

Several members of this Wonder Y team, based at Tring, are also regular paddlers. Tom is built like Sir Steve Redgrave, with the rippling muscles and long reach, but he likes to raft because he says it's more working class than rowing and is more open to people who have to work and can't spend several hours a day training.

'It's still competitive,' said Tom, 'but it still involves a pub afterwards, and we can do this and have a pint and a curry and it's not going to affect our form.'

They are well placed to talk about form, having won the Great River race which is open to all sorts of craft in London. Here on the Grand Union Canal, which was once a transportation route from Birmingham to London, the Wonder Y team train two or three times a week before racing at weekends. They also form part of the British dragon boat racing team.

And if you are wondering why they are called 'Wonder Y', needless to say it came about after a few beers in the pub in 1988, when a Welshman new to the area suggested they started building a raft to race down the canal. Several weeks later, back in the pub, cold and wet, they wondered why on earth they were doing it. Having been for one of their night time training sessions, I can definitely see why. It's a fantastic way to earn a pint.

To get involved find your nearest raft club or contact www.raftrace.org.uk. Further up the rafting ladder there is the white water raft race series, involving races on the country's white water courses.

This is where it gets more extreme, as you are battling against huge swirls and whirlpools, as you bobble down a course of white froth. Contact the British raft team on www.britishraftteam.co.uk

WATERPOLO

I have saved the most painful watersport until last. I am talking about the mayhem I had experienced when I joined the British water polo champions in Sheffield a couple of years earlier. The Rotherham Metro side wanted to show me what they have to put up with under the water, where there is a grey area around what's seen and allowed.

All I can say is that it's a good job I had already played my part in producing children. It was like being bitten by a toothless shark, and a gentle squeeze was all that as needed for me to willingly release the match ball. My eyes watered as if in an ocean of onions, but they had been opened to what a tough sport water polo is.

It is a contact sport, and while you are not allowed to deliberately hit, kick or punch your opponent, you have to be prepared for the unexpected and the occasional 'foul' that goes unnoticed. In all the splashing around a tackle, you can't always tell what's happening underneath. Despite my rude awakening, water polo remains one of my favourite sports for action and physical exertion.

It is sometimes called rugby in water and that's how the modern game started: played in rivers and lakes, in England and Scotland. The first rules were developed in the late nineteenth century in Great Britain by William Wilson, and in the early days, wrestling and holding opposing players underwater to recover the ball was allowed. Now that there is more control, it's perhaps closer to handball, but trying to dodge your opponents, so you can throw the ball into their net, while all the time treading water, requires immense lung power and athleticism. You can't push yourself up on water, so it's all about your core body strength to lift you up out of the water to get power behind a throw.

It is utterly exhausting and if you add to that, the tackling: the hit from an arm or charge or something less legal, it's easy to see why only the fittest and strongest athletes will survive for more than a few minutes.

The British team may have gone out of London 2012 at the group stage to the reigning champions Hungary, but their spirit in the face of adversity was there for all to see, and they are gaining ground with Rio 2016 to aim for. The British water polo league, which started in 2010, now includes five men's divisions and three women's.

For more information go to
www.swimming.org/britishswimming/water-polo

THE RISE OF THE ZORB, AND OTHER INFLATABLE BALLS

Dr Who has the Daleks and Cybermen, as his regular foes. Over the last seven years giant inflatable balls, often called zorbs, have been my nemesis. Each time I think I have mastered them, they have reincarnated themselves in an even more lung-busting, head-spinning, pain inducing form. They are the time lords of short, sharp, aerobic exercise and I am not surprised they have invaded earth with such force.

I blame the hamsters. The innocent looking rodents were the pioneers. Rolling around in their plastic spheres having so much fun, covering great distances around the kitchen since the early 1970s.

But the question is, how did this activity spread to us human beings? A Russian article from 1973 refers to a sphere similar to a human zorb. By the way 'Zorb' is a brand name, used by the one of the companies that started it commercially in New Zealand in the 1980s. It has spread across the world, but other names now include hill rolling, sphering or giant inflatable balling. What's all this got to do with water? We'll come to that. But first, here's a potted history of zorbing.

It is said that the Oxford-based group of extreme sport adventurers who called themselves the 'Dangerous Sports Club' first experimented with putting people into a giant ball in the early 1980s. The idea came from a Welsh artist and the first prototype was 70 foot high. Inside two deckchairs were suspended in the middle for people to sit on during the ride.

However, according to the club, they moved on to other ideas because their ball needed zero wind to be handled effectively, and it was left to the New Zealanders to pick up the concept later on. The Dangerous Sports Club, which included the legendary Graham Chapman from the Monty Python team, did have many successes though, and can be thanked for developing modern bungee jumping and other extreme activities. They remain a club more interested in innovation than marketing and can be contacted on www.thedangeroussportsclub.co.uk

The idea that an inflatable ball could capture people's imagination hadn't gone unnoticed and they reappeared on TV in 1990 in the *Gladiators* series. Admittedly these were steel balls, but the birth of the zorb as we know it today wasn't far away.

In 1994, New Zealanders Andrew Akers and Dwane Van Der Sluis finally designed a giant inflatable ball, in which people could safely move along in, and a new sporting craze was literally on a roll. So much so that by 2001, zorbing entered the Concise Oxford English Dictionary, and it wasn't long after I started my search for unusual sports in 2006 that I was contacted by a chap called Paul from Zorbing South, the pioneers of zorbing in the UK.

'It's the longest and fastest zorb run in the UK,' explained Paul. 'It's 200 metres from the launching platform to the landing point.' I think Paul sensed a wavering in my voice because he then added: 'we do have a 100 per cent safety record.'

Obviously the BBC takes safety very seriously and before every assignment there are forms to be filled in, risks to be assessed and signed off by your line managers. While this was to be an extreme adrenalin-draining descent, zorbing is a safe activity. There are two layers of flexible plastic with a solid cushion of air in between, softening any bumps. What's more you are strapped in for safety and comfort. Well that's the theory.

It might come as a surprise, but I am not a huge fan of roller coasters or theme park rides that spin you upside down and round and round. I used to get car sick in a dodgem and the only time I go on theme park rides is to give my eldest daughter Lucy moral support. But this was for work, so I had to grin and bear it. The *Breakfast* producers Julia and Katie seemed rather pleased by the fact that the activity had passed all the health and safety checks and so having stopped off at a Bournemouth pet shop to get some shots of a hamster for the opening sequence, I met the camerawoman Deirdrie at the top of a hill in Dorset.

Deirdrie and I were strapped to the inner ring of the ball opposite each other. Deirdrie had filmed all over the world. She was an action woman, always keen to give new experiences a go in the name of art. She was such a skilled operator that she was prepared to hold a small camera while inside the ball, to give the viewer the sense of what this new experience was like. There was a strap over it to make sure it didn't fly around. It was hot and humid inside as we rocked gently on the spot, before there was a shout and a push and we teetered over the edge.

A gentle roll became a tumble, a tumble became a bump and a bang, then a twist and a thump. Ouch – I needed to brace my neck and back for that next time. 'Urm…arghh …whaaaay…wooo …!' – sound like you are enjoying it, Bushell, I thought, but my reactions were out of control. 'Argghh! This is stupid! This is madness!' was all I could say, and hang on, where was Deirdrie? Actually, where was anything? Where was my head? Where was the earth? We were revolving head-over-heels gaining speed with every turn and the land and sky merged into one, giving us a feeling of weightlessness.

I could see now we had come to rest, but was Deirdrie awake? She opened her eyes looking as queasy as I felt. The camera was pointing down, but there was no red light. That was the least of our worries as a face appeared at the hole through which we were to escape. We spluttered out head and arms first and grappled with each other as we tentatively rose to our feet. Wow, what a feeling. We hugged, we broke into a smile – we had done it and we had loved it. We had conquered the world and it would surely make great television. Or would it? That little red light wasn't on the camera, and with an air of resignation, we scrolled back through the tape. There were lovely shots of us both getting in, and strapping up, and then the first bounce and then...nothing. The judder and jolt had been so strong it had turned the camera off.

I don't blame Deirdrie in the slightest for not wanting a second go, as it dawned on me what I had to do. So it was back to the top and I was ready to roll again, only this time knowing what was in store and this time with one of the expert zorbers opposite me, the camera strapped close to his body with tape over the on/off switch.

The second time is never as bad. 'We just need a different angle' was enough to get me in for a third descent, which really the strongest of stomachs aren't designed to cope with. I'll admit I did have to make a dash for the nearest bush after that one.

But don't follow my lead – just one trip down that hill will give you all the thrills you need, and it is worth it for the experience. And f you don't fancy the extreme ride, there is also a wonderful way to relax and get clean at the same time, while still rolling down in a zorb.

HYDRO ZORBING

Despite the idea of rolling down a hill still making me feel slightly queasy, I wanted to get a taste of hydro zorbing. I'm glad I did, because it was one of the loveliest feelings I have had. You enter the zorb, but don't get strapped in this time. Instead they throw in buckets of warm water over you. It's like hosing down an elephant at the zoo after it's been rolling in the mud, and eventually there is mammoth-sized puddle in the bottom of the ball. You then sit or even lie down and wait for the weirdest bath you will ever have. Imagine lying there, drifting off in the bubbles, but then suddenly your bath becomes a time machine, the world revolving around it as you slip and slide through the rotations. On this descent, there are no bumps and there's no dizziness, because you don't feel as if you are moving. It's the water that's spinning around you. I finally felt like the hamster who had invented the wheel.

ZORBING RECORDS

- The Guinness Book of records acknowledges two world records to give the hamsters a run for their money.
- The longest ride in a large inflatable ball on dry land was 570 metres.
- The fastest time in a zorb over 100 metres was 26.59 seconds, set by former England cricketer Andrew Flintoff for BBC Sport Relief. Meanwhile Keith Kolver recorded a top speed of 32 mph in one.

The zorbing invasion of Great Britain had only just begun, though. It was a couple of years later at a swimming pool in Southampton that they appeared again.

This time they weren't called zorbs. There was just one layer of flexible plastic. If you have been on an activity holiday in this country, or to a theme park, you will have seen these balls designed for tiring you out on the water, and might have paid £5 or so for a five-minute ride. You step through you a gap which is zipped up behind you and then roll onto a swimming pool or small lake. The aim is to stand up and run, but at first you go nowhere, except onto your face or your bottom.

Yes, it looks hilarious to your mates watching and filming on the side, but inside it gets hotter, sweatier and the air gets thinner by the minute. With a bit of practise, the technique will come and by leaning forward and going full pelt on your toes (if Usain Bolt was a hamster he'd be good in one of these) you will turn the ball underneath your feet and may even move very slowly across the water.

I defy anyone to do more than just a few of these sprints before collapsing to the base of the sphere in absolute exhaustion. The air in there eventually will run out, so the instructors will haul you in after a maximum of six minutes. Most people stay in for just three or four minutes, and it has proved to be an effective way of getting children who thought swimming was boring into a pool.

At the same time it is now sometimes used by professional swimmers, to build up their fitness and aerobic stamina. It's a great way to work on breathing techniques. It still goes down as one of the most complete workouts I have tried.

THE ZORBING MILE

For Sport Relief 2012, producer Katie McDougall had one parting shot at me before she left the BBC to go freelance. She would let the *Breakfast* viewers decide how I should do the Sport Relief mile. In previous years I had completed the mile down the Mall on a space hopper...it took one hour 37 minutes, because for every two bounces forward there was one bounce back.

Then there was the Manchester mile on powerbocks. These are highly-sprung stilts, which are brilliant for giving you the legs of a kangaroo, and they elevated my sporting prowess, making me nine feet tall, until I stumbled into the railings to chat to Tony Livesey broascasting live on the John Inverdale programme on BBC 1.

So for 2012, we had to find something to top that, and the nominations were: bog snorkelling, yes for a whole mile; stand-up paddle boarding, which is a way to walk on water across the sea, and is a combination of punting, rowing and surfing; horseboarding, which involves riding around a field on a mountain board being towed by a horse; street surfing, where you wiggle your hips to get moving on a bendy board along the streets, and finally a lung-busting mile across open water in a giant inflatable ball.

I thought another trip to the depths of the bog and a reunion with the water scorpions would be bad enough, but I guess the viewers, wanting to see pain, thought that would be over too quickly, as a mile was only 35 lengths of the murky trench. A mile in the ball, however, would be more of a physical challenge in every way. The ultimate revenge for the zorb, as it would literally suck the air and life out of me.

It had never been done before. The Waterwalkerz coach, Angus Lancaster, didn't think it could be done at all, as the balls aren't designed to go forwards or backwards. Even when you get your legs going, the thing just tends to spin around on the spot. Nevertheless, this was for Sport Relief and reassured by the presence of a support boat, with an oxygen tank, I rolled off the jetty at Willen Lake in Milton Keynes.

The plastic surface slides beneath your feet like a giant ray trying to slide you off its back. It was even harder to stand up on the lake water than it had been in the swimming pool because even on a calm day, there was a constant wave, and so more resistance. The key to success here was to stay on my feet, lean forward and sprint as if life itself depended on it.

I was feeling nauseous, and the world beyond my plastic dome was starting to blur into a foggy delirium. This was the warning sign that it was time for the support team to reel me in, using the line of rope that trailed behind the ball to the boat.

The fresh air that poured into my lungs as I thrust my head

through the unzipped hole was like pure nectar, and I lay back in the sunshine, waiting for confirmation that I had covered my first third or maybe half a mile. Not a chance. I had managed a mere 200 metres. Usain Bolt can run that in 19 seconds.

It wouldn't have been possible to complete this challenge without coming up for air. The oxygen gets finer and poisonous gases eventually build up, and so I was only able to push my stay to the limit thanks to the tank of oxygen waiting on the boat.

The crew would watch each time I went back inside for the telltale signs that the air was running out – whether it was me slumping to the base of the ball, or talking nonsense. The trouble is I do this at the best of times, especially in my sleep. I once turned to my partner and wished her 'Happy Goatmas'. I was fast asleep and it was October, and I was dreaming about goats celebrating their version of Christmas. Back in the ball I was murmuring 'Slowly, slowly, catch the monkey'. I got that phrase into my head as I tried to pace myself over the mile and when I kept repeating the word 'monkey', the team hauled me in again.

I was starting to cover slightly more distance with each spell in the ball, but the last 250 metres were completed at more of a crawl. My back was like wood, but my legs had become jelly. I had spent two hours, one minute and 14 seconds inside my spherical prison, and thanks to my eight air breaks, when I finally stuck my head out into the crisp March sunshine I had completed what surely has to be the most draining challenge I have faced.

I am told it is a new world record, but it's not officially recognised and I don't know why anyone would ever have the desire to break it.

FLYING ZORBS

That was my most tiring brush with the giant ball, but then the zorb materialised again in Milton Keynes to inflict an even more powerful bite.

I was at a wind tunnel at Airkix, one of the venues for indoor skydiving (which still goes down as one of the most exciting and exhilarating experiences out there). There are places to try this now at Milton Keynes, Manchester and Bedford. From 2013, there will also be a new indoor skydiving tunnel at Basingstoke. You drop into a gushing jet of wind fired up by giant turbines below, with just a tightly sprung net in between providing reassurance. Then with the help of a guide you learn to balance on your tummy and fly gently around like a fledgling bird. All the time, your cheeks and jowls flap in the wind, contorting your face into the funniest of formations. The professionals demonstrate what can be done when you have conquered the laws of gravity, and they jet about like Superman, at times slowing to walk upside down around the perimeter of the tunnel.

For some, though, simply flying around is not extreme enough. So on my next visit to the tunnel, I was to tackle a new challenge. The tunnel was now occupied by a sinister-looking inflatable ball. The zorbs were back, set for a new invasion, and this time they were even bigger and had changed their name to air spheres.

'It's not for the faint-hearted,' the instructor warned, beckoning me to dive through the hole and into the ball, which was hovering inside the wind tunnel. There were three of us in there, including the instructor who had brought in a mini-camera to capture the inflight experience. There was no harness to climb into, just two strap handles to cling on to as suddenly at tremendous speed the ball was lifted up the tunnel by wind, which had been turned up to 170 miles per hour. A screeching whistling noise wiped out any other sound, and it took all of my strength to stay holding on.

The ball ricocheted in a furious frenzy up and down the tunnel, ping-ponging randomly off the walls while spinning and twisting at the same time. Inside it was like being in a washing machine. I was told that in the 45 seconds that we were airborne, we travelled the equivalent of four times around an athletics track. So that's 1,600 metres in 45 seconds, and upside down and side to side.

I had managed to cling on with my arms, but my legs had enjoyed a life of their own and at one point my knee had connected with the instructor's nose. I am not sure how much pain she was in, but she said it had been worth it to watch the sheer terror on my face. The others trying out this sport that day agreed that it was also one of the most extreme activities they had sampled. 'Terrible, but I loved it!' said one girl.

At the time of writing, 'airsphering' isn't offered as an activity at Airkix anymore. A spokeswoman from Spheremania told me it wasn't proving economically viable. 'But we are doing "snow-sphering" at the Chill Factor in Manchester'. She added: 'It's the most extreme ball of them all, and I have tried them all.' She added and told me they reached speeds of 30 miles per hour down the frozen slopes. So the giant inflatable balls have even invaded winter sports too. Is there no stopping them?

BODY ZORBS

In Bristol they have now got into the schools as well. Their power it seems is limitless. They are doing what football, cricket and rugby have all failed to, tackling those children still turned off by mainstream sport who don't get any meaningful exercise.

These seemingly lost souls have been drawn from their slumber and pulled into physical activity by the zorbs, and this time it's the 'Body Zorbs'. These smaller spherical creatures don't swallow you whole like the airspheres or downhill zorbs, and you are not zipped into a dome as you are when you roll across the water. The body zorbs slide over your outstretched arms and sit around your head and body. You hold on to two handles inside, and there's a hole in the top through which you can breathe and one in the bottom through which your legs stick out.

It means you can run around in them, and charge full pelt at your friends, who are also wearing the body spheres.

Like a crash of rhinos you collide and keel over, but you don't feel a thing. Once you have mastered the roll you can also use the force and momentum to go head over heels. You don't feel a bruise or bump because the inflatable ball around you takes all the impact.

In Bristol they have provided less sporty children with an extreme physical workout, and for the first time the zorb has also been used in team sports. I joined pupils from Victoria Park School for an inaugural game of body zorb football. The protection of the inflatable ball which every player was wearing meant age, ability and size counted for little. We were all on an equal footing.

On the pitch there was an eight-year-old, some children aged 10 and 11, and an instructor and teacher. We were chasing a giant beach ball, and the tackles were flying in immediately. I am ashamed to say that I went steaming into the eight-year-old on the opposing side, not realising it was him in the steamy ball, and over he went. No foul though, because in body zorb football, you bump and bounce into each other all the time, safe in the knowledge that no one is going to feel pain.

'Sometimes when you play football, you fall over and get tackled and get injured, but in this you don't get hurt,' said one girl, who said she never normally played team sports.

A 14-year-old lad panted: 'they are really comfortable, and when you hit someone and they go over you feel really proud.'

Their teacher explained why they had been using this sport, as part of the school curriculum. 'Some kids don't get into mainstream sport, but this gets them running around. It gets them outside and it's healthy'.

The only danger is exhaustion. It requires so much energy, that after ten minutes the pounds are dripping off you and you need half time, just to cool down.

It's hard to think of a sporting workout that kids have loved more. It was 2-0, both goals coming from headers which bounced past or over the keeper.

Body zorbs are widely used at theme and holiday parks, schools and leisure centres now, and if you are ever offered a go, try and persuade them to set up a game of football, because it will be the weirdest match you will ever play in.

The inflatable ball has come a long way since it was just an activity for hamsters. The fact that it's now involved in team sports, guarantees it a pumped up future and it's emerged as a major weapon in the battle against childhood obesity. Watch out later for the zorb's final appearance, when we work together in a battle against 'the Bison' coming soon in the book.

9
OLYMPIC SPORTS

'**W**e got away with it!' Surely this was the biggest understatement of 2012. It was the answer Lord Coe, Chairman of the London Olympics Organising Committee, gave when asked to look back on the fantastic success of the games he oversaw. He was speaking at the Lord Taverners' charity Christmas dinner. In truth the games produced so many sporting and cultural highlights that made the hairs stand up on the back of your neck: So many 'where were you when?' moments.

For me, the build-up to London 2012 has had the biggest impact on what I've covered over the last seven years. Sports which had been out of reach for Great Britain suddenly had the funding to mount a challenge and more importantly attract new talent for the years ahead. There were also new initiatives to get more people into established sports, like Rush Hockey and Street Volleyball. Over this chapter I will reflect on some of the Olympic sports which have captured my imagination and got people off the sofa. I will also take a look at some of the spin-off sports that have made us mere mortals feel like true Olympians. I couldn't possibly get them all into one chapter, so have given running and cycling their own sections later in the book.

TRUE OLYMPIANS

ARCHERY

There's only room in this forest for one of us, the lean earthy man, announced, as his wispy goat of a beard twitched threateningly, in a beam of sunlight. He drew back his bow and with a condescending sneer, released his arrow. Before I had time to focus on the target, I heard the thud announcing its arrival in the centre.

It was the proof I needed that the actor playing Robin Hood, Jonas Armstrong, really had been practising for the role. I had spent a couple of days in the forests of Hungary on the set of the BBC drama, to film a couple of behind the scenes features with the cast. It was a brief departure from my role in sport on *Breakfast*, although much of the reports were on the physical challenges in the forest.

To earn us special access it was decided that I should get into character and dress as a peasant, just to make it a little bit different from the normal TV previews you get. Producer Katie McDougall had scripted a mini extra episode for *Breakfast*, and so it was her right to cast me as a peasant.

It was one of the more surreal assignments I have been sent on. I was chained up by Richard Armitage (as Sir Guy of Gisborne) and chased by the Sheriff, played by Keith Allen, who improvised the line 'a basket of vegetables to the first peasant to bring me the witless buffoon Bushell', and we were told the true story of how actor Gordon Kennedy had been cast aside in a local hospital when he went in with an injury picked up during filming. He had arrived wearing no trousers and they thought he was a tramp.

The cast seemed so much more relaxed and willing to open up because I was dressed in rags and dirtied by the forest. But you can't take the sports reporter out of the peasant and so I challenged Robin Hood to an archery contest to see how fit and skilled these actors have to be. The answer was that they had obviously spent hours in the gym and practicing with their arrows.

We heard stories of ruptured groins, torn hamstrings, the Sheriff's broken teeth and Jonas' broken metatarsal, which held up filming for several weeks. But he still beat me in a race through the forest paths and then hit gold straight away.

I was told how important sport was to the cast, as it helped build essential team spirit. 'Off to a pub in Bucharest to watch Man U tonight,' said Robin Hood, (alias Jonas), as we said goodbye.

Shows like *Robin Hood*, plus films such as *The Hunger Games* and *Brave*, have made archery cool again. They have led to youngsters queuing up to join clubs up and down the country. One reason is they can all taste a bit of history when they draw back a bow for the first time.

Historians believe people first started using bows around 25,000 years ago, and it's one of the oldest sporting skills known to human beings. In Britain, a bow dating from around 2690 BC has been found in Somerset. However, according to archery historian Hugh Soar, it was only after the Norman invasion of 1066, when Duke William had defeated English king Harold at Hastings, that the longbow was developed into a weapon of war, and archery became widely practiced.

Royalty realised the importance of the skill, and in 1457 James II of Scotland banned golf because too many of his subjects were 'wasting' time when they should have been practising their archery. At other times, kings have banned games such as football and bowls in order to refocus their people on archery. In 1541, Parliament even passed a law ordering every town and village to provide archery butts so that all able-bodied men could practise in case they had to go into battle.

The introduction of firearms in the following centuries cut the need down for archers, but it didn't quell the sporting side, and the first clubs were formed in the 16th century, with target archery starting in the 18th century.

At the 1908 Olympics, in London, the British team was represented by 25 women and 19 men in the archery tournament, and yet these were the only Games that British archers competed in, until 1972. It has been regaining its place in our sporting consciousness ever since, though, and London 2012 was the country's most famous archer, Alison Williamson's, sixth Games. This put her up there with fencer Bill Hoskyns (1956–76) and Tessa Sanderson (1976–1996) as British athletes who have appeared at six Olympics.

Having filmed an archery piece with youngsters at a taster day in Northamptonshire, I saw at first hand the technique and strength you need to draw back the bow with enough control to get your shot on target. The arrows can travel at 240 kilometres per hour, and you are against the clock, because Olympic archers have just 20 seconds to load and shoot at the target which is 70 metres away.

Of all the Olympic tickets I applied for ahead of London 2012, the ones I got were for an archery session at Lords. It was a great example of how to bring a sport to life for a live audience. There were no Brits involved in the session I went to, but you could cut the tension with a knife as the Mexican and Korean women fought for individual gold.

The athletes were way down to the left and the target a similar distance to the right. It was breath taking the way we heard the release, then followed the rush of air as the arrow passed somewhere in front of the hushed stands, towards the big screen, then down to the coloured rings. My teenage daughter Lucy, who'd expected it to be boring, was transfixed and leapt out of her seat, arms in the air, to celebrate every time the Korean archer scored a 10.

Archery's role in society continues to hit the spot other sports can't. In 2011, it became the first sport to be hosted on the Speaker's Lawn at the Houses of Parliament, as MPs queued up for the opportunity to have their first go with the arrows. Across the world it has also opened doors. At the Asian Games in Doha in 2008, I met a lady called Nada Zeidan, who had broken through religious and cultural barriers using archery and has since helped more Muslim women across the Middle East get into sport. Archery also helped her realise her dream of eventually being accepted as a rally driver, and she was the first woman to get sports sponsorship in the Gulf.

Back home the opportunity to get involved has also never been greater and to find a club, contact www.archerygb.org.

There is also still a version of the sport that keeps alive the hunting element, one that takes archery back to its roots and to a time when dinner depended on the accuracy of your aim. This is for those who like their arrows wild, who want to stay closer to nature and can keep a steady hand, even after walking through woods, clambering up steep slopes, or wading through rivers. In field archery you have to get around a cross-country course, shooting at 24 targets along the way. The distances vary and are often unmarked. So it's all about your instinct and judgement. You have to shoot across water, fire up and downhill, and if you have just climbed a muddy bank, tiredness can make it harder for you to keep your aim.

Field archery came into the UK with US forces stationed here during the Second World War, and it's been growing steadily over the last decade. What's more, Britain's Alan Wills got gold at the World Championships in Hungary in 2010. To find out more, go to the website of the National Field Archery society – www.nfas.net.

HORSEBACK ARCHERY

The thunder of hooves, the swish of a tail, and then the fizz of an arrow. It's a stirring combination, but if you want your archery to be even more extreme – if you can fire while travelling at 40 miles per hour – then add a galloping horse. Horseback archery takes us back to the days of Genghis Khan.

It has been used in combat ever since people could ride. Cave paintings show mounted archers shooting in battle, or for pleasure. Having a horse was a great advantage over your enemies on foot.

In the early years, the likes of Genghis Khan would use horseback archery to gain wealth and power, while in Europe around the 9th century, people lived in fear of the tribesmen from Hungary on horseback.

The man who has brought this back as a sport is also Hungarian. In the 1980s Lajos Kassai, couldn't understand why 'this martial art which once created and crushed empires was almost forgotten forever.'

One of the problems was that armies eventually worked out that mounted archers were ineffective against a mass of warriors on foot. A man on a horse provided a larger target than a person on the ground. The arrival of guns then fired another arrow into the heart of this sport.

While its renaissance originally started at festivals in Mongolia, after the country had gained independence in 1921, it fully emerged as a sport when the modern rules were drawn up at Kassai's archery school. The comeback has now reached the UK, and in 2010 the inaugural horseback archery championship was held in Sussex.

It is a staggering mix of sight and sound as rider and horse set off at a gallop along the 100-metre course. They have 12 seconds to complete the journey, but on the way, they have to load and release arrows at three targets. It felt like we had stepped back in time as the decorated UK champion from 2010, Neil Payne, swept past, turning around to collect an arrow while travelling at racehorse speed down the dusty track.

He was wearing traditional Hungarian costume, which included a white headdress, and his run was over in a blink of an eye, by which time he had hit three targets.

'Obviously it's going to be a bit more challenging than playing tennis, or riding a bike,' he said. 'You're bringing two sports together and you have to learn to ride well too.'

So well, that you need to be able to gallop at full pelt without reins. You grip the horse with your legs, but you need to keep enough mobility to swivel your top half around to reach for the arrows. They are held at the back of the horse. Without stopping to think it's then a case of getting the arrow into position, aiming and firing, as your mount gets you down the track.

You are judged on accuracy and speed. If you take longer than 12 seconds to complete the run, it's a penalty, and the nearer you get to the 10 with each shot, the more points you score.

It's a well-rehearsed drill. As soon as your horse is into its stride, you line up and fire forwards to the first target. Within a split second, you reload and aim for the second, which is now to your side. By the time you are drawing back for the final shot, the target is behind you so it's a case of firing over your shoulder. At this point you are not looking at where you are going, so this is when trust and your relationship with your horse is crucial.

'It's exciting, and there's a great buzz around it,' Neil said, as he assured me that this wasn't as impossible as it looks. 'You do feel like you are rediscovering a part of history, and with a bit of coaching, I promise, it's possible to get the basics, and it's not that out of reach.'

It starts with a lesson on foot, because you shoot in a different way from normal archery. My instructor Dan showed me to bring the arrow onto the other side of the bow frame, and then hook it back with my index finger.

My first shot was into the gold, but my beginner's luck was then going to be tested on a horse. If it's a first go, you won't expect to trot, because firing at walking pace is enough to think about. At this stage, it's just getting used to moving and firing at the same time.

'Elbow back, head up!' my instructor bellowed, as I watched my arrow land wide. I reached for another and re-loaded, and then realised I had already forgotten about being on a horse. The first base camp had been reached. Even experienced riders start at slow speeds, before building up to a trot and gallop.

Teenager Anna Folwell was hooked after her first lesson. 'The fact that you are on a moving animal, while trying to shoot, is unbeatable, plus you have to allow for the speed of the horse. Because it's taking you away from the target, you need to be able to shoot further.'

'It's simply a beautiful sport,' added Zana Greenwood from the Centre of Horseback Combat. 'The imagery is just fantastic, and the feeling of being on a horse and firing is something so natural.'

It's one of the greatest feelings of power I have experienced in sport, and that was still just at walking pace. For more information go to: www.bhaa.org.uk

POMMEL HORSE

Feet in a bucket and upside down, I tried to turn around and around on a mushroom. It wasn't elegant, it wasn't dignified, and under the chuckling but sympathetic gaze of Olympic silver and bronze medallist Louis Smith, I wished I had started 30 years earlier. Actually, make it 40 years.

Louis himself started gymnastics when he was just four years old. He told me he was a handful for his mum and was in danger of getting into trouble, so he was taken to a gym to burn off his energy and give him more structure and discipline. He was diagnosed with ADHD as a child, and sport proved to be far more powerful and effective than any drug.

So when he was seven, Louis had learned to spin around with his feet in a bucket suspended from the roof of a gymnasium near Peterborough.

When I first arrived at his current training gym in Huntington 15 years later, he was in full flow. Not in a bucket, or on a mushroom, but on the piece of equipment this trains you for: the pommel horse. It is one of the most difficult of all the gymnastic disciplines.

My eyes were fixed in disbelief on the chalky hand of this incredible athlete. A hand which was supporting his whole body, as he spun over and around the leather horse with such grace. Louis was pushing the human body to places it shouldn't go. I was amazed as I watched him power feet first into the air, swishing his legs to propel him off the horse. Without a stutter he planted himself back on the gym floor. Such poise, such presence, such power.

The pommel horse was originally developed many centuries ago, to train soldiers to mount and dismount horses at speed, during battle. It is said that Alexander the Great used one in training, while it's believed Roman soldiers also had wooden horses for practice. It's only been a competitive sport for around the last 300 years, and there has been another spin-off as well – some athletes still do their routines on a moving horse.

Before we get back to the Huntingdon gym, here's a quick guide to the sport of equestrian vaulting. In Roman times, there are records of acrobats displaying their skills on cantering horses, and since the 1950s the sport has been on the rise again, firstly in the USA and then the UK. It's something I tried near Andover in Hampshire, and I would suggest that this activity is a lot more accessible than you might think. Admittedly I could already sit on a horse, but my rising trot has always been random and erratic. However when it came to horse vaulting, I was able to stand up on the horse, with my arms in the air, during my first lesson. Admittedly my trusty steed was on the end of a rope being held by an instructor, and I was only cantering around in 15-metre circles, but it was a start, and as I flexed those arms I forgot that I was on the back of a moving horse.

It helps if you have a history in gymnastics, because simply standing on the horse isn't going to win you any prizes. There are all sorts of somersaults and flips and moves to perform, and in the team competition, you sometimes have two athletes on board at the same time, meaning you can get extra height.

One of the most impressive parts of the routine is the

mounting and dismounting, because it all happens while the horse is still cantering around. You run alongside until you can match the speed of your four-legged friend, and then with a hop and a jump, you get up on top.

Louis Smith would no doubt be able to master such moves, but it's not an Olympic sport, and his life has been in the gym. The wonderful thing about Louis is that his feet are still firmly on the ground, and he still trains in Huntingdon, alongside the six- and seven-year-olds who are taking their first steps in the sport. They too start with their feet in the bucket, trying to propel themselves around, but whereas I resembled a harpooned seal, they were flicking their legs like little fish, back and forth in the blink of an eye. After just a few weeks, they cast off the bucket and are able to support themselves on the mushroom, which is only a couple of feet high, with just their arms and upper body strength.

This is how you start your journey towards the pommel horse. Once you can keep yourself turning with just your wrists as anchors, you graduate to the real thing, and start learning the moves that have earned Louis Smith three Olympic medals. They are also why he made such an impact on the dancefloor, winning the BBC's *Strictly Come Dancing* with some extra-ordinary moves of superhuman upper body strength.

His body may look perfect, but in reality he says it's often in pieces. We have no idea of the pain he has to go through.

'Sometimes my body is so sore, I find it hard to get out of bed in the morning, the pain is so bad, but I keep pushing,' he told me.

The physical punishment is bad enough without the mental pressure he is also under. With the world watching, all that work comes down to the finest of margins, and your fate is decided in less than a minute. The slightest of distractions can throw you, as Louis found out at the European championships in 2011, when a stray camera, which he hadn't clocked before, took his attention away for a millisecond and he was off.

'All those years of hard training, twice a day, six days a week, and I have just 50 seconds at the end of it to prove to everyone what I can do,' he added.

He showed his deep pools of reserve, though, by managing to bounce back to win silver at the Korean World Cup event in the July. He must be made of steel, and remains one of the toughest athletes I have ever met. In Beijing 2008 he made history as the first British gymnast since 1928 to win an Olympic medal, and this inspired those around him to win a team medal at London 2012. Louis himself was rewarded with a silver.

To get involved in pommel horse and gymnastics visit www.british-gymnastics.org and for horse vaulting it's www.vaulting.org.uk

DIVING

In some sports it pays to start young, before wisdom and fear move into your brain. I remember jumping off the high diving board at my local swimming pool as a child, but here I was in Southampton dragging my chewed nails along the surface of the 10-metre board like a cat on its ninth life.

Teeth grinding, I peered over the edge. They must have raised the board, I thought. That's far more than 10 metres. This is the Empire State Building, and that's a paddling pool below.

I was reassured it wasn't just me who gets the jitters. Even Peter Waterfield, an Olympic silver medallist and Tom Daley's diving partner at London 2012, admitted it's different now from when he first started.

'When I first went to the top of the board, I was young and

just wanted to get up there and jump off. It's only now that I am nearly 30 [this was 2010] that I am thinking "what on earth am I doing up here?" You have got no fear when you are younger. It's only when you get older you think about it more.'

Diving is now one of the coolest sports around. Most of us can only gaze up in wonder at the higher boards, where some of the finest specimens of human beings, launch themselves into the air. They are the Greek sporting gods of our time, with bodies and nerves of steel and the flexibility of a gymnast. You need the full box of tricks to be able to hurl yourself off what is effectively a three-storey building and then somersault and twist on your 40 mile per hour journey down into the wall of water.

It hasn't always been like this. The history of the sport goes back around 100 years, and in the early 19th century the only 'dive' was a simple forward plunge. The aim was to travel as far as possible underwater. In Britain, the National Plunging Championships were held from 1883 to 1937, and continue to this day in Yorkshire. Plunging was part of the 1908 London Olympics, too, alongside other now defunct pool events such as underwater obstacle races.

It was gymnasts rather than swimmers who changed attitudes. At the beginning of the 20th century, some Swedish and German gymnasts started practising their landings in water, rather than on hard floors and mats. In summer, gymnastic equipment was then transferred to the beaches so that the gymnasts could perform acrobatics and land in the sea. It soon developed into a recognised sport which was called 'fancy diving', and for some years separate competitions were held for plain and fancy diving.

You wouldn't dare accuse the likes of Tom Daley of 'fancy diving' today. He's taken complex, gravity-defying routines beyond the pool and into the living rooms of a whole new audience. Having competed at the Beijing Olympics at the age of just 14, he's given the sport a new lease of life, and it's led to a surge in popularity.

And what he and Pete Waterfield do may not be as impossible as it looks. Pete is proof that you don't have to be born half sea-bird to dive. At nine years old, he was an ordinary kid who couldn't even swim. It was certainly a challenge, but luckily for Pete and his two brothers, their committed father could see how sport was a route to a better life for them, and way of keeping them out of trouble. So he got Peter into sports such as judo, karate, and then fishing. This was the turning point, because to go fishing young Peter needed to learn to swim. It was during a lesson in the pool that Pete's head was turned by the super humans diving into the water next door. Different sports often complement each other, and the agility and mobility Pete had learned through martial arts gave him the perfect springboard for his switch to diving.

Back in 2010, Pete scampered to the top of the 10-metre board in Southampton as if he was walking out to bat at Lords – with purpose, supreme confidence, and his head held high. Then, with a flick of his feet, he became a kaleidoscope of pink, spinning and turning like a catherine wheel, and before I had time to take it all in, he was into the water as straight as a dart. There is no room for error. Hitting the water at such speed means if you get the entry wrong, you are likely to be heading for A&E.

I was told it would be far too dangerous for a novice to dive straight off the 10-metre board. I would be risking all kinds of damage to my eyes, head and other vulnerable parts of the body. So it was down to the five-metre board instead. Like an army of caterpillars, my toes wiggled their way over the edge and into the air.

'Just remember what I told you,' Pete shouted. 'Stretch your arms up and squeeze your ears,' he had smiled. It does feel rather strange at first, as you lock your hands together to form the shield that will take the impact and dilute the force from of water.

He'd seen me go off the one-metre and three-metre boards, and had nodded sympathetically. If you are a beginner it's all about getting a nice clean, straight entry, and while each time it had felt like a perfect 10, my legs hadn't been singing from the same hymn sheet. Kermit would have approved as my frog legs trailed in behind me. Learning to keep everything straight, from the tips of my fingers to my outstretched toes, was something I had to work on away from the water.

Indeed it's all the work out of the pool that enables Peter to perform such mind-boggling, gravity-busting manoeuvres. It's the endless hours of practice in the gym that enables him to become a blur of pikes, twists and tucks, which he packs into just two seconds.

'We are not just doing five hours in the pool,' he added. '50 per cent of our training is in the gym and on trampolines. It's strengthening, stretching, and training our bodies to take the impact of hitting the water at 40 miles an hour.'

Not only that, but in synchronised diving, Peter has to match Tom Daley inch for inch. They have to be in perfect time with each other. It's a high-speed, complex dance routine, which they perform while falling through the air.

Back at the other end of the spectrum, my toes were the first to go as I dropped like a stone into the water from five metres. In this sport you have to build confidence slowly, and it was a challenge enough keeping my legs straight while entering the water feet first. The diving could come later. Even at just 20 miles per hour, the air gushing past gave me a rush of adrenalin that the professionals probably don't have time to appreciate as they concentrate on their routines. And after all the months and years of work they put in, it comes down to two seconds in which their hopes and dreams can vanish into thin air.

If you can swim, are flexible, have a good head for heights and are utterly fearless, diving could be the sport for you. There are now over 100 diving-friendly pools across Great Britain and Northern Ireland, and to get involved go to the website www.swimming.org

CLIFF DIVING

For some divers, going off a 10-metre board is like dipping your toe into a paddling pool. They are the extreme adrenalin junkies who tease the grim reaper with their death defying leaps off towering cliffs, which can be as high as the ninth floor of a tower block.

It's never likely to make the headlines in the way indoor diving does, because it's just not as accessible to us all. But it has become more mainstream thanks to the Red Bull Cliff Diving World Series, which takes the top cliff divers on earth to beautiful locations around the world, where thousands stare in disbelief. The divers make it look so graceful, but the forces battering them are anything but, as they perform their somersaults and twists on the way down into the ocean. It's certainly not one to try yourself next time you're on holiday.

Norwegian skiier Fred Syversen holds the record for the highest cliff jump, but it wasn't intentional. He dropped 107 meters, that's 351 feet, off a cliff while actually getting ready for a different and lower jump. He survived with hardly a scratch!

The current highest cliff dive was record by Oliver Favre in

1987. He plummeted head first into open water from 53.94 metres, in France. That's 177 feet, and is the height of just over nine adult giraffes, all standing on top of each other.

More recently the king of cliff diving has been Britain's Gary Hunt. In 2012, as the Cliff Diving World Series came to the UK for the first time, he won the competition for the third time. In the British leg, 14 of the world's best divers launched themselves from a man-made platform, 27 metres above the Irish Sea off the coast of Pembrokeshire. It's not just about height, but also what you do on the way down, and the way in which you perform those somersaults, twists and turns. Hunt clinched his third successive title by winning the final stage in Oman, with his trademark triple-quad dive, to set a points total of 506.85. He said it was the best competition he had ever taken part in. He had been an Olympic hopeful before switching to cliff diving, leaving the boards to the men and boys who have gone onto become household names. Let's hope Gary gets the recognition too. For more information on cliff diving, visit www.whdf.com/www.redbullcliffdiving.com

COASTEERING

While it's a wonderful feeling jumping off a rock into the sea, if you can find somewhere safe enough, only a select few have that special kind of brain that can switch off fear when stood at the top of a cliff, with rocks and the rolling waves beckoning below. To get a taste of this sport without such heights then the increasingly popular actvitiy of coasteering combines swimming with traversing and scrambling over the lower levels of sea cliffs, as well as cliff jumps which can range from one to 10 metres.

It tests your climbing skills and stretches your nerves. I experienced the sharp intake of breath you take as you drop into the sea, off the coast of Jersey in the island's Ultimate race. The feeling of freedom as you plunge feet-first into the salty sanctuary between the rocks is matched by the overwhelming waves of relief. It can't be stressed enough that you should never do this on your own with your mates. Only ever go with a qualified coasteering guide who knows the coastline like the back of their hand and knows where it's safe to jump.

Someone like David Harriss, from the British Coasteering Federation, who told me: 'It's an adventure which is all about getting from point A to point B. Whatever is in the way, be it a cliff or a cave, we climb or try to get through. The jumping into the water is only a small part, but sometimes it's safer to jump than climb down a rocky face.'

You do wear a wetsuit, buoyancy aid, helmet and suitable climbing footwear, but this is an extreme adventure activity that can be high risk, depending on sea and weather conditions, and as I stress should only be done with qualified instructors. Check out www.britishcoasteeringfederation.co.uk.

GHYLL SCRAMBLING

A similar sporting experience, but inland, is ghyll scrambling. This one isn't just for adults, as teenagers can take part too, under close supervision. It takes place along a river which cascades down a hill or mountain. Again, following the lead of a qualified instructor, you negotiate your way down the water assault course, by climbing, sliding on your bottom and at times jumping down waterfalls into deep swirling pools.

You are wearing a wetsuit, buoyancy aid and a helmet, and it's so important to do exactly as you are told. As long as you follow the safety instructions, though, it is an exhilarating way to descend a mountain.

I took my daughter Lucy down a course near Keswick in the

Lake District and while it was stomach-churning telling your 'little girl' that it was a good idea to jump off the top of a seven-foot waterfall, by the end she was glowing and didn't stop talking about the 'amazing' experience.

There are good locations in Wales, Scotland and the South West – for more information go to www.ghyllscrambling.co.uk.

WATERBOMBING

At the other end of the diving pool from our cliff and Olympic divers, there's a board event which is also all over in a second or two, but which makes far more of a splash, especially for all the coach potatoes out there.

In fact, extra potatoes, or even pies, might just help you in the World Water Bombing Championships, held each year at Ponds Forge International Sports Centre in Sheffield. It was originally inspired by a beer advert starring Peter Kay, and in 2007 when I went along there were plenty of Peter Kay lookalikes lining up at the opening parade, alongside people dressed as the Village People's YMCA crew, men in Borat mankinis, and a robot.

'Style isn't really the important thing,' said MC Simon Frances, 'it's all about just going for it, making the biggest splash you can and looking as silly as possible.'

It started in 2005, and has grown ever since. Competitors go off a three-metre board, and it proved just how powerful the impact can be even from this height. A Henry VIII lookalike slapped the water so hard, his wig and false beard scattered far and wide. The robot's lavish costume, which had taken weeks to build, was a floating mass of debris as soon as it landed, and so I went for the minimalist approach, wearing just the budgie smugglers.

At 11 stone, I was never going to wet the judges with my

splash, though. I ran at full pelt and spread my body out like a swan learning to fly, but couldn't get my knees up and plopped into the water, emerging to the shame of a 2, a 2 and a 1.5 on the judges' scorecards.

It's true to say that some took it seriously, and with a world title at stake, the Peter Kay approach looked out of date. The winner was a silver-suited diver who back-flipped before splashing the water with such force that fountains seemed to shower the applauding crowd.

'This year, I had to be so well trained,' he glowed. 'You've got to be a bit of an athlete, and now I am thinking I will have to get an agent, and a costume designed for next year. I will do radio, TV and hopefully go to a few celebrity parties.' I wondered if the impact had gone to his head.

Still, there are also prizes for the best costumes and it's all about raising money for charity. So to get involved go to http://www.pondsforge.co.uk/events/view/Worldwaterbombing championships

10

THE PARALYMPICS

If the London 2012 Olympics became a new benchmark for future games, the same is arguably even more true of the London Paralympics which followed in hot sunshine in late August and September. The following chapter is about the sports, which before 2012 some of us hadn't heard of, but which are now opening doors to a whole new generation of athletes, and which have shown what's possible rather than what's not.

PARALYMPIC SPORTS

'The Paralympic games were the defining image of the summer' – not my words but those of Lord Coe, speaking at the Lord Taverners in December 2012. 'We won't see the world in the same way again,' he added.

An unprecedented 2.8 million tickets were sold and those lucky people soon realised they were witnessing a historic event. One that would change attitudes forever. I was honoured to present BBC *Breakfast*'s coverage of the Paralympics, morning after morning, from the studio overlooking Olympic park.

I have always had a particular interest in Paralympic sport, having covered the Winter Paralympic Games in Canada in 2010. I realised what a landmark games London 2012 would be, when my nine-year-old daughter Sophie, who has virtually no interest in sport, kept asking me, 'Daddy, will you meet Ellie Simmonds?' Her school had done a project on the swimmer.

Then it was Noel Thatcher, the former multiple gold medallist, who strengthened this belief, saying that he thought London 2012 had seen Paralympians achieve parity for the first time. Hannah Cockcroft, who won ParalympicsGB's first track gold, was getting the same headlines on the back pages, and the same media coverage, as Jessica Ennis had during the Olympic Games.

London 2012 went further than any games beforehand in changing attitudes towards Paralympic sport. It was a new frontier with 4,200 athletes representing 165 countries. Most events were sold out, which had also never happened before.

There is still a long way to go in some parts of the world. There were stories of hardship which demonstrated the work that needs to be done, but these also showed the true spirit of the games. Student Liam Conlon was a volunteer who went to meet members of the Burkina Faso team at Heathrow. He found that they had nowhere to stay or train. So he took them home to his parents, found a local school for them to train at, and helped upgrade their hand cycling equipment to competition standards.

It's not just countries with a lack of funding, that need to catch up though. Some major nations were still criticised for not offering sufficient coverage. .

But it's thought that the London 2012 games will show the way forward, 64 years on from the birth of the Paralympics at Stoke Mandeville hospital.

'London 2012 was incredible, and different from previous games,' Helena Lucas told me after helping to win ParalympicsGB's first sailing gold medals.

'In China after the Olympics, certain hoardings were taken down and it felt a bit like the party was over, but here the atmosphere just got more and more amazing.'

It's been a long journey since the German doctor who had escaped Nazi Germany and fled to England, started advocating sports therapy to enhance the quality of life, for those injured in the Second World War. He organised the 1948 International Wheelchair Games to coincide with the 1948 London Olympics, and the Paralympic movement was born.

For me there were so many highlights. Up there on the main scoreboard was 'M Bushell wins gold'. Sadly I can't claim Mickey Bushell, the wheelchair sprinter, as a relative, but it's an honour to share his name.

There was the most incredible comeback I have ever seen by Richard 'The Monster' Whitehead in the 200 metres, and the staggering success of Sarah Storey.

I also asked a protection officer, who was inside the Olympic stadium day after day during the Olympics and then Paralympics, what his best moment had been. He said it was when a Paralympic athlete from Djibouti, Houssein Omar Hassan, finished more than seven minutes behind the winner in the T46 1,500 metres. The crowd got to their feet to applaud what they thought was his final 100 metres. It wasn't.

Djibouti's only athlete at the games had hurt his Achilles tendon and still had another lap to go, and so 80,000 people clapped and cheered and stayed on their feet throughout that final circuit.

One of the big successes and moves forward by the Paralympic movement in the last decade has been the way they have opened up a whole range of sports to everyone, and made them more inclusive. The more people understand Paralympic sports, the more they will want to follow them. The best way to make anyone appreciate what an athlete is doing, is to put them in the thick of it themselves.

MURDERBALL (WHEELCHAIR RUGBY)

I was strapped into a wheelchair at a school in Norfolk and told to brace myself. I drew a sharp breath and grimaced as two of ParalympicsGB's wheelchair rugby team raced towards me. They had earlier told me that when they had done this to a *Blue Peter* presenter, he had been sent flying from his chair. I held on and absorbed the shudder juddering through my bones, which felt like they had all become momentarily unhinged. Then another hit came smashing into my chair. It was part of a programme to spread the word about this fast and very physical game before the Beijing Olympics. A group of able-bodied secondary school children had also been invited in.

The aggressive, full contact nature of wheelchair rugby is why it's also known as murderball, which was the name of a film about the rivalry between the Canadian and US teams in the build-up to the 2004 Paralympics. The film shows the ferocity of the sport, in which wheelchairs collide at high speed, and it's credited with changing the way people view disabled sport.

Empire magazine reckoned this alone stripped away the

layers of delicacy with which the able-bodied treated Paralympic athletes. People could suddenly see what they *could* do, not what they couldn't.

According to the US wheelchair rugby star, Scott Hogsett, everyone who saw the film immediately wanted to play. But he had to then break it to them that to qualify, they had to have limitations in all four limbs. So some were turned away. 'They tended to think that we are fragile, that we are made of glass. Then all of a sudden there is this wheelchair rugby where we are hitting each other, knocking each other out of our chairs, getting right back up again and not getting hurt.'

It's not surprising that this is one of the most popular Paralympic events. It's a mixed team sport, invented in Canada in 1977 by a group of quadriplegic athletes who were looking for an alternative to wheelchair basketball. According to the International Federation of Wheelchair Rugby, the athletes wanted a sport which would allow players with reduced arm and hand function to participate equally. It combines basketball with elements of rugby and handball.

There are four players in each team, trying to pass and carry the ball up the court and across their opponents' goal line. Contact between the wheelchairs is an important part, as players use their chairs to block and hold opponents.

It was recognised by the International Paralympic Committee in 1994, becoming a full medal sport for the first time at the Sydney games six years later. It's now become one of the most played Paralympic sports around the world, with more than 40 countries participating.

I was with the British team just after the first woman had been picked to play for ParalympicsGB.

It was Josie Pearson, the athlete who won discus gold at London 2012. Back in 2008, her all-round sporting talent meant she was a key part of the murderball team. 'It's very tactical,' she told me. 'Yes people see the big hits and think that's what it's all about, but you have to very switched on and have it upstairs as well, and be mentally as well as physically fit.'

There is an element of chess about the way you position your players across the court, to protect and then to attack. There are two types of chairs in play, too. One has wings on the side, to stop attacking players being taken out, while defenders have picks on the front of their chairs which can help them get underneath an opponent and even turn them over. It's common in a match for people to come a cropper and end up on the floor. And it has to be one of the most ferocious sports I have witnessed, with head-on collisions at speed as metal smashes into metal. While the chairs do protect you from some of the impact, it's a force that the school children and I took some getting used to.

'It's weird,' said one, 'it's shocking at first but once you get used to it, I wanted it more and more,' while her friend added, 'incredible though, what amazing athletes.'

They certainly are, with rippling upper body muscles that give them such speed and force. ParalympicsGB have come so close to medalling in the past, coming fourth in Athens and Beijing, and following a sixth place at London 2012, the team will now focus on getting new talent in for the build-up to Rio.

To get involved and to follow wheelchair rugby, go to the website www.gbwr.org.uk. They are looking for men and women, whatever your age. If you have upper and lower limb disabilities and a thirst for action, then maybe it's about time you gave this a try. There are loads of opportunities to play your part on the sidelines too, as they need coaches, officials and people who can give them a hand at clubs across the UK.

SLEDGE HOCKEY

For many of us it's the highlight of any cold snap that engulfs the country. Getting out the sledge and sliding down a hillside. I remember my 75-year-old nan rolling head over heels across the snow after we'd run into a deeper drift. It's one time of year when it feels acceptable to be a kid again.

So imagine my excitement on the morning of my trip to join the British sledge hockey team in Nottingham. What a combination, sledging and hockey. It is the murderball of the Paralympic winter games, and is also opening up to the masses.

Sledge hockey was the idea of two men from Sweden, who wanted to carry on playing ice hockey regardless of any physical disability. It became part of the Paralympics in 1994, when fittingly Sweden won the gold. Norway were the next champions, followed by the USA and then Canada. Despite being one of the first nations to form a team, Britain has never medalled, and failed to qualify for Vancouver, but as I will explain this should soon change.

It has all the aggression, the collisions, the raw speed and bone crunching slams of ice hockey, but all the players are sitting on sledges resting on two blades. It's one of the top draws at any Winter Paralympics and the crowd I was in, winced and took a sharp breath as sledges collided and players were crushed up against the wall.

'It's so physically demanding and there's an awful lot of hitting involved,' one of the American players told me. 'We have to generate a lot of speed just using the strength of our arms and so you have to do so many upper body workouts.'

A lack of ice time and funding has hampered ParalympicsGB's efforts to qualify, plus with London 2012 coming up, some sledge hockey players were tempted away into summer sports instead. However the seeds of change were already in place, which is why I had gone to Nottingham. The team had started a campaign to spread the word beyond the ice rink and had invited local school children to come and join the national squad for a training session.

'It's a matter of raising the profile and getting as many people onto the ice as possible,' said Gary Farmer of the British team. 'Then we can develop more as a nation.' Also since 2010, teams have been able to pick female athletes too.

At first it felt like gliding on a kayak, especially as you use your small hockey sticks like punts or oars to propel you along. I could get up a decent speed, but at first turning involved a few collisions with the other beginners. The biggest challenge, though, was summoning enough strength to lift the puck and get it flying through the air. Shots along the ice seemed to lack power, and my trouble was that the movement I needed to get my arm back and under the puck would also tip me over onto my side. This is where upper body strength comes in, and the top players can get the puck travelling at 100 miles per hour.

It's all very well talking about getting lots of practise in, but that can be difficult when you are competing for ice time with other sports. So the British have invented a new version of the game to give themselves a chance. It was Paralympian Matt Lloyd, who competed in sledge hockey at the 2006 Winter Paralympics, who came up with the idea of 'in-line' sledge hockey. The first match was held in Surrey in 2009, with a league set up a year later. It's played with the sledges resting on roller skate wheels instead of blades, which means the sport can now be taken into sports halls across the country.

It's all inclusive because people of different abilities can play on mixed teams. Once you are on the sledges you are pretty much equal and so it's all down to talent and skill. You still have the helmets, the gloves, the goals and the pucks – and according to the 15-year-olds beside me, having their first go at the sport, the excitement too.

'It's just surprising how fast you can go, but I want to hit the puck as hard as those professionals,' said one lad, grinning from ear to ear. 'It's amazing that I have only fallen over 15 times!' said another.

By spreading the word in this way, British sledge hockey hope to unearth more talent as they target qualifying for the Paralympics in Sochi in 2014, and then the goal is a medal in South Korea in 2018.

The inline school experience is only part of the master plan. While I was in Canada I saw the future. A group of injured ex-servicemen were there to be given a taste of sledge hockey. They were on a scheme called the Battle Back programme, which had been launched in 2008. It's a Ministry of Defence initiative, supported by the charities Help for Heroes and the Royal British Legion.

A significant number of serving and veteran military service personnel, injured in Iraq and Afghanistan, were selected for the London 2012 Paralympics. The Battle Back scheme is run from the Defence Medical Rehabilitation centre at Headley Court and enables wounded and injured soldiers to use sport as part of their recovery. There's clear evidence that sport can accelerate rehabilitation and lead to greater mental and physical strength. Plus the evidence so far is that the drive and strength of athletes with a military background means they often have what it takes to reach the top in sport as well.

Major Martin Colclough says Battle Back has already helped 1,500 people from the Forces get back into sport, and of the 88 people that have been to one of the Paralympic talent days, well over half were singled out as potential athletes. 37 are now in a Paralympic sport. It's already bolstered the developing British sledge hockey team, which came eighth at the Paralympic winter cup in 2011, despite having eight players who'd been involved for less than a year.

Tyler Christopher and Lee Coupe have both come through the Battle Back scheme, and Coupe plays sledge hockey for the Battle Back Bisons, based at Basingstoke. Other newcomers to the British team include Caroline Bonner from the Coventry Honey Badgers.

There are now 12 league teams across the country, and 150 players, compared to one team and just 16 involved in 2009. So the sport has come a long way, despite the national team being completely self-funded. That medal target for 2018 doesn't look that far-fetched at all.

To get involved and to support your team in this action-packed sport, contact the British Sledge Hockey Association at www.sledgehockey.co.uk.

WHEELCHAIR TENNIS

It's like patting your head and rubbing your tummy at the same time, or is it the other way around? Either way, trying to push a wheelchair while hitting a tennis ball requires extraordinary powers of coordination and strength.

One of the driving forces behind making this sport more inclusive over recent years has been the hosting of taster sessions for all. The more people you can get to sit in a chair and try a sport like tennis, the better an idea everyone will have of the skills required.

So in the summer of 2012, the Lawn Tennis Association ran an All Play experience on Clapham Common during the Wimbledon fortnight, and one of the highlights was a chance to try wheelchair tennis.

'We want to get more non-disabled people trying this

version of the sport,' said ParalympicsGB wheelchair tennis coach Geraint Richards. 'We want them involved because this game is fully integratable with non-disabled tennis. We now play what we call one up, one down, and this is doubles with one player on each team standing and the other in a wheelchair. The other reason we want to get all people into a chair is so they can see how hard these guys have to work to push the chairs around on court.'

The strategy seems to be working. At London 2012, the wheelchair tennis was second to sell out behind murderball, and it is the fastest growing wheelchair sport in the world.

It was 1992 when wheelchair tennis first came into the Paralympics and after the 2000 Paralympics, which boosted public awareness, it was added to the Grand Slams as well. And I couldn't have been in better hands as I strapped myself in alongside the two best wheelchair tennis players in the women's game, the British numbers one and two, Lucy Shuker and Jordanne Whiley. I wouldn't like to say who's number one at the moment, because they keep swapping. Peter Norfolk, nicknamed 'The Quadfather' because he competed in the quads competition, may have put the sport on the map in this country, but Lucy and Jordanne are set to dominate the next generation.

Jordanne was only 20 when she competed at London 2012, and is one of the youngest players ever. She's lean, agile and one of the fastest around the court, and she first picked up a racquet aged just three. 'It was just after my 3rd birthday and I had broken my leg [she has brittle bone disease] and a stranger just handed me this racquet and after that I just wanted to play,' she explained. Jordanne got to the quarter-finals at Beijing in 2008, aged just 16, and in the summer of 2012, got to the doubles final of Wimbledon.

'Holding a racquet for someone just getting into a

wheelchair is difficult, so it's important you get a knowledge of what we have to do. It's so you get the jist.'

I realised how it's so much about positioning and reading the game. You also have to be so fit. On one hand you need to be light, so you are quick and more agile in the chair, but you also need strength in your body and arms to get the lift and power to smash home a winner. The top male wheelchair tennis player has a serve of more than 100 mph. Have a go at trying to serve while sitting in the park and you will get an idea of the technique required.

I found it demanding on my arms and hands, which were gripping too tightly around the racquet. I could return the ball if it came to me, but often I misread its path and found myself stranded too far forward as another whistler from Whiley sailed past my reach. On other occasions I would get the wheeling right, reaching the spot in time to hit the ball, but then I didn't have the power or control to send it back in the right direction. The ball is allowed to bounce twice, which gives you a chance to chase after it, but that only works if you have the skill and speed.

The message from Lucy was 'don't give up'. She started playing when she had just come out of University, after a motorbike accident. She was already a decent badminton player but the transfer to tennis wasn't straightforward. 'When I first started I had numerous tantrums and found it really difficult to push the chair at the same time,' she confessed. 'But now I really recommend it; whether you are disabled or not, it's a fantastic support to get into.' Fancy a go? See for yourself : www.tennisfoundation.org.uk

GOALBALL AND SPRINTING

I don't know what is more terrifying: running a sprint race despite not being able to see the track in front of you, or lying on the floor in the dark waiting for something that's just been compared to a cannon ball to hit you where it hurts. Both are right up there and both were part of my introduction to Paralympic sports.

I will come to goalball shortly, but one of the most impressive athletes I have ever met is Libby Clegg. Training six days a week, and then being quickest out of the blocks when it matters, is still not enough for Libby. Every step of her sprint for the line in the 100 metres or 200 metres must be in perfect sync with her guide Mikhail. The pair won Paralympic silver for the second time at London 2012, with Libby running the 100 metres in a time of 12.13 seconds. Later in the week she set a new personal best in the 200 metres, 25.10, and yet Libby only sees a slightly blurred image of the stadium through the corner of her left eye. The track in front of her as she sprints flat out is blocked out by a deteriorating eye condition known as Stargardt's Disease. That's the technical bit, but the reality is, when you meet and chat to this bubbly star of ParalympicsGB athletics, you'd have no idea that she has any visual impairment at all, let alone one that affects her view of the track.

So this is a team effort; it's raw instinct. One step out of time or out of line by either Libby or Mikhail, and they will lose time and the race. They are joined at the hands by a loose piece of cloth, but it's mainly down to Mikhail's vocal instructions.

'Mikhail is very important to me. He's my eyes on the track,' Libby explained as we jogged along at an indoor training centre at Loughborough. 'He helps me know where I am, every step of the way.'

The corners in the 200 metres must be especially challenging as they have to bank round at an angle.

'Yes there's so much communication,' Libby continued. 'I

don't speak, it's just Mikhail telling me where we are and when to lean. It is pretty scary with the speed, so you need to have a good relationship with your guide and trust them.'

For the first time at London 2012, guides like Mikhail were also rewarded for their effort with medals. 'I'm chuffed to be part of the team and the process,' he beamed. 'People at home don't understand the training and the kind of commitment from both parts.'

'Come on drive, push, push, let's go,' he said gently into Libby's left ear as they went up and down the track, learning to read each other's breathing and heartbeat as well as recognising the vocal instructions. There was only one way for me to appreciate what Libby was dealing with here. If you have space and there are no obstacles around, place your hands over your eyes, but allow just a bit of peripheral vision on your left side and you get will an idea. On the track, I wore goggles that Libby had partially obscured. Once they were on I could just make out an image of Mikhail on my left side, but because I was facing forward I couldn't make out any detail.

I set off into the unknown with tentative strides. I could hear a bit of laughter as Mikhail and Libby told me 'Come on, move the left arm more, control it, chin down, get the chin down, control it control it…!' Then before I ran into Simon the cameraman (yes, Simon the bravest cameraman in the world) I heard, 'Dip, dip – there you go!' Mikhail's voice trailed off to a low finish and then I felt a reassuring pat. I had been going at a fraction of Libby's speed, and it had felt so disorientating.

In sprinting, then, you listen to your guide, but in goalball, you are waiting for the ball to get louder and louder before there's a thud just in front of you, and then perhaps the crunch of the vulcanised rubber ball against your body.

Goalball is an adrenalin-packed team sport, played by three each side, and with two goals at either ends of a sports hall. The idea is to throw or bounce a large heavy ball, which weighs 1.25 kilogrammes, from your end of the pitch past your opponents and into their goal at the other end. Then you wait for them to throw it back, and you try to stop it. It sounds easy enough until you add the blindfolds, which everyone wears. Inside the ball there are bells, so it's all about listening for the approaching jingle.

The sport has come a long way since it was developed in 1946 to help rehabilitate Second World War veterans left blind or visually impaired. Thanks to the blindfolds, anyone, regardless of their level of visual impairment, can play on the same side or against each other. Indeed many of the European leagues have mixed teams including blind and sighted players. The only ability that matters is your skill on the ball.

'Most team sports involve being able to see teammates and the ball,' said Anna Sharkey, one of the stars of the British women's team that won the European championships in 2010. 'This is different, and everyone is on a level playing field. It takes any disability out of the equation and you are just an athlete just doing what you do best.'

The sport's inclusivity means it ideal for schools. My first game with members of the British team also came at a session where children were getting a taste of the sport.

'It looks easy, but it's really quite hard,' said one girl. 'It's faster than you think, and so when it hits you at full pace and with no padding, you are doomed!' added another. It does take some getting used to, but after a few minutes your hearing feels more acute and the court is also marked with tape so you can feel your way around.

I was on the edge of the pitch. I could tell that much by the line of tape that eventually met the bottom of the goal frame. With that in mind, on all fours, I backed a yard away into the centre of the goal area, and spread myself wide. Behind me, a teammate indicated that she was doing the same, while facing the other way and in front of us further out from goal was our third player, covering the middle.

The whistle went and the sound of the bell began to get louder and louder. It was still quite faint, but I realised it was close. One, two, three – and dive. I went down, using my arms to protect my face. The impact on my elbows was less than I had feared, but it was an ineffective block and the ball bobbled off my elbow and into the goal behind me. Other shots followed. Sometimes the bouncing bombs would only make one noise on the floor before the bells were pouncing on me. I took one on the edge of my face, and one on the thighs, but again no damage was done and I started to judge the path better, clutching the ball gratefully with my outstretched fingers and then bringing it back into my chest.

I had the ball, I had stopped a goal – but now I had just 10 seconds to find my bearings and deliver it back. I reached for the tape, tapping furiously at the floor. It seemed a mile away, but there it was and using that as my guide I ran my fingers back towards the goal again. I pulled myself up on the post and then rested on the top of the low crossbar. I moved along and rocked back, before rolling out forwards and releasing the ball. I waited for a whistle and applause for a goal, but instead there was a brief silence before the noise of the bell came back at me again. The action feels non-stop and it leaves you panting for breath.

The GB women's team had gone easy on me, but they told me how much it does sometimes hurt as they shared stories of their injuries. Don't be put off though, because it only really gets painful at the top level, when medals are at stake and when the athletes are in full flow. It's only then that the ball is travelling at up to 60 miles per hour.

Luckily Mr Knott in Hampshire wasn't put off when he saw it featured on BBC *Breakfast* one morning. His teenage son Adam remembers: 'My Dad Phil was watching BBC *Breakfast* when the item on goalball came on. The first thing he did was rush upstairs to wake me up, and he made me fill in a form which he had printed off. Then a few months later I went to Brunel University to try out blind football, blind judo and goalball and luckily for me the British assistant goalball coach was there and he took my details.'

The rest is history. Adam and his younger brother David are now part of the developing ParalympicsGB men's team. Before the Paralympic games in London the whole team based themselves at the Knotts parents' house near Chandlers Ford, sharing a room and living, breathing and dreaming the sport. London 2012 came too early for them to threaten the top nations, especially China, but they will be a force to be reckoned with by Rio.

If you want to join the Knott brothers then get involved: www.goalballuk.com

As well as contacting the governing bodies for the individual sports, you should check out the umbrella website for parasports, www.parasport.org.uk. This is all about inspiring, educating and pointing people, towards the sport that is right for them. From just having a go at a Paralympic sport, to getting involved at the top level, this website will put you in touch with the right people. It will help anyone find the sports which best suit their abilities.

11

RUNNING CRAZY

It's free, it's addictive and you always feel much better afterwards, even if putting your trainers on does feel such an effort at times. This chapter is dedicated to one of the great loves in my life, running. Whether you are a fun runner who likes the social aspect or a hardened endurance athlete who's focusing on a PB there are so many ways to get involved, even if you'd prefer to go backwards.

One of my earliest sporting memories, and the moment I fell in love with running, was watching Sebastian Coe and Steve Ovett race in the 800 and 1,500 metres, establishing Great Britain as a dominant force at middle distance running. It's a distance we can all relate to, I guess.

At primary school it was the 1,000 metres for me, and at this point I had better get a skeleton out of the cupboard. Long distance running was always one sport in which I could beat the bigger kids.

When I was around nine years old, during the time of the *Daily Owl*, I used to organise runs from Ashwell to the neighbouring village of Hinxworth for my mates, knowing I would stand a good chance of winning. I don't know that in today's world of computer games, and more perceived danger out there, I would have the freedom to stage these runs if I was nine years old today. I was equally dominant at school, until my moment of shame. I had always employed a very risky tactic in the 1000 metres, which involved endless laps of the playing field. I used to make a break for it early on, and then try to hold on, out in front, relishing the fact that the others couldn't catch me.

Anyone with experience will tell you this is a bad habit to get into and it doesn't work as you get older. Each year my rivals would inch closer, until in the final 100 metres of the steeplechase in the summer of 1976, I could feel the presence of Peter Neeves right on my shoulder. A tall, friendly lad, his long strides now seemed effortless compared to my frantic kicking for the line. Panic set in. I tried to stop my legs from veering to the left into Peter's path, but it happened so quickly. Before I could re-align my body with my legs, I was swerving back over to the right, once again into the way of Neeves, who lost his momentum as he huffed in justified disapproval. One, two, three more strides and I was there, victory once more, but there was no feeling of pride this time. 'Shame, shame on you', my conscience was baying.

What made it worse was that my dad, John, was the school headmaster. So I had not only brought shame on myself, but also the family. I still don't know to this day why the race wasn't just awarded to Peter Neeves. Perhaps it's because he was such a pleasant young man who didn't throw his arms around complaining to the teacher in charge. Instead, the race was re-run and this time I didn't have to cheat to win at a canter. I know, I should have let Peter come past me to make amends, but when you're young, you make mistakes, and my punishment was the guilt that slowed me down in the years that followed.

Peter I am sorry, but I learned then that cheating never pays, because that was the last race I ever won. I got my just desserts in the Hertfordshire County Championships the following Autumn. I had been chosen by my school to enter the county championships and this is a great way to get experience. Find your nearest club or team by visiting the website of UK Athletics, www.uka.org.uk.

Top tip, though: always make sure you tie your trainers on tightly! Back in the Hertfordshire mud and the gold medal was in sight. The conditions on the ground, though, were getting murkier and in the mud, disaster struck. Right foot, left foot, right foot...squelch. As I looked down, my left foot had disappeared into a brown underworld. As I pulled it out, I was greeted by my sock. My left trainer had abandoned ship a stride behind. I could have run on, Zola Budd style, but decided to retrieve the shoe. My humiliation was complete as I toppled sideways, and by the time I was on my feet again, not only had any chance of gold disappeared, but silver too. Disappointment dragged me home in third place, and it felt like defeat.

The next serious running was that marathon journey from Yorkshire to Hertfordshire some four years later, which, yes, was life-changing, but after 180 miles in six days, it was time to hang up the trainers for a while and football became my passion. The blisters, and a bout of pneumonia three months after the multiple marathons, meant I just got out of the habit of training, which as any runner knows is a slippery slope. However, decades later I was to fall back in love with distance running thanks to a hare and a ponytailed Scotsman.

BEST FOOT FORWARD

HASHING

Some runners relish a slippery slope. They call it 'shiggy', and it was thanks to a Scotsman who was wearing hare ears, and a high court judge shouting 'petrol', that I was infected with the running bug again 20 years later.

'On, ON', was the cry as a white-haired former army officer, who called himself 'Fruit and Nut', blew his hunting horn. 'Petrol' was a warning that a car was approaching. There were several hounds, well, dogs to be precise; a golden retriever, a white Jack Russell and my own mutt Basil. Hel thought he was a pedigree Labrador, but in reality his mother had run off with a farmer's lurcher, therefore polluting his blood line.

So there was a hunting horn, we had hounds and we were charging through the countryside on the trail of a hare, but this is certainly no blood sport. We were following the trail, left by a human hare, a headmaster who answered to the name of Straddle Various. It was our first taste of the sport known as hashing, which had arrived in the Hampshire village of St Mary Bourne with Scotsman Alan Watters. Soon after he moved to the area, he claimed he wanted to introduce us all to the hash. You can imagine the reaction around this sheltered, rural community as eyebrows and frowns gathered in suspicion.

But this had nothing to do with drugs. The roots of the Hash House Harriers go back to the old English schoolboy game of Hares and Hounds. Some boys would go ahead and leave a trail of paper scattered along the route for the rest of the pack to follow. The Rugby school in Warwickshire held its first 'Crick Run' in 1837. The sport, then better known as paper chasing, became popular on Wimbledon Common in the 1860s, but it wasn't until just before the Second World War that the modern hashing movement started.

An accountant called Albert Stephen Ignatius Gispert had been introduced to paper chasing in the Malacca area of Malaysia. He then relocated to Kuala Lumpur and got a group of expats to join him.

They would dine together at the Selangor Club, where the food was so bad, the establishment became known as the Hash House. They would spend their lunchtimes laying trails of paper for the rest of the group to follow, and they soon discovered that it was a great way of making the jog around the block more interesting. In 1938 they drew up a charter, and at the thousands of hash groups now all over the world, the principles are still the same: To promote physical fitness, to develop a good thirst and to satisfy that with beer, and to persuade older members that they are not as old as they feel. There are several strange hashing customs that have been added since. Every member has a hash name, and I was soon known as Kate Adie, purely thanks to the BBC connections. I had no choice in the matter and journalistically speaking it was an honour. Then there are the forfeits – anyone caught taking a short cut, or cheating, drinks a half pint of beer or something soft if they don't drink alcohol. And woe betide anyone wearing new shoes on a run. I found out early on that new trainers don't make very effective or sweet-smelling pint glasses, as you are asked to baptise your new running footwear by drinking from them.

Despite such oddities, I have enjoyed countless wonderfully bizarre adventures with hashers over the years, and thoroughly recommend it as a fun way to get fitter. They describe themselves as drinkers with a running problem, and while most are as fit as fiddles, they are first and foremost a social club. For a start, it's not competitive. The person who volunteers to be the hare goes out before a run and lays a trail of flour, which has replaced the bits of paper. The idea is to also lay lots of false trails to give the pack a challenge. It's a communal effort for runners of all abilities, and there are 'regroup check points', when the pack stops to let everyone catch up.

Having said this, the better runners still get to cover more distance, and this is how. When the hare gets to a point where two, three or four paths cross, he or she will lay blobs of flour going off in each direction. It's up to the quicker runners to discover which is the right trail and which are false ones. You know you are on the wrong route if the blobs of flour run out after two, or if there is a bold line of flour known as a bar across the path. But this could be half a mile up the wrong route, and so these advanced search parties will have done an extra mile by the time the slower runners and walkers reach the crossroads. Indeed by the time the whole pack has regrouped, the faster runners will have already done the hard work and found which is the right trail for the next stage of the journey. Then the process can start again, with the hare trying to outfox the faster ones with false trails along the way.

Every hash has its own system, but this is the most common, and I found it was a wonderful way to see the nooks and crannies of towns, villages and countryside that I never knew were there. It reminded me how running is the purest way to get fit and see the world, and how it's so accessible to most of us, and is sociable and free.

The hash runs generally start and end at a pub, which is the venue for the downing of those drinks. A run may involve wading across a river and anyone who doesn't follow the exact trail, for example taking a bridge instead, would be guilty of 'sinning' and so would risk being nominated for a liquid punishment in the warm down at the end. As the sinners swill their drink, they are accompanied by a rousing rendition of the hasher's song.

This weird and wonderful world took me to the roots of hashing in Kuala Lumpur, over a weekend in October 1998. It was the bi-annual international gathering, in the 60th anniversary year, and 6,000 hashers gathered inside a football stadium for the opening ceremony. There was also an Olympic-style election for the hosts of the next inter-hash in 2000, won by Hobart in Tasmania.

At an inter-hash you can choose between several different runs daily, varying in degrees of difficulty, from a four-mile jog, to what they call a ball-breaker of 20 miles or more. I chose a middle distance run, which took us through a vast bat cave on the edge of the city and out into the jungle, across swamps, and through bewildered villages, the inhabitants of which were drawn from their dwellings by the haunting hashers call of 'on, on'. This cry is a way for the pack to stay in touch as they spread out across the trail. There is a whole language in fact. 'On back' means a false trail, and 'on inn' means you are finally within touching distance of the pub at the end.

The problem here in the thick jungle was that the cry of 'on, on' had been smothered, and silenced by the trees. I was alone, and smelling like a bag of chips too. To dissuade blood-sucking leeches from picnicking on our flesh we had been advised to cover legs and arms with salt and vinegar, and for once this wasn't a strange hashing ritual but very practical advice. It must have put off any tigers too, because I stumbled and tripped my way through the vines without any wildlife for company, and arrived at a clearing where dozens of cheering fellow hashers were gathered around a block of ice. They weren't cheering for me, but for the hasher who had been caught running through a white line. The forfeit in hotter climates is to pull down your shorts and sit on a block of ice while downing your beer (I never said they were sane) but I am happy to report that it all went down well with the locals.

'I want some of what you are on' is what must have been going through the mind of an elderly gentleman who tottered into the circle from nowhere. He was a grey-haired, spindly man, about 80 years old and chirping away in Malayan he made straight for the ice, pulled down his dusty beige trousers and plonked his bare backside onto the ice. Letting out a yelp he stayed rooted to the spot, gleefully lapping up the beer and the cheers. I wonder what he told his grandchildren.

If hashing sounds like it could tempt you into getting fitter, and believe me some people walk their dog around and do it just for the social side, then there will be a hash group near you. Go to the website www.hhh.org.uk

I have seen all ages on a hash run, too, from those in their 80s and 90s to my daughter Lucy, who was just one when she came around on my back.

Hashing had brought me back to running – It is also one of the few sports that enables ordinary people to feel like their heroes, to enter the same races and rub shoulders with the elite.

THE MARATHON

Take the London Marathon, now one of the world's great sporting occasions. It helped get the ball rolling and has led to countless similar events around the planet. In what other sporting event do you have novices and people dressed as rhinos, Big Ben or a yellow submarine, all on the same course at the same time as the stars; the Paula Radcliffes and the David Weirs of this world.

It should be on the list of the top 100 things to do before

you die, and for me the London marathon 2011 will go down as one of the best days of my life. Let me point out right now that I wasn't especially fit going into it. Yes, I could plod around six miles in an hour and five minutes, but it was tough going. Like everyone else I drew up a training programme in the autumn, but when the rain and wind are lashing the windows before you even leave work, and when the Christmas mince pies are begging to be eaten, well, the 'training regime' is easily filed away.

I met up with Olympic marathon runner Liz Yelling for a December training run on the beach at Sandbanks in Dorset. She spoke of the need to keep a little bit of running going over the festive period, but added that you had to allow yourself Christmas Day as a day off and that I could have a couple of drinks.

One other useful idea she had was this. To keep your training going on those days when you are off to see relatives and friends, simply get your family to kick you out of the car when you're halfway there, so that you have to run the rest of the distance. It didn't quite work in my case as I was driving to Yorkshire and the only others in the car were my three daughters. I can see the idea working, though.

I am sure I wasn't the only one who didn't start their London Marathon training until after Christmas. Finally, in January, I managed to drag my sorry carcass over six miles in the Chilterns, and while the beautiful crisp winter landscape was inspiring for the soul, my right knee and thighs had their blinkers on, and I was soon being jabbed by sharp, shooting pains. In the past we might have been encouraged to rest, or soldier on, but trying to sort things out yourself often leads to more problems, and so my top tip for future marathon runners is to get any early niggles looked at by a physio straight away.

It's also wise to have your gait analysed. Not the rusty thing at the front of your garden, but your bio-mechanics, your running style. I am flat-footed and bow-legged, and I wasn't surprised to discover that I had the gait of John Wayne and that this would obviously impede my efficiency. But having my gait monitored meant I could then get the right training shoe and exercise routine for my individual running style.

Pain of some description is common among marathon runners. I attended a marathon work shop at Eton Dorney where there was a lady with shin splints, a man who had once run the marathon with a broken pelvis and a former party girl who said she had just cut out the booze and the fags. Definitely painful. Then there was me, with my post-six-mile limp, caused by runner's knee, or to give it the technical term, IT friction syndrome. So I went to seek the advice of top sports physiotherapist John Green, who hit my knee and the proverbial nail on the head with a series of twists and bends.

'Everything looks good on the surface, you look reasonably fit, but you can't build a great house if you haven't got a good foundation. It's going to be a vulnerable structure.' What he meant was that I wasn't strengthening my running muscles, while asking them to work smoothly over a distance they weren't used to any more. It's one of the most common problems for anyone preparing for the marathon. You finally pluck up the will and energy to get out there for a training run, you make sure you you're your watch and iPod on, and quicker than Flash Gordon you are out of the door, without having properly warmed up your muscles.

The prescription for my pain, then, was simple. Ten minutes of stretching exercises before I set off to warm and loosen me up. I had a routine of five simple movements which I had to stick to before I went out, and when I came back, and this helped build the foundations for the weeks ahead. It was so important for me to spend time doing this, even if it meant cutting down on the length of my training run when I did step out.

The other top tips that got me through the pain and helped build up some stamina over the coming weeks were these. Firstly, start taking any energy gels and drinks that you think you will use come marathon day early on, so your body can get used to them. Secondly, get a proper marathon vest that's not going to rub and make your nipples bleed. That's as important as getting fitted trainers a month or so before the big day to get your feet comfortable. Finally, download the Marathon Talk podcast. This got me through the longer training runs, when my mental strength was waning. It's free from the Marathon Talk website and is a weekly programme presented by Martin Yelling (Liz's husband) and Tom Williams. It includes more tips, advice and features, and it makes you feel like you belong to the wider running family. I may have been alone pounding the streets in the driving rain, but I realised I wasn't the only one, and I wasn't so aware of the miles passing.

It might sound as if I was out regularly, as winter turned to spring. If only. It was at most once a week, and the furthest I went was 17 miles, after which felt like my legs were going to drop off. Admittedly the few runs I did were on the slopes of the Chilterns or Hampshire's north downs – another tip must be to include hilly terrain in your training. After this, the London Marathon course will feel so lovely and flat.

It was like the night before Christmas on the eve of the London Marathon 2011. I took Michel Roux's advice. He's the marathon-running chef and patron from Le Gavroche restaurant and *Masterchef* on the BBC. Boiled chicken and basil on a bed of spaghetti, with one small glass of wine, was his recipe for a good night's kip. OK, I had two glasses, Michel, but only for medicinal purposes – and it worked.

Sophie Raworth, Iwan Thomas, Nell McAndrew, Michel Roux and Stella from *The Apprentice* were famous faces I recognised near the start line, on the sunny morning of the race.

I took my first energy gels, and then rubbed muscle-warming lubricant into every part of my body that I could feasibly reach. I had seen bleeding nipples, and had heard the stories of chafing, so wasn't taking any chances. Then after a live interview for the BBC News channel, we were ready, 35,000 poised, waiting for the moment when the months and weeks of training would prove their worth.

The gun fired and we were on our way. The first few hundred metres was a blur as wave after wave of legs and colourful vests broke over me. The one piece of advice I was determined to follow was 'don't go off too quickly'. Everyone is worried about hitting the dreaded wall of pain at some point, and your chances of getting over it can be determined by how far you push your body's limits in those early stages. What made it easier to rein myself back were the crowds; the thousands of supporters lining the route. Every step of the way there was a smile, a cheer, the call of a name and an outstretched hand. It seemed obvious to me that if touched every hand I could get to, it would help me stay nice and slow. The whole world seemed to be overtaking me, but I didn't care because I was in Wonderland, soaking up the music, the tapestry of faces, the sense of euphoria.

I couldn't stop smiling, and while my tactic wouldn't suit the more serious runners going for a personal best, for a first-timer, a middle aged man whose body was stepping into the unknown, it paid real dividends. For 13 miles the waves of people had swept past me, but the tide was about to turn, and at around the

14 mile mark I actually passed someone else who'd stopped for breath; hunched over, hands on knees. Then there was another one, then several more, and now it felt like *I* was in the fast lane. The Blackwall tunnel came and went, but still no wall; still no pain. My brain must have been affected, though, as I nearly undid all of my good work by biting off more than I could chew. Volunteers were handing out sweets, and at one point what looked like energy crystals. At the next corner, I took a scoop of what I thought was energy gel from the palms of more outstretched arms. I didn't stop to consider that it was odd that they had squeezed the gel out of the sachets and onto their hands. I just nodded, took a handful and shovelled it into my mouth. I swallowed whole lumps, waiting for the sweet taste to trickle down from tonsils to toes, but there was nothing sugary about this pick-me-up. It was oily, almost petrol-like, and it was only when I noticed people around me smearing the gooey substance into their calves and thighs that I realised that it had been a lubricant stop, and I had swallowed some Vaseline.

Luckily I suffered no ill-effects, and actually the last six miles were my fastest. My wall was a molehill compared to what some of the faltering fallers around me were facing, and I really felt for those who had gone off too fast, or suffered an injury along the way.

The finishing line was the only anti-climax in the day. I don't know what I expected. A 26.2-cannon salute, or dancing unicorns? But instead we were ushered into lanes to collect our medals and then on to the area where we'd pick up our bags. It was brilliantly organised, but I guess what I am saying is that I was really sad it was over. Having been on such a running-induced high, the wildest party in paradise would have seemed like a come-down, and a cup of tea and a laze on the sofa that evening were the perfect way to celebrate.

My time was 4:42, just outside my target of four and a half hours, but at least my running foundations had been solid enough for an average semi. From this point, you can expand and strengthen your running in other areas to improve your time, but for me it was a good enough starting point. I had seen for myself why this event has become so famous around the world, and why it's so hard to get into. Keep trying, because it's well worth the wait.

I was back home in a hot bath that night by the time a chap called John Farnworth finally crossed the line. It was after 10pm, but he had just become the first man in the world to complete the distance while keeping a football up off the ground. Yes, 26.2 miles of continuous keepy-uppy. I was rather relieved that he had finished, because just two days earlier I had almost scuppered his record attempt.

I met him for a training workout on the Embankment by the Thames for a Saturday *Breakfast* piece, and he had shown me the skills he had spent months working on. He knew every contour of his lucky football, every stitch of the one that would stick with him all the way around. He invited me to see how difficult it was to keep the ball up while jogging along the bobbly pavement. One touch, two touches, and soon I was up to six in a row. Getting cocky I turned to ask John a question, and out of nowhere managed to smack the ball with my left foot. If it had been on a pitch in a game, I could have been celebrating the goal of the century, a rasping curler with the outside of my left foot. What's more I am right-footed. So why now, why here by the Thames, with John's special ball, did I make the connection of a lifetime with my left? The ball soared past wide-eyed cyclists, past tourists posing for a photo, and over the wall.

'That's my...that's the...' John could hardly speak. We dashed to the wall just to see the inevitable. Goodbye ball. It was now 100 metres away and drifting off towards the Thames barrier. Goodbye potential world record, goodbye all the months of hard work that John had put in. He was very polite but he must have been seething inside.

There are times in life when nothing will stop you and at that moment, wild tigers with their teeth around my underpants wouldn't have dragged me back as I raced along the Embankment looking for a solution. I was a man possessed as I looked to the sky, willing the wind to change direction. The power of the mind never ceases to amaze me – because change it did. I hung from a footbridge leading to a barge restaurant, and with a fishing hook on the end of a stick, clawed the ball back from the brink. John was able to go and do the London Marathon with his lucky ball after all. He's now a world-famous professional freestyle footballer and completed the 26.2 miles, while keeping the ball in the air, in 12 hours and eight minutes. It helped him raise over £10,000 for charity.

In April 2013, just before this book went to press, I attempted the Virgin London Marathon for a second time, and this time didn't give this beast the respect it deserves.

In mitigation: my full-on life travelling north and south between the studios at Media City, seeing my daughters and spending time at my partner's house, meant I didn't have much time for training. You are meant to be out there doing three or four runs a week, but I was lucky if I did that a month. Plus it seemed like every time I had a run planned, there was thick snow or ice on the ground and a phone call or email came in with a story idea I had to respond to.

But it had been such a pleasant experience the first time that I thought I would be fine. I did manage a 17-mile trek across the Chilterns and was drenched by every passing lorry in a tidal wave of puddle water on the main road near High Wycombe, and it was torture. However, I still thought it would be all right on the day.

I discovered while collecting my race number at the exhibition that the former World Superbike champion, and now musician, James Toseland had also eaten Vaseline during his first London marathon. He was looking supremely fit as he limbered up at the press call, alongside other sporting greats including former England cricket captain Andrew Strauss and former Olympic medallist in the heptathlon, Kelly Sotherton. They were nervous – it was a completely different physical challenge from anything they'd been faced with before.

On race day itself there was a humbling collection of familiar faces in the celebrity tent beforehand, with Iwan Thomas stretching one side of me and Katherine Jenkins, some of McFly and Amy Childs on the other. Then there were the representatives from the House of Commons; Graham Evans MP, and Shadow Chancellor Ed Balls MP. But at that moment it didn't matter a jot who we were: we were united by one aim, running 26.2 miles. This is an individual race, a battle against yourself using your own will power, but you are part of a 40,000-strong team. It's a great leveller; a unique collective challenge, in which the likes of Mo Farah enter alongside mere mortals dressed as fairies, beer bottles, rhinos and camels.

I positioned myself at the front of the green start next to the towering model Sophie Anderton. I had a camera in my hand, a small go-pro 3, with the intention of recording the journey from a runner's point of view. It was the idea of my colleague Dan Curtis. I didn't want to let Dan down and wanted the first bend to be a sea of cheering faces, not a jiggling tapestry of backside. So I sprinted. We were off and with the wind in my sails I bounded like a performing gazelle to the first bend. I kept shooting forward, focusing on the road ahead, but where were the masses? Where were the crowds?

Of course they were starting the race at a sensible pace and so it was a full 600 metres, maybe more before I heard footsteps and then saw the well-oiled machine, James Toseland, gliding past on his way to a fantastic time of 3 hours and 3 minutes. Next there was the uplifting and beaming smile of Tony Audenshaw, from Emmerdale, who does the Tony's Trials feature on the Marathon Talk podcasts. As a regular listener this was a special moment, but he told me to ease off the pace. We'd glided through the first mile in just over 7 minutes; 'stupid boy', I thought, as Andrew Strauss pounded past me before finishing in 3:51. The next 12 miles were a sea of jubilant faces and hands that I had wondered at the first time. The support – from the pubs in the East End south of the river, to all the volunteers with their water and energy drinks – is like a jet engine strapped to your back. I stopped a few times to wipe water off the camera lens and change the batteries, which had been jiggling around in my pocket, but I'd made it to halfway.

Then came the 14-mile mark. I couldn't talk to my new running friend Rob, who had slowed down to accompany me, any more. My legs became stilts, it felt like I was balancing a basket of heavy washing on each hip, and there were still over 12 miles to go. How on earth will I finish this, I wondered? The knees wobbled, and so I slowed even more to avoid cramp taking hold. At one point a walker overtook me which gives you an idea of my speed. I was looking out for Chris Lord, an inspirational man whom we had met the night before. A year before to the day, he hadn't been able to walk across the room to watch the marathon go past his City of London apartment. He was in the middle of a fight against cancer. 12 months on and he was running the London marathon for the same

Leukaemia and Lymphoma research charity as I was. It was an incredible journey for him to take and sadly I found out later that he had been clipped at mile 12, had fallen and broken his knee. At the time of writing he is still planning to finish the marathon. What an inspiration to us all.

It's the charities, the crowd, and thoughts of your loved ones and a cup of tea that keep you going through 12 miles of tiredness and pain. You are meant to go quicker on your second marathon as you try to beat your personal best, but I came up the Mall over half an hour slower. It was still the most fantastic feeling. The Monkees were playing on the Tannoy and those around me danced and sung as we staggered past the grandstands and I felt far more emotional this time, as I waved and screamed to Emma, who I'd picked out in the crowd. It had felt like more of a journey. At least I had still beaten the pantomime camel, and the footage I had shot was actually useable and made an interesting little video for the BBC website and for *Breakfast*. But take my advice: do not take the marathon for granted.

IRONMAN AND EXTREME TRIATHLONS

Despite that heart-in-the mouth moment, the running bug had truly taken hold again, and I dipped my toes into more extreme events. The Patagonian Adventure race takes teams over hundreds of miles in South America – in kayaks, on bikes and on foot. You are on the go for days and nights on end, and in Wales, I got a glimpse of what this marathon for insomniacs can be like. I joined the GB team for a night training run near Chepstow, and listened to their tales of the monsters they see as they stumble through forests, with lack of sleep taunting the shadows of their mind.

For those who have built the strongest of foundations, there are the Ironman events, and Chrissie Wellington, who came onto the *Breakfast* sofa with her gnarled and ravaged feet, has to be one of my all-time sporting heroines for her four world titles in the Ironman event.

It involves a 3.4-mile swim, a bike ride of 112 miles and then a full marathon run. Chrissie wasn't from always from a running back ground and only ran her first triathlon in 2004. She was world Ironman champion just three years later and set a new world record while suffering from shingles in 2009.

It doesn't end there. She fractured bones in her arm and hand after a bike accident a year later, but still returned to obliterate world records again in 2010 and then in 2011, with an Iron-distance world record at the Challenge Roth event of 8:18.13.

Chrissie told me that it would take a year of my sort of training to build up the strength and stamina required for such a distance, so it's something to work on, but in the meantime, there is a much more accessible multi-discipline sport that has boomed in popularity over the last decade.

TRIATHLON

I was breaking into a sprint on the home straight at the end of an Olympic-distance triathlon at Windsor. I was just a few hundred metres behind the new champion and I was actually ahead of elite athletes. Admittedly I had set off on my swim section some two hours ahead of these front runners, but the fantastic thing about this triathlon was that us amateurs were still doing our 10-kilometre run at the end when the proper athletes caught us up. I was rubbing shoulders with the medal contenders as I reached for the line. It was like being on the pitch at Wembley with the FA Cup finalists.

An Olympic-distance triathlon is a 1.5-kilometre swim, a 40-kilometre cycle ride and a 10k run. For beginners who find this daunting there is a sprint race as well, which is half as long.

My training had consisted of a couple of six-mile runs, a solitary bike ride, and a swim up and down a local pool. I had run out of time for a more thorough workout, before I entered a chilly River Thames at 7am in early June. The furthest I had ever swum was 500 metres, and now I was challenged with doing three times that distance.

The start of a triathlon is a whirlpool of arms, rubbery wet-suited legs and brightly-coloured caps, all clawing away in a quest to find clear water. I was left by the pack in my first triathlon, as the other competitors pulled away up the River Thames. I was in clear water, but because the first 1,000 metres was upstream, I was slapped in the face by a procession of rippling waves and the odd passing weed.

As a beginner, my aim was to complete the swim in whatever way I could, and I freely confess that at one point I even resorted to doggy paddle. At least this meant that I could draw breath and nod to the spectators supping their mugs of tea on barges and cruisers moored at the side.

The new Olympic champion, Alistair Brownlee, completed his swim en route to gold at London 2012 in 17 minutes and four seconds, eight seconds off the lead. My swim would take a whole 40 minutes longer, but with my neck aching, I eventually emerged decorated by weeds, having at least set a personal best.

Trying to get your wetsuit off while running to the next discipline should be a sport in itself, and triathlons can be won and lost during the transition stages. The wetsuit comes off, followed by your goggles, and with cycling shoes already attached to the pedals, you are ready to go: all within around 30 seconds if you are quick. Having everything ready and rehearsed beforehand is crucial. Baby oil and petroleum jelly can also help with peeling off the wetsuit. I wish I had known that as I tugged, pulled, stamped and stumbled on the grass, trying to free myself of the rubbery skin.

The cycling stage was all about stamina. Pedalling in the rain on open roads, as lorries thundered through puddles, meant I got almost as wet as I had been in the river. The weight of the water made the long and winding road seem even further and my mind started playing tricks on me. When I asked a marshal if I was nearing the end of the 40-kilometre slog, he punctured me further when he replied: 'You're nearly a third of the way!'

It was nearly two hours before I entered the second transition phase leading into the 10-kilometre run. Having done the London marathon this felt like a pair of comfy slippers, and I was buoyed along by the presence of the elite athletes. Alistair Brownlee's best time, set at London 2012, of 1 hour 46 minutes and 25 seconds, was a world away from my time of three and a half hours, but I had lost so much ground fighting the wetsuit and freewheeling on the bike. If it's your first time, under three hours is a realistic target, and I hope I have proved that fun runners can take part alongside the elite.

BACKWARDS RUNNING

For the final part of this chapter on running, we need to stop, turn around, and 'retne eht dlrow fo gninnur sdrawgninnur'. Luckily it's far easier to try running backwards than writing it in reverse. Take another look at that previous sentence and see if you can work out what it says.

Backwards, or retro, running is not just a new novelty sport that has spread across the world in recent years. It's an attitude; a way of life for some now too. It's claimed the Chinese have been practising backwards walking and running for thousands of years. They are said to be the pioneers and the first who realised its enormous benefits.

Several American sports stars then picked up on it in the 20th century: wrestler William Muldoon, and boxers Gene Turney and Muhammad Ali are said to have used it in training. Other converts include Ed Schultz, the athlete, and Gary Grey, the sports therapist who developed retro running as a way of rehabilitating athletes.

Jon Voight, the Hollywood actor, thinks it helped him deal with age. 'As you get older you have to do something to keep fit. You have to watch what you eat, and I have a little regime that I don't tell anyone about. A couple of times a week I go running backwards,' he is quoted as saying.

It may seem surprising that it has stayed a secret for so long, but not anymore. Since the start of the new millennium it has taken off in the way jogging did in the 1970s, and around the world, footballers, basketball teams and tennis players all use retro running as part of their training.

The first UK backwards running race was organised by James Bamber from Wacky Nation, and it took place in Manchester in 2009. Three years later, 150 lined up at the start. It made its Welsh debut in the summer of the same year, at the World Alternative Games, where the star attraction was the world record holder in the backwards half-marathon, Garret Doherty from Dublin.

I met Garret for a training run in a park in Crystal Palace, as he was getting in the miles ahead of the world championships in Barcelona with a group of new recruits.

'I was jogging around a park in Dublin one day,' explained Garret, 'but the sun was behind me and I wanted the light to warm my face and so I just turned round, and for some reason kept on running. It felt good, it felt natural and I got a great reaction from other people in the park, so I kept going.' Garret thought he had found something new, something to tell the world about, but on websites he found that the world already knew.

Garret has now conquered that retro world. He's the three-time UK champion, a world champion, and his record time over a half marathon is 1:39 minutes. Most of us would struggle to beat that going forwards.

After limbering up on the spot, Garret shouted 'go' and we swivelled round and teetered through the giant oak trees of the park. It's an odd feeling at first, rotating your head like a nervous owl to see where you are going, but as long as it's an open space, you get used to that and learn to trust your natural instincts.

Doing a few neck exercises first helps loosen the muscles and makes the movement easier.

I may have looked daft, but with my head up and more alert, I felt my lungs open up more and I was less out of breath than when running forwards. I also felt lighter, because it was my toes and the balls of my feet hitting the ground first. This gave me more spring in my step, and so the rest of my foot only skimmed the surface. I was taking shorter strides, but more per minute, so it still felt quick. As you gain confidence you can increase that stride length.

The sport makes bold scientific claims. Apparently you take over 20 per cent more oxygen into your body when running backwards. It increases your cardiovascular system and burns off one third more calories. Retro followers also believe it develops greater balance and stamina and reduces the impact of the ground on your joints, therefore reducing the risk of injuries. They claim it also exercises the right side of the brain more and therefore benefits memory and concentration.

It can also help you go forwards, too. Gary Gray, the US physiotherapist, is quoted saying: 'It's truly a cross-training exercise. It can significantly enhance your ability to move forwards.'

Meanwhile Sally Raynes from Wacky Nation says:

'Forward running is not bad for you, but like most things in life, too much of one thing can be detrimental. This is particularly true for runners with poor biomechanics where every stride adds extra stress to their joints. Backward running restores a balance to the lower leg muscles. It works those muscles that often get ignored like the calves, shins and front thigh muscles.'

I failed physics O level, and biology was more about mice and locusts, so I am not in a position to make scientific judgements. All I can comment on is how I felt as I finished my first backwards mile, which included a section weaving through the trees. I was firstly relieved that none of us had fallen over. But I also felt energised, sprightly, and strangely even slightly taller. I maybe fantasising, but I was aware that I had tapped into new parts of my body. It's a bit like when we suddenly start to kick a ball with our other foot. It feels strange and alien to begin with, but there's a wonderful balance to footballers who can use both feet.

I am told it takes four or five runs to start noticing a big difference, but what you will feel the day after is how stiff the backs of your legs will be.

I can now sometimes be seen running along the paths of Hampshire or Buckinghamshire in what some would describe as the wrong direction. There are obvious limitations. Don't try this on a road or in a built-up urban area. It's also wise to have a friend or two with you. But as long as it's safe, the next time you are out for a jog across the park, why not turn around and take a few steps backwards. If you enter one of a growing number of races, like the annual UK championship every May, you might want to wear a vest that suits the occasion, like the curly-wigged runner who wore the numbers 811 811 on his. Read it backwards and you will get his joke.

For more information go to the website www.reverserunning.com and also check out www.wackynation.com/event-management. They also organise the UK rock-paper-scissors championship.

ON YOUR BIKE

12

ON YOUR BIKE

The bicycle has been the sporting success story of this century, especially for Great Britain. We are a nation obcessed and inspired by so many gold medallists and more recently the sideburning speed and stamina of Bradley Wiggins. This chapter is all about different ways to get involved and what can happen when you don't keep your eyes fully on the route ahead.

ON TWO WHEELS

THE RISE OF THE BMX

One by one they locked me in a steely stare. With helmets on I could only see the whites of their eyes and they meant business. I was lined up in gate one, with Kira in two, and then came Sam, William and Will. They rocked on their bikes, itching to start, eyes now fixed on the BMX track ahead at the national cycling centre in Manchester.

A push of the legs and in a storm of spokes we sped down the ramp, jostling for position as we tried to keep up the speed, up to the first whoop – that's the name given to the bumps on a BMX track. Kira was over first, while Will even managed to get some air, such was his spurt up to the summit. They were off to the first berm (which means bend in BMX language) and while they could continue their momentum, I was too big, too heavy, and had to stand and walk myself up that first slope. It was only a couple of feet high, and I had better explain my shortcomings. You see Kira was only four, while William was even younger, just over two years old. Yes, two years old, and already he had me beaten on the balance bike World Cup course. Dan Walker, our pal from *Football Focus* fame, had teased me enough after I was defeated by a 14-year-old in sumo wrestling, so what would he make of this?

The toddler racers did have size on their side. Balance bikes are really only meant for little ones as they learn to ride. They have no pedals and so are low enough for two-year-olds to put their feet down.

They push themselves around with their little legs until they get up speed, when they can tuck their legs up and cruise.

That's something not even a small adult can do. I had only agreed to race the toddlers because they'd been so good in training and the older ones (aged four and five) were desperate to put me in my place. None of the dads or mums would volunteer to join me against their competitive little racers. For the record I did come last, but it had got them giggling in a way normally reserved for Mr Tumble.

There is now a World Cup series of races for two-to-five-year-olds. It started in Manchester in the summer of 2012, and proved so popular a second one followed in the November, involving hundreds of riders. Some parents may worry about their child competing at five years old, let alone two, and may wonder if this is not just the parents living out their own sporting dreams through their children.

Seeing the determined, smiling faces of the children wheeling around this prestigious track went a long way to dismissing such concerns. Every child who'd turned up for this training session didn't want to stop, and in the races they all get a medal. Even when two-year-old Will burst into tears when he fell off, nothing was going to stop him getting back on after a quick cuddle with Mum, and on the whole they didn't seem to notice who had come first, second or third. In fact, the only time the riders seemed concerned was when this BBC reporter came over to ask them a few questions. I wasn't after a Jeremy Paxman-style interrogation, just a little word about how they had found the race, but the large fluffy microphone appeared to spook them, and so instead the parents did the talking.

'There is really nothing else like it out there for kids of this age', said Elle Robinson, Mae's mum. 'All the kids had a great time and in that last event they were flying over the bumps and racing against their friends. She wants to come back again.'

She will get the chance with weekly balance bike sessions now held in Manchester, Birmingham and Kent.

There are two main aims of the classes and the World Cups. One is to teach children how to ride at an earlier age. Some find it easier to learn on a balance bike rather than with stabilisers, because they get used to balancing themselves rather than relying on extra support. The pedals, which are the last bit of the cycling jigsaw, are then apparently straightforward to get used to. The other spin-off is the development of talent at an even younger age. If they can get around one of the national BMX tracks at the age of two, what on earth will they be like in 10 to 15 years' time when they start to realise their potential? Already staff at the track are noticing a difference.

'The whole team can't stop talking about these little riders,' said Nicola O'Neill from the National Cycling Centre.

The top toddlers go on to get international experience as well. The winner of the first event in June 2012 went off to represent Great Britain at the world championships in Florida. Ashton Heron may not remember much about the week he rode for his country at the age of three, but his dad will.

'I'm not sure it has quite sunk in yet for both me or Ashton,' said Adie. 'It's these types of events that will really leave a legacy from the Olympics.'

Ashton came onto the *Breakfast* sofa with his dad and is the youngest sporting guest I have introduced to date. He brought his bike and had so much confidence that despite the glare of the studio lights, which often scare young children, he did answer my questions. He said he liked going fast and that I was rubbish, and nodded 'yes' when I asked if he had been watching the likes of Sarah Storey, Victoria Pendleton and Bradley Wiggins over the summer. By starting so young on the Manchester BMX track, Ashton has taken his first steps towards joining them. It's claimed that the earlier you can programme in skills such as balance, the more it will be embedded into the subconscious.

He can also learn from the best, because he's already training alongside the British team and the likes of Shanaze Reade. 'It's an amazing opportunity,' she said; 'events like this not only give our youngest riders the chance to get on a bike around here, but they're against their friends on the same track that I train on.' Shanaze started racing she was 10, so some of these kids have an eight-year head start.

I have seen first-hand what it will be like for the youngsters when they graduate to full sized BMX bikes. You need incredible balance alongside raw nerves and a rare combination of physical attributes: the explosive legs of a racer, plus the strength and flexibility of an acrobat.

A race starts by throwing yourself and your bike, down a near vertical eight-metre ramp. You want to get to that first whoop before the other riders, because you know there could be carnage: you know you could be taken out by someone else through no fault of your own, and that all those years of preparation could end in intense pain.

The BMX bike only made its debut at the Olympics in 2008, but it was an instant hit. The races are all over in 40 seconds, but the journey is littered with impossible-looking box jumps, those sweeping berms and whoop after whoop. The balance bikes are so small that it's not going to hurt those that fall very much, but that's not the case when you reach Shanaze's level. Injuries are part of the job description in this aggressive form of cycling. She has broken bones in her foot, her elbow and at the base of her spine. Then just a few months before the London 2012 Games she was lying in hospital with a suspected broken neck. She says she is so well known at hospital that the staff joke 'oh no, not you again'.

Not that you will ever hear her moan. She is so down-to-earth and takes everything in her stride, even when asked about the time an Olympic medal was just around the corner in the final of the Beijing 2008 race. She crashed on the final berm when she clipped her rival's wheel, and failed to finish the race.

'Yes, it hurt, but it just made more determined to get gold in the future,' she says. 'Even when I am knocked out, and don't know who I am, you can't let injuries get to you and affect your confidence.'

The top riders never let the fear of further injury throw them off course.

It started in the 1960s, when children began racing their bicycles on dirt tracks in California, drawing inspiration from their motocross superstar heroes. BMX stands for Bicycle Motocross and both involve speed, skill, jumps and acrobatics.

I got stuck in the mud in the motorised version of the sport, when I was trying to get around a track near Salisbury. You have to get up enough speed to get through the quagmire, but I wobbled on a bend, got the throttle all wrong and was left looking for a push. You don't have to worry about that in BMX. It's just you working with gravity and it feels so free, and so simple, with just the single gear and one brake. Like in track cycling, whether you get around the banked curves or not depends on maintaining your nerve and speed, but within a lap or two even beginners can build up enough confidence to get around a circuit, just like three-year-old Ashton.

For more information on the balance bike World Cup, contact one of the centres offering sessions, www.nationalcyclingcentre.com, www.birminghambmxclub.com or www.cyclopark.com, and for BMX information go to britishcycling.org.uk.

CYCLO-CROSS

If the obstacles aren't quite extreme enough for you in BMX, there is a sport which feels like doing an army assault court on your bicycle. Add a bit of mud wrestling, and you have cyclo-cross.

I went down to the cycling track used for the 1948 Olympics, at Herne Hill, to see how this is not so much a case of 'get on your bike', but 'get on and off, and on and off your bike again'. Key to success is being able to mount and dismount smoothly and quickly without stopping, and having broad shoulders to be able to carry your bike over the larger obstacles.

It first started in France in the early 1900s and one theory is that road racers decided to race each other home, but went cross-country, overcoming any fences or hedges that got in their way. Today it's used to keep the road racers fit during the winter months and provides competitors with an adventure playground of cycling. There are bumps, hurdles, huge drops and climbs and the obligatory mud baths. Some events even take place after dark.

I got off to a good start, building up speed around the first corner on a gravel path, but ahead of me was a hurdle about a foot high. I tried to time the squeeze on my brakes to slow me sufficiently to jump off while still moving, but like a gymnast making an awkward dismount, I stepped backwards and lost a split second. By the time I had regained my composure and climbed over the obstacle, I had been overtaken.

I was then warned about the first big drop. Keep up the speed to get through the mud at the bottom had been the advice, and they were right, because any wavering and it was straight through the bush and fence hugging the base of this tight sloping turn.

After weaving through bushes and along the tram lines in a bog, we arrived at what they called 'Death Hill'. Only the mountain goats of this sport could get up while still pedalling, and even with my bike over my shoulders, climbing was a battle against the slime that wanted to take me back down.

The British champion at the time, Jody Cranforth, had got to the top. 'You have to be able to ride in all sorts of ways, coping with the road, the off road bits, the getting on and off slickly. It's a bit of everything and is pretty technical,' he observed.

The best bit was the bath that felt so well deserved afterwards, and also the stop at the pub on the way back. For information on cyclo-cross go to www.britishcycling.org.uk/cyclocross

ROLLAPALUZA

Here's the deal. You want to go for a bike ride, you need to get fit, but you pass the pub, and the fire's burning, the music is pumping. Well stop right there, because there is a fantasy land, a paradise in which you can get fit in the pub, and on a bike. What's more the music is still thumping and the crowd are urging you on, calling for more.

When I went to a rollapaluza evening in London, I had no idea what to expect. I was told to meet the other riders in the Horseshoe pub. Not only that, we were upstairs, and there was a retro vibe as the 45" vinyl 'Beat the Clock' by Sparks was on the turntable.

Up on a temporary stage, two men in Lycra shorts were adjusting themselves in their saddles as a crowd started to gather. The needle went back to the start of the song and the lights dimmed. The men on their static bikes, mounted on special stands, flexed their muscles, nodded to the crowd, and waited for the signal from the referee, who had set the hands on a giant stopwatch on the wall behind them to 0. Then they set off, pedalling as if their lives depended on it. The wheels were turning so fast that they were an invisible blur, but the riders never left the stage. The sweat built on their foreheads as they pushed every muscle, getting up to speeds of 50 miles per hour. The noise was deafening as the raucous crowd screamed their encouragement and blew on horns. It was a race to the line over 500 metres, and then they flopped onto their handlebars, exhausted.

It was as if I had gatecrashed the coolest of parties, where an extreme session down the gym was in bed with a night at the disco. This is the world of rollapaluza.

It's a unique cycling sport. The quicker you can work the pedals, the faster the hand on the dial will move round. This is why the crowd gets so excited, because they can see the red and blue hands on the clock face ticking round to the finish. Add in the MC and the blasting music, and it certainly livens up a ride around the block.

The sport was very popular sport in the UK back in the 1940s and 50s. Then roller racing nights would draw huge crowds to ballrooms, cinemas and even luxury hotels. Then the accompaniment was more refined, led by dancing girls and big bands. As cycling took off, with more sophisticated bikes, the sport took a back seat and was almost forgotten in the UK. That was until 1999, when some bike couriers took a break from their jobs on the streets of London and went to Zurich, for the European Cycle Messenger Championships. They attended a gold-sprints night, the European name for roller racing. The London pose liked what they saw. This would bring the courier community back together, they thought. It would help keep them fit on cold winter nights and give them a bit of breathing space away from the gridlocked roads.

Road racer Greg Tipper had seen the idea at cycling clubs, but wanted to bring it to the wider population and so in 2000, the rollapaluza movement started. They brought in DJs and bands to recreate the old roller-race format, but in a contemporary style.

'It's gladiatorial,' said Casper Hughes, one of the organisers. 'You are facing off against your opponent on stage and with the crowd going wild.'

'Don't pedal backwards' was his top tip, as I got comfortable in the pedals for my beginners' race. If I did, the bike could fly backwards off its rollers, causing injury and carnage. In truth there's little danger of this, because once you start pedalling, your legs develop a mind of their own. Whipped up by the crowd, mine were spinning in a frenzy, so fast they left my other senses behind. But in a moment, the short, sharp race was over and I slumped over the handlebars searching for breath. I had been set a beginner's target of 25 seconds, and so I wasn't too downhearted to have done it in 26.

It's bringing the velodrome to your local and 12 years on, Casper and fellow creator Paul Churchill are staging over 200 races a year, with 18,000 people now taking to the stage annually in a bid to 'beat the clock'. They've included Olympic gold medallists Victoria Pendleton, Dani King and Sir Chris Hoy, while Sydney Olympic medallist and London 2012 Paralympic gold medallist Craig McLean smashed the world record in 2008, with a time of 18.94.

Overseas France, Belgium, Germany and the Philippines are some of the countries to offer an international challenge.

More recently in the UK, this stage cycling event has spread to the wider public, featuring at festivals, school and community events. There's now a university tour and schools programme, with roller races being set up in PE lessons. Some competitors haven't ridden or owned a bike before, and at least in rollapaluza, there's no danger of falling off (unless you pedal backwards). To find out where you can go to 'beat the clock' go to www.rollapaluza.com.

OLYMPIC CYCLING AND THE TOUR

2012 was the greatest year ever for British cycling, with continued Olympic success and history made in the Tour de France. It just shows what can be done with investment and a long-term strategy. British cycling got the funding and foundations in place at the start of the century, and the harvest a decade later has exceeded expectations.

It was one of those 'where were you when...' moments as Bradley Wiggins wore the yellow jersey across the finish line to win the Tour. With Mark Cavendish winning the final stage again, Great Britain ruled in Paris. Wiggins wouldn't have got close in the Lance Armstrong years, for reasons that have now been made clear, but now the sport can move on and hopefully we can talk less about dope tests and the past. Bradley's win and the recent success of British riders have been a breath of fresh air for the sport. Thanks to them the Tour can look to the future with a much cleaner bill of health.

A few weeks later on the streets of London and Surrey, the speed, stamina and emphasis on team tactics were there for all to see in the London 2012 Olympic road race. I was lucky enough to be at Box Hill to see the teams come past nine times. Most of us would be proud to climb this summit a couple of times, but even after nine ascents the pace seemed unrelenting. Thousands turned out to cheer on the riders, with hundreds camping overnight to book their space on the verge. Being so close to the action helped a whole new audience understand the strategies at work in these races. Team GB flew past, protecting their queen bee, in this case Mark Cavendish, by cycling in front of him to create a slip stream, so he would use less energy on the climbs.

On this occasion for Team GB, the tactics didn't work, but Mark's world championship win the year before, and Wiggins' heroic victory in the Tour, have led to a massive surge in interest, with the masses finally understanding the intricacies of these cycling marathons. Mark has been quoted since saying he wouldn't change anything about what was an unforgettable day. The million people lining the route, five deep for most of the way, meant the team found it hard to communicate, but Mark said he wouldn't swap the atmosphere for any medals. It was a sign of how far this sport has come. The fact that Bradley and Mark came from ordinary backgrounds helps enormously, too. We can all get on a bike, whether it's a balance one, a BMX, a mountain bike, track or hand-cycling bike, and that means we can all appreciate what the athletes are going through.

Well, almost. I have had my eyes opened twice to the extreme demands on cyclists' bodies and minds.

The last 22 kilometres of one of the stages of the Tour de France is a continuous climb to the top of Mount Ventoux. From quaint Provence villages, you rise on a beanstalk of tarmac through winding forest before a restaurant marks the top of the tree line. Then it's up through a desert of rocks and scrub, as the wind pummels your weary limbs. This has become a beacon for cyclists everywhere. It's where Tom Simpson, one of the great names in the sport, died in 1967. He was Britain's most successful road racer in the post war years, until the Bradley Wiggins generation changed all that in 2012.

Simpson was just 29 years old when he died of exhaustion on the slopes of Ventoux. The post-mortem found that he had taken alcohol and amphetamines. It was common at the time for cyclists to take alcohol to help them through the pain of endurance riding. In the shadow of the mountain's peak, there is a memorial to Simpson, where caps and water bottles have been laid in respect. It's a timely reminder of the challenge the riders who climb here have to face – and to think, this sprint to the top is only a fraction of the whole Tour de France stage which starts over 100 kilometres away.

Those not doing Le Tour can still live the dream, and many try to become part of an elite group called the Club de Cingles du Mont-Ventoux. To earn your place, you have to ride up the mountain via three different ascents in the same day.

'It's without doubt, in my view, the hardest of any mountain in France,' said the leader of the group I joined.

They were a party of keen cycling enthusiasts from London, who had decided to attempt this challenge the week before the 2009 Tour arrived. It was a fitting time to try, because the route was already lined with caravans, motor homes and fans who'd booked their roadside seats early for the arrival of the professionals.

We set off soon after dawn and the first six kilometres from the town of Bedouin consisted of a gentle slope up through fields and hedges. Then it was a sharp left and the real work began. As someone who doesn't really get time to ride, apart going to get milk from the shops, each turn of the wheel was a mini achievement for me. The key was getting into a rhythm and thinking of being on a treadmill at the gym. I may have looked like a pecking chicken, rocking back and forth from saddle to handlebars, but it was working. Just don't stop, I thought, as I thrust my bottom out and my head forward.

A bearded Frenchman, clapping as he emerged from the trees, provided a welcome diversion from the burning thighs. Then to my left, there was an orange oasis: a Dutch party bus with 30 revellers all drinking beer and singing. That wasn't quite as motivational, and possibly distracted the lady in front of me, who wobbled and fell from her bike. She soon overtook me again though, as we climbed through the trees. It seemed an eternity of endless exertion before the steep road finally levelled out. A spot of lunch, a cold drink and a stretch of the legs felt like paradise.

Through the alpine air, we could see the summit: our holy grail, bathed in blue sky. The winding road to the peak looked like a mythical meander leading to a fairytale castle as we started our final ascent to the promised land. Reaching the Tom Simpson memorial is another milestone, a final chance to take in some water before the push for the top.

The team pulled me along with their constant cries of encouragement. My producer, Iain Marshall, himself a keen cyclist, had persuaded the campers on the road side to paint 'Allez Bushell' across the tarmac. I could see how this must lift the professional riders in their moment of need, and seeing cameraman Nigel Craze pass me in the comfort of the group's support car made me even more determined to conquer the beasts now biting my legs.

The wind was howling as the final corner beckoned. A final push and I was counting each pedal turn. Around and up, one last draw from the dry well of energy, and there 100 metres away was the finish line where Nigel was waiting with his camera. The red light was on, and I was ready to deliver a piece to camera. Nigel gave me the signal that he was recording, through a bustling crowd of cyclists and supporters. They were oblivious to the dragon I was about to slay. After all, cyclists crossed that line in the sky every minute, and I was just another rider completing the first of my three ascents. But for me, at that moment, this was a bit of history. I had rehearsed what I was going to say, and fixed my eyes on Nigel's lens.

I was now almost close enough to see my reflection in the lens, and was gearing up for the final couple of turns of the pedals, when it suddenly went dark. Nigel had disappeared. The world was tipping on its side, and I couldn't release my feet from the pedals. I was over. I had fallen off, just a metre from the line. After spending six hours in the saddle, I had come crashing down at the last. I had started delivering my reaction to the camera, but instead of rolling those last few feet, my front wheel had got stuck between the legs of a beefy German tourist. He'd appeared from nowhere and suddenly my face was engulfed in his bushy beard. He murmured something unsavoury in German as he pushed himself free, leaving me to fall to the side. I wouldn't like to say whether he'd crossed my path, or if I'd inadvertently strayed into his, because it was a Piccadilly Circus of bikes and people. It didn't matter who was to blame. He continued walking as Nigel helped me and the bike off the floor, and by the time I asked if he was OK, the German man was out of earshot.

So it was back 100 metres down the hill to try again. Unbelievably my second attempt to reach the finish also ended in disaster. This time the laces on my trainers got entangled in the pedals. It was a case of third time lucky, and there wasn't much time to stop and think with the group still hoping to make two more ascents.

I found freewheeling down the mountain even tougher than coming up. It stretched muscles in my hands and feet that I didn't know I had. The speed you pick up is awesome and terrifying at the same time, and I developed a close relationship with my brakes. The day was running out, and so to ensure the more experienced members of the group could get into the Club Cingles, I became part of the support team. It was a good job too. On the second ascent the afternoon's burning sun was an issue, and on the third, high winds blew people backwards into the railings and off their bikes completely. Nevertheless, seven out of 12 in the group made it into that special club, having conquered the climb three times in a day.

'Doing it three times is absolute madness,' said Petra from London, 'but it's a big tick in the box.'

'So, so tired, what an ascent,' said her friend, while another lay on the floor. 'My legs are in pieces – and I thought rowing was tough,' she exclaimed. Meanwhile Tracey, another experienced cyclist, was in the car. 'The heat stroke got the better of me, along with the wind, and I fainted on my bike. I think I overcooked it on that third time,' she said.

A few days later we were back home, watching the Tour de France riders go up past the same vans, the same passionate fans, at my downhill pace. Thankfully 'Allez Bushell' had been replaced by 'Go Bradley', who just held on to fourth place overall on that day in 2009. It was a fantastic feeling knowing we'd been there, tackled the mountain and got a short sharp sense of the agony these riders have to go through. For a life-enhancing, magical cycling experience and to find out more about the ride up Ventoux, check out www.clubcinglesventoux.org.

Having seen how tough just this little bit was, made Bradley's 2012 Tour de France win extra special. It's 47 years since England won the World Cup and 77 years since Fred Perry won Wimbledon, but no British man had won the Tour in 109 years until Monsieur Wiggins showed up – an athlete with true grit, who'd grown up with his mum on a London housing estate, but who had inherited his dad Gary's professional cycling genes.

I spent time with Bradley at a London 2012 launch party outside Buckingham Palace, as the Beijing Games came to a close. We were having a drink and listening to Boris Johnson's 'wiff-waff' speech, and it was genuinely like chatting to an old mate down the pub. By this time he had already won three Olympic golds, and was a household name, but even he probably couldn't imagine that within four years he would have won the biggest cycling prize of them all, Le Tour de France.

But a professional cyclist's season is about so much more than the Olympics and Le Tour. They are punishing their bodies day in, day out. I saw this at first hand when I spent a day cycling up Mount Etna with Mark Cavendish, ahead of the Giro D'Italia in 2011. He'd flown into Sardinia the night before, after a day cycling up some Italian hillside. We had fish for dinner, a glass of water and then it was time for an early night. He spoke about how hard it was being away from his family, yet cycling had been his passion ever since he got a bike for Christmas when he was 12 and living on the Isle of Man.

Mark is not a specialised climber, but even though I had a lift some of the way up the misty mountain (so that I didn't keep him waiting too long at the top) he still had time to have a cup of tea before finally welcoming me into the café at the summit. Like Bradley, he seemed so down-to-earth and honest. He told me when he thought I had asked a stupid question. I had wondered whether doing the Tour de France ahead of the Beijing Olympics had affected riders' chances of a medal. His honesty was refreshing. Some sports stars can seem mechanical with their rehearsed responses to questions, but Mark spoke from the heart. He felt too much emphasis was put on Olympic cycling by the public back home, which is why his world championship achievements hadn't got the recognition they deserved in the UK. Yet in other parts of the world he was a household name.

Thankfully that was to change just a few weeks later, when he was on the Queen's birthday honours list, and then later that year, after winning the green jersey at the Tour de France, he was voted the BBC Sports Personality of the Year.

I haven't yet mentioned much about track cycling. You could easily write a whole book on the success of Team GB over the last decade. It's almost beyond my understanding how they get around those steep banks at such speeds, in tightly packed groups and with no brakes. The tightrope between success and carnage is so thin, and some of the Paralympic GB cyclists go around on tandems, having to be in perfect sync with each other as well. This sounds like a heart-racing challenge for me to try in the future, but to explore all cycling opportunities, go to www.britishcycling.org.uk.

BIKE POLO

The success of British cycling over the last decade has helped revive another sport too. Bicycle polo featured at the 1908 London Olympics as a demonstration sport, with Ireland winning 3-1 against Germany.

It is said to have been invented by an Irishman, Richard J Mecredy, in 1891. The game reached its peak in the UK in the 1930s, with many regional leagues and 170 teams with over a thousand players, and was mostly played on grass. Unfortunately the Second World War saw the start of the sport's decline, but the traditional game is still played, and a European Cup featuring club teams from Great Britain, France and Ireland is an annual event.

Bicycle polo is similar to the horse version of the game, except bikes are not that expensive to feed or clean. It's a chance for people who can't ride a horse, or who aren't rich enough to buy a polo pony, to experience the thrills of mallet and ball. That said, the bike polo I played couldn't have felt more different from the clink of champagne glasses and thunder of hooves on the polo field.

There are two types of bike polo, grass and hardcourt, and they seem to come from different stables. There is traditional bicycle polo, played on grass, but I was about to play hardcourt bike polo, which has taken the sport into the inner cities. The modern version of hardcourt bike polo started in the USA in 1999, when a group of couriers started hitting a ball around on their bikes in breaks between deliveries. Word got around and by June 2010, the sport had spread to 380 cities, with 8,000 players around the world. It was brought to London in 2006, and began to thrive in the Brick Lane area. The London scene is now the largest in the world, thanks to the tournaments organised there which feed off the boom in cycling culture within the city.

Although some of the original couriers in Seattle had an awareness of grass bike polo, the rules of the hardcourt game have more in common with ice hockey as the creators were big followers of this sport. The rules use the same terminology as ice hockey and the only link to polo seems to be the mallet.

That all explains why the polo experience I had, on a school playground in an urban area of central London, as the snow was falling on a freezing March evening, was a world away from the polo I had previously seen and played on grass. Hardcourt bike polo is as physical and rough as full-on horse polo, but all you need is a few sticks, a ball, your bikes, and a hard area like a playground or basketball court. 'It's poor man's polo,' one enthusiast muttered through the muffle of his scarf. 'It's raw, and hardcore, and has really grown on the back of Olympic cycling success in Athens and Beijing.'

It will push your riding skills to the limits. You need speed, ability, enough technique to turn your bike on a sixpence, and the courage to get stuck in where it hurts.

'I love it, I have toughened up. I have had to, to get used to the bruises, but it's such a buzz,' said a new recruit in her mid-twenties.

It was a three-a-side match I was in, and despite my caution in the sleety conditions, I was told not to put my feet down. This is a foul and you are sent to the side of the court as a punishment before being allowed back on. The best way to keep your balance is to use your stick. You can rest on it, or use it as a pivot to turn on. But beware. An opponent can hook your mallet away from underneath you, even if it sends you tumbling. There was plenty of contact, whether it was mallet against mallet, bike smashing into bike, or body charging into body.

I was relieved to be told that I couldn't be hit over the head with a mallet. That's alright then, I thought, and when I didn't have the ball I was safe, because I couldn't be taken out. I could still be blocked by my opponents, though.

It was full of adrenalin-pumping action, but hitting the ball with enough force to score while moving along was a huge challenge. I did connect a couple of times, but they were tricklers rather than thunderbolts, and it would have taken me ages to score the five goals a team needs to win. I was also bamboozled by the movement of the ball. The key is to keep moving, but I found myself stopping to see where the ball was, and then I got in the way of my teammates as they came racing back down the court. Like in many sports, it takes time to adjust to the pace, and practice is the only way.

Thankfully there are now more opportunities to do this, because of the way the sport has thrived thanks to a growing online community. The internet has enabled different groups across the world to get together, and now clubs in the big UK cities like London, Birmingham and Manchester have leagues and are starting to take the sport into schools. For more information go to: www.lhbpa.org for hardcourt and www.polo-velo.net/english for traditional bike polo.

13

ANYONE FOR TENNIS?

Tennis at London 2012 was one of the major success stories, with gold for Team GB's Andy Murray, and silver for Murray and Laura Robson. It came in a historic year all round for British tennis, with Murray breaking that Wimbledon men's singles final drought stretching back to the 1930s, becoming Olympic champion, and finally winning a Grand Slam at the US Open all in the space of a few months. Add to that the rise of the women, with Heather Watson winning an event on the WTA tour for the first time in Japan, and both Watson and Robson rising to verge of the top 50 in the world and you feel we are at the start of a golden new era. What's more there are now more ways than ever than can get us calling for 'new balls please'.

For instance, what has a giraffe got in common with Andy Murray? It's why the Olympic champion might also have gone for a 'boomerang', or even a 'poop', had he been playing several hundred years ago. Before I reveal all, it's confession time. I have finally joined a club myself, in the vain hope that I will at last improve if I practise all year rather than just for a couple of weeks during Wimbledon. The pressure to hit a decent shot, and the embarrassment of getting it wrong, really intensifies when on the other side of the net, there is a tennis icon, someone who I am normally used to watching in awe on the television...

GAME, SET AND MATCH TO THE STARS

I paced up and down the hotel room, trying to calm myself by remembering the time I had partied on the beach with Usain Bolt. He was still in the shadow of Asafa Powell at this point, and we were in Athens at the Jamaican team's Olympic launch party in 2004. The reggae music was pumping as Asafa and Usain walked onto the stage and started strutting their stuff. They'd been just as relaxed in the interview earlier. Talking to Usain was a soothing experience; he stretched, smiled and in his surprisingly deep voice talked about his barefoot training on the mountain paths back home.

The mood on stage was infectious. It was more like a music festival than the build-up to an Olympic Games, and I found myself joining in the dance moves with the man who would become the fastest on earth.

Aware that the big man might have his eyes on me, I felt under pressure to control my jiggling legs, and so I switched to default mode. I slipped into the one dance move I remembered from school: one hand on my hip, the other pointing diagonally away from my body and towards the sky. Saturday night fever had broken out on the sand. Thankfully my producer Robin Marks, one of the best in the business, brought me back to my senses and dragged me off to the side to protect my vanishing dignity.

A few years later, Usain Bolt adopted a similar pose after winning gold in the 100 metres at the Beijing Olympics. It's now an iconic sporting gesture around the world. I wonder…!

The memory of Bolt in the sand had eaten up some time as I twiddled my yellow tennis racquet and stared at the door. Then a young public relations man strode into the room, with a black folder under his arm.

'You will only have 10 minutes, you know that, don't you?' he asked.

I nodded and in she glided with the aura and style we have come to expect from the one and only Serena Williams. She was dressed for dinner, with a floral dress and matching shoes. She shook my hand warmly and, realising that she was taller than me, sat down on the sofa. It was the Thursday before Wimbledon, and she was here to talk about the power of the women's tour and other changes in the game.

It wasn't like talking to a sports star, though. Serena had the presence of a Hollywood A-lister, a movie legend. Maybe it was her accent or the way she conducted herself, but I felt so inferior, in a way I never normally do in interviews.

But that was nothing compared to how I felt a few moments later. We were chatting about her top tips for amateur players, about what we could all do to improve our game and serve. So I stood up, and making sure that I was far enough away from the china ornaments on the mantelpiece to swing my racquet, I served an imaginary ball. Serena broke into a chuckle. Holding a hand up to her lips, she sniggered. 'Mike…why do you play with a child's racquet?' I froze, lowering my eyes like a scalded dog. It was yellow. Mine was red. I had somehow picked up my daughter Lucy's racquet instead.

I had spent so long working out the right questions to ask,

dressing smartly, and getting there with plenty of time to spare, but that didn't matter now that I was standing in front of the multiple grand slam winner holding a child's racquet.

'Tell me about your superstitions, Serena...' I sought the safety of a different subject. 'Hey, don't worry about it,' she chortled, and went on to tell me how she always ties her shoelaces in the same way, uses the same shower before each match and bounces the ball five times before the first serve and twice before the second. If she forgets any of these things she is convinced it affects her mentally.

Luckily that year, in 2008, she wore the lucky socks, had the spare dress, and did all she needed to, because for the first time in six years she was Wimbledon champion again.

The second time I was left red faced in the company of a tennis ace, was not entirely my fault, but I always now approach cooked tomatoes with far more respect.

I had arranged to do a behind-the-scenes feature with Elena Dementieva. The idea was that I would pick her up in a cheesy sports car, have a game of tennis, and then take her for dinner in the plush restaurant at the Roehampton club.

I saw her in the rear view mirror as I rehearsed my Russian greeting, which sounded something like '*prevy-atsa*'. There she was – a vision in pink and a few inches taller than me. And as I repeated my pidgin Russian, she nodded her approval. 'Oh hello,' she greeted me, 'oh thank you, very impressing'.

These days, the stars of Wimbledon are so much more than tennis players; they are fashion icons, famed for their glamorous lifestyles, and so I had to set the right impression. At first Elena couldn't stop smiling and giggling. Maybe it was my £1 Blues Brother sunglasses, or perhaps because her boyfriend was keeping an eye on proceedings from a distance. I believe he plays ice hockey in Russia, and his steely glare made me nervous.

So much so that I stalled the car, having left the handbrake on. The boyfriend could relax; this buffoon was more Austin Powers than Pierce Brosnan. 'Oh my God,' Elena shrieked, followed by more rapid-fire laughter.

The second attempt to start the car was more successful and we arrived at the club for a knock about. She thrashed me, of course and there was a fair bit of grunting (good job that sentence is in context...!)

'You make me sweat' she said as she came in for a chat at the net, and told me about how it always took time, for her to find her feet on grass.

'It's all about confidence. It's a very mental game when it comes to grass, because everything is very fast and unpredictable, so you have to rely on your instincts.'

The rest of the afternoon was spent with her showing me the exhausting training schedule that she has to suffer every afternoon – and watching me toil. To be fair she didn't want to risk injury, and I think she also relished her chance to get her own back on a reporter.

'Ha, this is my chance for all those questions I get asked about my serve, this is it, and you are going to work really hard, come on come on, you can do it!' she ordered. She had me cycling, lifting, stretching, doing press-ups and squat thrusts, and then she turned the speed up on the running machine so fast that I fell off the end. Luckily I landed on my feet. She said she'd never had so much fun.

She might have thought what happened over dinner was revenge, but I swear it wasn't.

She was trying to teach me the Russian for 'bon appetit' when the baked monkfish, with luscious vegetables, came steaming out. Distracted by my new Russian phrase, I ignored the vast plumes of steam rising from the plates plunged my fork in. A jet of fine liquid red lava ejected from one of the juicy roasted tomatoes and *splat!* landed on Elena's pink tennis top. To make matters worse I couldn't speak to apologise because my mouth was on fire, having stuffed the scalding tomato in.

Thankfully, Elena called for help, and some water arrived as she collapsed into her chair, now in unbridled laughter. I take pride from the fact that she may still tell this story in distinguished tennis circles around the world.

There wasn't much I could do about my third most embarrassing moment with a top tennis player. I'd had knock-ups with greats like Boris Becker and lived to tell the tale, and been beaten by a 13-year-old called Evan Hoyt, who's a star to watch out for in the next few years.

But nothing has compared to facing the serve from one of the fastest racquets in the game, held by the big serving Australian Mark Philippoussis. He may be a gentle giant to talk to, but on the few times I did manage to make contact with his deliveries – which can reach speeds of over 120 miles per hour – they either twisted the racquet in my hand or knocked it out of my grasp completely.

We have no idea, when we watch from the comfort of our seats, the reaction time and wrist control you need to be able to return such shots. What I needed was to play Mark at a version of the sport that isn't so reliant on power and pace. A sport which is a leveller, and which enables players of different ages and ability to have decent rallies together.

Luckily there are now several sports like this, serving up opportunities across the UK.

REAL TENNIS

If I could tempt Mark Philippoussis inside, then I could maybe outwit him with a boomerang or outfox him in the penthouse. I might stand a better chance if we had a game of real tennis. It includes the leading contenders for most bizarre terminology in sport, with other names including 'railroad', 'poop', 'bobble' and 'piqué'. It certainly makes for great questions in the sports round of a pub quiz. So what do Andy Murray and giraffes have in common? Well, they can both produce aces.

Real tennis is how the sport used to be played 500 years ago, although we have to go back even further to find the original roots of the game. It's thought the name comes from the French word '*tenez*', which means 'take heed' – a warning from the server of the rocket about to fly at you.

There are reports that a form of tennis was played in Roman times, and it was certainly popular in France by the 12th century. But there were no racquets then. Players would strike the ball with their hands, in the way they do today in other descendants from that first game, like fives and one wall handball. More on these later.

As for real tennis, by the 16th century the hand and glove had become a racquet. The game moved into a court, and rules were drawn up. But it's still very different from the sport of tennis most play today. The courts are enormous, 90 feet long by 30 wide, and there aren't the cries of 'out!' if the shot is outside the baseline. You can use the four walls to play off, and three of those have sloping roves known as penthouses. Then there is the buttress (called the tambour) that intrudes into the playing area, and finally there are various window-like openings called galleries which you try to aim for. One is called the wining gallery and has a bell inside. Get a ball into one of these and far from having to make an insurance claim, you might win the point. The ball itself is handmade, heavy and solid, and so is partial to a bit of spin. This just adds even more unpredictability to the bounce when it comes off a wall or penthouse.

There are many other intricacies as well, including a so-called chase, when the ball is allowed to bounce twice, but there's only so much you can take in at first.

This sport has the ability to make even the top players look silly at times. Some describe it as a cross between tennis, squash and chess, because it's as much about the tactics and strategy as it is about power.

Royalty and the landed gentry, who could afford to build the large courts, loved it and by 1596 there were 250 courts in Paris alone and the game was spreading across Europe. In England, Henry VIII was hooked and he built a court at Hampton Court Palace. There is still a newer court on the same site in use today. Indeed, get a ball into the window (called the grille) that Henry's portrait is gazing out from, and it's an especially satisfying point.

Henry played the game with such enthusiasm that he ordered more courts to be built at other palaces, and he was so caught up in the game that he was busy playing a match when news of his second wife Ann Boleyn's execution was brought to him.

The problem for real tennis, though, was finding enough courts. By the age of Napoleon, the French ruling classes were under fire, and finding new real tennis venues fell by the wayside. In England, other racquet sports like squash and rackets started taking over, and by the 1890s the outdoor game of lawn tennis, with its smaller courts and simpler rules, would win the public's affection game set and match.

It's not quite 'match', though, because the giraffes and the boomerangs have forced a tie break. Real tennis has been making a comeback over the last few decades, and this isn't a case of a bunch of old sports enthusiasts trying to keep an eccentric British tradition going. The court at the Oratory school near Reading is one of several built around the country to get a new generation into real tennis. There are now 26 in all, and the Oratory school is where I met former multiple world champion Charlotte Cornwallis.

She was the same height at me, with long brown hair and lean strong arms, and she studied the court as a general might study the battlefield. Well, she had gone unbeaten for four years.

'Keep the flat bit of the racquet facing the floor,' she advised as she dinked a serve up onto a penthouse roof. The ball scuttled along the top edge, and then, slowly, teased me as I shuffled along on the floor like a cat waiting for a bird to fly off from a tree. Then it took off, dropping onto the back wall and bouncing down on the court, but luckily at a height at which I could make clean contact. I had returned the serve and we were into a rally. Speed around the court is key, along with mind reading skills. You have to think about where your opponent is trying to place the shot, before then waiting for it to settle. It's like being in a giant 3D pinball machine, and you have to be patient before pouncing.

'You have to have a brain in this sport,' said Charlotte. 'If you don't engage it, it just doesn't work. It's not just brawn, but brains as well. I like the fact that I can go on there with the guys, and make them run around the court, keep them on the end of a piece of string and send them packing.'

She soon had me dangling too, as an inch-perfect shot landed in the window opening, ringing the bell that was hanging there.

Since I met Charlotte, her reign at the top has come to an end, but a new generation has become hooked. In 2011, Claire Vigrass, became the youngest ever World Champion at the age of 19. It's no longer just a sport for kings.

The World Champion is an Australian call Rob Fahey, who

has held the title since 1994. However, his unbroken sequence of victories in the British Open has just been brought to an end by a young British player called Bryn Sayers – very appropriate in 2012, a year of British success.

Real tennis is no longer the domain of the privileged classes, as over 75% of the best players around are from state schools (or their overseas equivalent). For more information contact www.tennisandrackets.com

PADEL

There are more modern versions of tennis that also help you compete with players much better than yourself. One might well enable average club players to return those Philippoussis serves, because in padel you get a second chance.

Millions of people play this version of the sport in Spain and South America – and now in the UK in places like Huddersfield in Yorkshire. If you have ever been on holiday to the Costa del Sol, you have probably pressed your face up against the glass of a padel court. It's a glass box that goes around the outside of a tennis court, which means the ball stays in play. That's why it was invented in Mexico 42 years ago.

'This Mexican man was pretty wealthy,' explained Toni Salord-Monserrat, who's a padel coach in the UK. 'He had a big house on an estate and was bored of going to collect all the balls [which suggests he wasn't the best of shots either] and so he built walls around his court. A new sport was born, a game of tennis in which you do get that second chance.'

It means that if a serve whizzes past you, don't panic. You can bide your time, let it bounce and let it hit the wall before finally returning it. The side and back walls take some of the power out of the ball too, and this why it's a leveller. Speed, strength and power are not as important in this version of tennis and so I ended up playing against a 75-year-old and a nine-year-old.

It wasn't stop start, though, as you might expect with players of differing abilities. Far from it. The rallies would often last for 10 to 15 strokes and were only decided by a mistake or sublime bit of skill, like the deft shot executed by my nine-year-old playing partner just over the net.

'It's quite easy to get the hang of, and fun,' she said. 'I guess it's a mix of squash and tennis, but mainly tennis,' added her mate.

The tennis balls you use have had some of the pressure taken out, so they are more suitable for the plastic padel bats, which have shorter handles. It's all about making the game easier to pick up, so anyone can get involved.

'This gets young kids on the court and they can rally immediately,' said Peter Vann of the Huddersfield club. 'They can rally straight away because there is no pressure. It's a very easy sport to learn, so it's good for confidence and developing the all-round skills that apply in tennis, like the hand eye coordination, the ability to move forward and volley, and the slow lobbing game.'

All the skills, that is, except the serve. Again, to make it easier, all serves are underarm at first. So you don't have double fault after double fault holding you up, and I wouldn't have had my arm nearly taken off by Mr Philippoussis. One word of warning, though – the rallies can go on and on and on!

The sport now has established world championships around the world, and is set to grow further in the UK. There are still only a handful of courts, but that looks set to change. The organisation that looks after padel in the UK says that it's now in a position to part-fund 100 courts, all over the country.

For more information go to www.padelengland.org/

TOUCH TENNIS

This must be the only sport started by a goat. It's also one of the few at which I excelled, and actually took points off a former Wimbledon star.

One of the sporting highlights of 2012 was Andy Murray winning Olympic gold and the US Open, as well as becoming the first British man since Bunny Austin in 1938 to reach a men's singles final at Wimbledon.

He did that thanks to victory in a remarkable semi-final match against Jo-Wilfried Tsonga. It was a contest of enthralling tennis, of dramatic dives across the grass, of stretching for every ball, of returning shots from impossible angles.

There is now a version of the sport called touchtennis, which promotes this kind of play and enables us all to throw ourselves around like the great serve and volley stars of the past. It's similar in some ways to padel, in that it's accessible, easy to pick up, is a leveller, and the rallies can go on for ages. But you don't need special walled courts, just simple markings in the local park or your back garden. It's played with softer foam balls, on smaller courts (for singles, it's 12 metres by five) and the racquets are shorter too, like children's ones (perhaps I should have told Serena I was a touchtennis star!) The emphasis is on speed of mind and delicate touch.

It was started by Rashid Ahmad in 2002, in his garden in South London. He was so fed up of getting thrashed at his local tennis club that he took out his frustration by setting up a game he could play with his daughter in his back garden. She only was five, but because the court was small and the balls softer, they could enjoy rallies together. Rashid still thrashed her every time, though, and boasted to his mates at the club that he was now the self-proclaimed 'greatest of all time', hence the name GOAT. You can't argue with the fact that at that point in history, Rashid was indeed the GOAT at touchtennis – he was number one in the rankings, which included just him and his daughter.

Perhaps foolishly, with his self-confidence restored, he opened up the game to his mates from the local tennis club. Sadly his GOAT days were over. Rashid's reputation may have been in tatters, but his sport was now going from strength to strength. There are now over 1,000 players on the world touchtennis tour and what's more the number ones in the men's and women's game are both British.

'The key is not manipulating the ball with sheer power,' the British world number one Elliot Mould explained as we knocked up at the All England championship at Home Park tennis club near Windsor.

'It's more about deft stroke play, clever angles and chess like manoeuvres. In mainstream tennis, I over-thought everything, and had too much time. I couldn't execute what I wanted to do, but in this, its close, it's so fast, you don't have time to think, and I just respond instinctively to what's coming at me.'

The women's number one Nikki Withers admits it enables her to beat players who would thrash her on a larger court.

'I can out-think them, whereas on a real court I would be overpowered,' she explained.

Rashid Ahmad can still beat his daughter, but he is now just busy keeping the world tour and ranking points up to date.

'We try to make it as fun and inclusive as possible', he said. 'It's like the five-a-side of tennis and anyone can play, as long as you can hold a racquet.'

Well that just about includes me then, and what's more I managed to win points against a famous face from the grand slam circuit who is now playing on the touchtennis tour. It proved how much of a leveller this game is when I found myself leading former tour player and current BBC Radio 5 Live commentator Jeff Tarrango.

He seemed alarmed. 'No one is going to believe at Radio 5 Live that I am actually losing,' he complained – and then after a dramatic pause and with horror taking over his voice, he screamed, 'and look who I am losing to!'

To find out more about touchtennis go to: http://www.touchtennis.com or you can buy equipment to play a similar short tennis game at many retailers. Just type short tennis into a search engine.

CARDIO TENNIS

If you are struggling with your game as a whole, if you are fed up of chasing shadows, just not getting enough of the ball against better players, and not getting the exercise that tennis is meant to be, maybe it's time to pump up the music, dance, play trebles instead of doubles, and to keep moving on your toes for a whole hour.

These are some of the highlights of cardio tennis, which helps you get fit without being held back by the failings of your own game. It doesn't matter where the ball goes, in fact at first there's no ball at all. It's more about getting your heart rate up than skills.

You start by doing a series of tennis-based exercises and drills, alongside up to 30 others on court. You sweep, you stretch and you spring from side to side as the coach calls out the moves. It's like a fitness class, but with tennis moves thrown in. After the initial workout, balls are introduced – and lots of them, so no one really notices or cares if you hit a wayward shot.

'It's all about repositioning tennis as something that's a lot of fun and high energy,' said Sam Richardson, Cardio Tennis UK lead and LTA coach, 'because a lot of people, especially beginners, when they go out to play tennis, find it difficult, and so they don't get very long rallies, and it breaks down quickly. But with cardio tennis, there's lots of people, the music is blasting, and it's a party atmosphere.'

It is non-stop. You have to keep moving, otherwise its press-up time. You jiggle around on the spot, waiting in turn to run out to play a ground stroke back to the coach, who's feeding the balls from over the net. Then it's a volley, and the next time you run in to the net and it might be a drop shot or a winning smash that you are asked to deliver. Once warmed up, you then play competitive points in doubles, pairing up with whoever is next in line. The winning pair stays on until they are beaten. At one point I struck lucky, and seemed set to stay on court with a talented partner for a record number of points. Until, that is, I started delivering a piece to camera and my forehand flapped a straightforward shot into the net, proving I can't speak and play at the same time.

The reaction from other first timers was encouraging. 'Some-times in tennis you get creaky, can't get that serve in, or get a rally moving, but this just keeps you moving and moving,' said one lady, while a more experienced club player claimed, 'It encourages you to try your shots in a more flamboyant way, but I am surprised how high it's sent my heart rate'. Another regular warned, 'it keeps you on your toes, with so many people and balls flying at you. You have to concentrate and think very quickly.'

Other exercises during the hour included a game with three players on each side of the net, and why not then bring everyone on for a game of volleyball tennis? At the end of it all, hundreds of calories had been burnt off and we weren't left cursing our backhand.

Cardio tennis is an initiative by the Lawn Tennis Association to get more beginners into the sport, while sharpening the skills of existing players. There are now 1,000 coaches in the UK trained to teach Cardio tennis, at 500 different clubs. Look for your nearest at www.allplaytennis.com

NO RACQUET REQUIRED

FIVES AND WALLBALL

So that's what became of one side of the tennis family tree: real tennis, lawn tennis, and their offspring, padel, touch, and eventually cardio. What about the distant relations on the other side of the family? What about the other descendants of the game played by the Romans and later in France, using just a hand or glove.

Whatever the origin, the legacy has spread far and wide, and two related sports today are known as fives and wallball. This second one was originally called 'One Wall Handball', but it led to confusion with the team game of handball that we see at the Olympics, and so is changing to wallball. Fives has developed into six different versions, but there are three main ones, Eton, Rugby and Winchester Fives, depending on where each root took hold. There is a theory that the name is from the slang expression 'a bunch of fives' (meaning a fist).

You don't need a racquet in any of the variations. Instead, you hit the ball against a wall using just your hands. A glove cushions the impact, and in some games there are hazards like the jutting-out section of wall known as the 'buttress' that invades the court in Eton Fives. There is also a step, and between the two is what's called the 'pepper pot'. This is a dead area for the ball so it is the place to aim for if you want to deal your opponent a shot they can't return. In Winchester Fives there is a smaller version of the buttress, but in Rugby Fives there isn't one at all and so this version is played in what's more like a squash court.

Fives started out as a working-class game, because it's so easy to play in a yard or against any old wall, yet its revival has taken place in well-known public schools like Eton, Rugby and Winchester. Its spread to the wider population is gaining momentum (the public school courts are usually available to anyone to hire), but its journey back into the inner city communities is being pushed along by its sister sport, the one that is now known as wallball.

If like me you spent hours as a kid whacking a ball against a wall in the backyard using just your hands, this will be trip down memory lane, but it is now a sport that is bidding for inclusion in the Olympics after 2020. It's now played in 37 countries and England were the European Champions in 2011. It's stripped the idea of the hand, ball and wall back to the basics. You don't need a special court, like in fives. Instead the court is marked out on the floor and wall with chalk or sticky tape, and all you then need is the ball, which you hit back and forth against the wall, alternating with your opponents like in squash.

'If you are striking the ball with your right hand, you should put your left foot forward,' the England star Peter Cohen advised me. It's fast and you have to be on your toes, and the bounce will sometimes deceive you. 'When people first come from tennis or squash they tend to miss the ball by the length of a racquet,' he mused.

St Paul's Academy was one of the first places to introduce it into the school curriculum. Over 20 have now followed in London. 'It doesn't cost anything, just a wall and two balls,' raved the Director of Sport, Niall McCann. I dived, and stretched and ended up on the floor. It was just like being a kid again.

To get into wallball in your area, contact www.ukhandball.co.uk, and to play fives, www.fivesonline.net is one place to look.

RACKETS

There is another branch to add to the tennis family tree; one with sinister beginnings. The sound of 'thwack', 'aargh', 'smack' and more 'aarghs' coming from inside prison walls might have indicated that some painful punishment was being handed out. But it was actually the latest version of the game of fives, starting up in London's 18th century debtors' prisons.

Inmates often played fives with stones, but wanted to speed up the game, and so they brought in racquets to whack the stones even harder against the wall. It soon spread beyond the gaols and into alleyways behind local pubs, but it's when it broke into schools that it really took off and four-wall courts were built to keep the sport contained.

Like in real tennis, the courts are huge, 60 by 30 feet. That's three times bigger than a normal squash court. The balls are still like stones, more like a golf ball than a tennis ball, and they fly around the court at 180 miles per hour, which is why this claims to be the UK's fastest ball sport.

I pulled on the special protective goggles you need to enter a court at Malvern college to face James Coyne, one of the top five players in the world. He also found it hard playing and talking at the same time, as I started the interview during our first big rally. 'It's one of the most exhilarating games I have ever...ah no, God, you...' he disappeared to the far end of the court, trying to reach my cunning drop shot.

'It's the sheer pace,' he panted on his return. 'It's scary at first, something I had never experienced before, but once you get to grips with it, and get the rallies going, it's the greatest game I have ever played, with those speeds of 180 miles per hour. The power, the adrenalin, there's nothing like it.'

At times it felt like I was chasing a bird, such was the speed as the ball raced back from the main wall. The racquet handles are longer, but the heads smaller, which makes it even more of a challenge to make contact, but at slower speeds I was able to play. When James showed me his full throttle serve however, the ball hit the front wall, then the back and was back around the middle of the court again, before I could properly see it.

There are now regular UK and world championships, and although it has been the domain of the public schools, in contrast to the days of debtors' prisons, it's now changing and the schools are opening up in the evenings with Rackets clubs for all. There are currently 26 courts in operation around the UK, and quite a few lying dormant. The last two years have seen the inaugural Ladies Open and schoolgirls championship.

Go to the website www.tennisandrackets.com but be warned, if you are an established squash player, that won't prepare you for the speed and bounce of these balls.

SQUASH

Squash can see itself as the son or daughter of rackets, and so is also a distant relation of tennis. But unlike tennis, it has not been included in the Olympics and for years the half a million or so people who play in the UK every week have wanted to know why. It's a question I often get asked.

If squash had been included at London 2012, Team GB would almost certainly have won two more medals, gold and silver perhaps, because James Wilstrop and Nick Matthew are two Englishmen who dominated the world rankings in the build-up to the Olympics. It has become one of the most popular sports for people wanting to improve their fitness or do a high-impact workout in a short space of time. Its smaller courts have helped it spread further and faster than its predecessor, rackets.

Squash was developed at Harrow school where rackets was being played. The students modified that game so it could be played more widely in cramped conditions, needing less space, and to make it safer in the smaller space, rubber balls were made. In 1883 the first purpose-built court was constructed in Oxford, and three years later the first set of official rules were drawn up.

The first British Open was held in 1922 for men and women at London's Queen's Club. In 2009, the world squash federation estimated there were nearly 50,000 squash courts in the world. Over 8,500 of them are in England, so it's not surprising that the best six English players are now in the world's top 12.

This just makes it even more frustrating for the likes of Nick and James. If they used a badminton racket, or table tennis bat, they would have been at the greatest show on earth, and if they had opted for tennis, they would be millionaires as well by now. Squash, it seems, has been the Cinderella of racquet sports.

'You can't help but cast a couple of envious glances at the benefits of everything connected to the Olympics,' said Nick in his broad Yorkshire accent as we waited to knock up in his home town of Sheffield. 'There are not many sports which had such a great chance of medals as this one.'

The reason it's been left out in the cold and restricted to tournaments like the British Open – the Wimbledon of the sport – is that it's not been seen as a great spectator or TV sport. The ball moves t up to 175 miles per hour, so fast that it can be hard to see, and rallies can take a long time and end in a 'let', which requires the point to be played again.

However, glass-sided courts have now transformed the viewing experience. Squash can be seen from all sides and multiple TV cameras in and around the courts have revolutionised the coverage, making it much more up close and personal to the fan.

'It has massively improved,' said James. 'Professional squash looks good now. You can see the ball, which has been changed from traditional black to white for TV, and you can see and feel how hard players are working as we strive for Olympic recognition.'

Nick then continues the argument. 'That old TV stigma can't be applied anymore,' he explains. 'Modern coverage shows the speed and dynamic action which were maybe lacking before. It looked easy on TV before but we can vouch that it's anything but.'

And I can too. They both challenged me to a run around on court for a while. I sprinted here, darted there, got to balls I never thought I'd reach. I dived, slid and stretched, while the world number one, James, hardly moved a foot. Working me from one side to the other with one hand, he may as well have been reading a paper with the other.

'It's a game about positioning, and trying to work your opponent out of position. To do this, you need accuracy and incredible fitness,' he says.

There is now a campaign going to get squash into the 2020 Olympics, and this time they hope the sport won't lose out as it has done to golf and rugby sevens more recently. With so many players now involved across the world, anyone who picks up a squash racquet needs to thank those prisoners in London years ago. For more information see www.englandsquashandracketball.com

TABLE TENNIS

A lot can happen at dinner parties when the wine is flowing, but how many guests have ended up inventing a new sport? That's what happened in Victorian England in the 1880s, when the passion for lawn tennis was growing.

Upper class families would follow dinner by lining up books in the middle of the table as a net and then using other books, or even cigar box lids, as bats. They would hit either a golf ball or a champagne cork back and forth. The corks, with their nobbly ends, made for some zany shots and it's worth a try at the next dinner party you go to. Just ask your hosts if they fancy a quick set of 'wiff-waff', 'gossamer' or 'flim-flam', as it was known. They will either call the police, ask you to leave or hopefully clear the table for a game.

It has been suggested that the idea was brought back by British military officers serving in India or South Africa, but the big development came in the early 1900s, when ping pong balls were invented, and when bats replaced those cigar boxes. It became known as table tennis. London hosted the first world championships in 1926 and in 1988 it made its Olympic bow.

Table tennis is no longer just a sport for those upper-class dinner guests; it is drawing in people from all walks of life thanks to its accessibility and low cost, which means it can be played in any small space. One of the UK's most high profile players, Darius Knight, learned to play in a garden shed and he reckons the sport helped steer him away from gangs and trouble in south London.

The close control and skill of top players like Darius is mesmerising. On the table they can get the ball to spin back on itself or rear up like a cobra, or simply hit it so fast that you hear it before you see it hitting the table. There's no special secret, though. It's simply about putting hours and hours of training in and just to show that this is a talent you can practise any time, any place, anywhere, Darius knocked the ball against whatever surface was there, as we walked and talked. He played it against the door, the wall, and even the sides of the lift. He kept going as we went down, and carried on out into the foyer, ping ponging away off whatever he could find as we shook hands and said goodbye. For more information about table tennis go to www.etta.co.uk

BADMINTON

The last racquet sport in this chapter also claims to be the most popular. With over 23,700 courts in England alone it comes as no surprise as it is played at clubs and courts at sports centres, schools and village halls up and down the land. The Olympic medallists Gail Emms and Nathan Robertson became household names after the Athens 2004 Games, and so this is a sport which needs little introduction.

However, it does have completely different roots from the other racquet sports in this chapter and instead grew out of the children's game 'battledore and shuttlecock'. This was popular in medieval times, but there are reports of shuttlecock games much earlier in ancient Greece. The game involved players using a paddle or bat, to keep the 'battledore' (which was a cork with feathers stuck in it) in the air for as long as possible. According to the wonderful book *The Badminton Story* by Bernard Adams, the record rally was 2,117 hits recorded in 1830. Surely it's time that was broken.

By the 17th century, the European and French upper classes were also playing battledore or 'Jeu de Volant'. Other variations of this centuries-old game were entertaining children in the Far East, and it's reported that British Army officers stationed in the Pune region of India helped it take the next step, in the 1860s. They introduced a net and for a time it became known as the sport of 'poona'. The officers helped bring it back to England, where in 1873 this new game, complete with net, was played by guests at a lawn party at Badminton House in Gloucestershire, which is now better known for its horse trials. The party was held by the Duke of Beaufort, and he introduced it to his friends as 'the Badminton game'.

The first set of rules were then drawn up in 1877 by the Bath badminton club, and the sport that we know today was formed. Nearly 100 years later, its popularity had grown to such an extent, that it was a demonstration sport at the 1972 Olympics before joining the Games in its own right at Barcelona '92.

If you have ever picked up a feather in the garden and let it go in the wind, you'll know that its flight is unique; so graceful and controlled, the way it can hang in the air, and so different from a ball. Apparently the best shuttlecocks are made out of the left wing feathers from a goose.

In a way badminton combines the best bits of all the racquet sports. It's accessible, pretty cheap, and easy to pick up, and it's not all about speed and power, but also cunning, tactics, co-ordination and angles.

It also enables players of different abilities to rally together. I had a knock up with Olympic medallist Nathan Robertson at the National Badminton Centre in Milton Keynes, and what struck me was his range. Yes, we could keep the shuttlecock in the air from end to end of the court, but then with a leap and flick of the wrist, he pounced, suddenly changing the whole speed of the game and I hardly saw his shot as it landed by my feet almost taking my racquet with it. The cock can be flicked, hit up to the rafters when it travels almost in slow motion, or smashed at furious speed, far faster than a tennis serve. Indeed it claims to be the fastest racquet sport in the world, with speeds recorded of over 250 miles per hour.

The success of Nathan and Gail Emms highlights one of the other big attractions, in that men and women compete in doubles on more or less equal terms. Even though Nathan retired in June 2012, he and Gail have ensured a new crop of talent is coming through, with a recent example being GB pairing Chris Adcock and Imogen Bankier, who won a World Championship silver medal at Wembley Arena in 2011.

Badminton, like squash, is also best experienced live when you get to fully appreciate the speed, skill and athleticism involved at the highest level. The Yonex All England Open Badminton Championships is the oldest and most prestigious event on the worldwide event calendar. For more information on badminton visit www.badmintonengland.co.uk

RACKETLON

If you have been tempted by some of the racquet sports above, but can't decide which one, there is now a sport that lets you play four of them. It's the racquet sports equivalent of the triathlon. You start with the smallest, playing a set of table tennis, then as soon as the last point is won, you dash to the badminton hall before then running to the squash court and ending with a set of tennis.

It's called racketlon and bills itself as one of the fastest growing sports. It claims to have boomed by 300 per cent in three years, and is now played in nearly 50 countries worldwide with 40 recognised national bodies. They include Finland and Sweden, where it started.

I went to Redbridge sports centre in East London for the World Doubles Championships and English Open singles event. Some of the Olympic badminton teams trained at Redbridge, but how would they have coped with suddenly switching racquets and hitting balls rather than shuttlecocks?

It is the player who wins the most rallies in total across the four disciplines that is the winner of the match. Each sport is played up to 21 points, so given equal weight. You are allowed two serves, and every point counts, whether serving or not.

I found the hardest part was the first few points in each sport. The touch I needed in table tennis was so different from the way I hit a shuttlecock, and so in the first few rallies on the badminton court, I kept landing it short. The bigger squash racket then took some getting used to before the greater range and power needed in the final showdown on the tennis court. I tried to play myself into a game, but by the time I found my length, I was several points down.

It seems though that the skills are very transferable. Judy Murray played in the first international event back in 2002, and Andy is reportedly a good all-rounder. Such talent usually comes out whatever shape of racquet or bat you are holding.

In 2013 there are 14 stops on the world racketlon tour, culminating with the world championships in Switzerland. There is more information on www.racketlon.net. The 2012 World Championships was hosted in Stockholm, home of Lennart Eklundh. He was one of the first people to play the sport and has now retired. There were 30 competitors from the UK in the World Championships and back home the sport now has 18 tour events in 2012 and several other smaller events. The English Racketlon Association is hoping Sport England will make it an official sport in the near future. The main UK website is www.englishracketlon.org. In this age, when we all multi-skill in everyday life, when there are so many channels on the TV and when our brains need lots of stimulation, racketlon ticks all the boxes, all four one and one four all.

14

AROUND THE WORLD IN BIZARRE SPORTS

Great Britain can claim to have invented many of the planet's most popular sports, and it seems there are Brits behind some of the world's oddest sports as well. Having said this, Finland can also claim to be wizards of the weird. This chapter is dedicated to some of the nuttiest global sporting acitivies i have come across, but they are not just to be laughed at. They go far beyond the chuckle muscle and have enriched, even saved people's lives.

GLOBAL SPORTING MADNESS

ELEPHANT POLO - A SCOTTISH AFFAIR
My voyage of discovery, uncovering the way bizarre sports have changed lives across the world, has taken me far and wide. How a sports reporter ended up covering the elephant polo World Cup in a remote region of Southern

Nepal takes some explaining, but this story begins in Scotland.

There are only three elephants in Scotland, but the chances of Blair Drummond Safari Park letting you sit astride Estrella, Toto or Mondula while wielding a big stick are slimmer than elephants featuring at Rio 2016. You can only stand there in awe and imagine, as you gaze at these magnificent beasts at Scotland's main safari park. Sadly there are no wild elephants north of the border. The nearest you can get to a wild elephant nowadays is a Red Deer – magnificent, yes, but the antlers would get in the way if you tried to strike the ball while bearing down on goal. Stag polo? Now that is getting silly.

As Toto sneered down her trunk and extinguished any hopes I still harboured of climbing on her back, I realised this mission was going to take all my journalistic powers. The burning question was this: just how could a country with no history or love affair with wild elephants win the elephant polo World Cup twice?

It's all Colin and Duncan's fault. Colin and Duncan Campbell – you know the family. The Campbells arrived in Argyll as part of a royal expedition in 1220. They put down roots on Lochaweside, and were placed in charge of the King's land in the area. Colin the Great, as he was known, may have been killed later that century in a skirmish but the clan was there to stay. His son became brother-in-law to King Robert the Bruce, and his great grandson, Sir Duncan, moved to Inverary and built the first castle there.

I know, I know – I have wandered a whole savannah away from our large grey big-eared friends, but I owe it to the villagers of Southern Nepal to explain how their greatest sporting spectacle came to be.

A sport which is partly the reason children there emerge

from their shacks in pristine school uniforms, and excitedly clutch their book bags as they stride with confidence into their new red-brick schools.

The point is, without Colin and Duncan, there wouldn't have been the current Duke of Argyll, Torquhil Ian, the current holder of the title. There wouldn't have been the castle that emerged like a charging bull elephant from behind the thick pine trees as I strode up the winding gravel driveway on a wet November afternoon.

I parted the ferns and peered through the grey slate air for my first glimpse of the magnificent castle. It was like stepping through the wardrobe into Narnia. The Duke was in the main hall – 'He's waiting for you with his trainer,' beckoned a wee from behind a step ladder in the entrance hall. They were having work done, so white sheets and ladders framed the relics of family history against a backdrop of 21st-century DIY.

I stepped into the room and once my eyes had taken in the hundreds of bayonets and muskets on the walls, I came to focus on a tall elegant, gentleman, who looked like he had stepped from the pages of a Willard Price Adventure.

'I am James Manclark,' he said. 'I'm giving the Duke a lesson in penalty-taking.'

Anyone who knows their winter sports will know James Manclark. He represented Great Britain in Luge at the 1968 Winter Olympics, which is impressive enough, but it's elephant polo that has more recently earned him sporting respect around the world.

He flicked back his mane – imagine a lion with highlights and you get a rough picture of the strong -jawed king of a man standing in front of me. With his giant hands, he gestured to the Duke, who was sitting astride a gold-plated statue of an elephant. Two elegant white trouser legs rose out of black boots, leading to the gold and black polo shirt worn by the grinning, raven-haired, handsome Duke.

It was quite a sight to take in. Up there on the mantelpiece the Duke, the man who owns a large part of Scotland, the man whose family has an integral part in the history of this land, was sitting on a gold-plated elephant. It was around a foot tall, the sort of souvenir you might bring back from a trip to Thailand, if you could get it through customs as hand luggage.

I jumped back to avoid the enormous polo stick that Torquhil swung down to connect with the ball, which was resting on a cushion in front of the fire. The ball flew several feet through the smoke-laden air into the wall, causing the lady in the hall to screech partly with shock and partly with spontaneous approval.

'Let the stick do all the work,' advised Manclark, 'rather than you trying to hit it.'

It all seemed so normal – as if this was the Scottish football team practising their free kicks right before a big game at Hampden Park.

The height of the mantelpiece added to the height of the statue elevated the Duke to the same size as a male Asian elephant. Crucially, it was the same height as the elephants the Duke would be riding in his attempt to win back the world elephant polo title for Scotland. He had captained the team to glory twice before, but had been beaten by Hong Kong in the most recent final.

'It's one of my practise stances, for my penalty shots,' said the Duke. 'They are hard to get right, and this mantelpiece helps. You know this sport is so competitive, when you are up there on an elephant and there are nine other elephants charging around, people take it so seriously. I am so proud to have represented my country in this sport, and to be a double world champion'.

The clatter of metal falling to the floor shook me to my senses. In his eagerness, Torquhil had bumped one of the 17th-century bayonets and it came crashing to the floor. After several more swings, cracks against the wall, and shrieks of excitement from the lady who brought us tea, Torquhil climbed down from his mantelpiece to talk tactics with Manclark in front of the fire. Here the battle lines for Scotland's world title assault would be drawn. Like an army general Manclark unfurled a great white sheet of paper and started mapping out team tactics in thick red pen.

The polo team had beaten National Parks of Nepal 12-6 the last time they won the world title that they had first captured in 2001.

'Obviously we go there to play sport,' continued the Duke, 'but by far the most important thing we're going for is the conservation of the elephants. By doing this we are putting money into the local economy and into charities there.'

It does cost around £12,000 to enter the tournament and I was to see at first hand the difference this money has made, but first I was taken outside into the castle grounds and into the sodden autumn air.

'We do normal training as well,' laughed the Duke as he climbed through the sunroof of his Range Rover. We had come outside for some wet weather practice, and in the absence of elephants, the Duke placed a cushion on top of his 4x4's roof and straddled the frame with one leg dangling down past the driver's window, and the other dropping through the sunroof.

'Take me to about 10 miles per hour please,' he called to Manclark, who was sat at the wheel as the Duke then proceeded to dribble up the wing, knocking the ball ten yards at a time. I was invited to give it a try and it was surprisingly difficult to connect at first. I found myself bending down so that my eyes were in line with Manclark's reassuringly bushy eyebrows. He was such a gent that he didn't mind having to reverse each time I missed the ball. I was starting to appreciate the skill involved, and the fact that I would need the tentacles of an octopus if I was going to make an impression when we got to Nepal.

'It may seem difficult here,' I said to the camera, as we crept along, 'but I am told it will be far more testing when we are in the heat of Nepal, with other elephants crashing into me'.

An elephant sandwich was common, I was warned.

The following week I was heading for Nepal to report on the progress of the team. It was mainly for a feature for BBC World, which has a large audience in Nepal, and despite the bizarre, whimsical appearance of this so-called sport, its impact in one of the poorest parts of the world has been staggering. It has saved and transformed lives, and I was about to find out how.

Apparently they used to send criminals to the Chitwan province of Nepal, because they were almost guaranteed to catch a vicious strain of malaria and die. Not anymore. Elephant polo has helped change all this. It all started in 1960, when a former butcher's delivery boy from Jersey, who was bored with his life, drove a Saab from Stockholm across Afghanistan and India. Albert Victor James Edwards, known as Jim, represented the island at badminton. He went on to work in a bank, but wanted to see more of the world, so he persuaded Saab to let him drum up publicity for their cars by taking one for a test drive: a test drive to India, via Iran and Afghanistan. At the Swedish embassy in Delhi, he became a good friend of the Swedish Ambassador's son, and was allowed to keep the car. So the pair drove along a track up to Kathmandu where he met the king and the car was sold for a princely sum.

It was the start of a love affair with the country that never ended. Several years later, Edwards returned with his brother and another partner to start up an eco-tourism business in the Chitwan province of Nepal. His aim was to get tourists to abandon fishing and hunting in favour of watching the wildlife which thrived in the swamps and jungles. He was able to buy an old hunting lodge called Tiger Tops and managed to persuade the Nepalese government to turn the area, some 360 square kilometres, into a national park.

This, though, is only half the story. Edwards was a keen sportsman and enjoyed tobogganing. So much so that in 1981, he was at St Moritz, having just completed his first Cresta run. It was here that he was introduced to Olympic tobogganer and British bob sleigh champion, James Manclark, who also happened to be an international polo player. Manclark's wife nudged him, saying, 'This Edwards chap is quite a nice man and he's got elephants'. 'Elephants?' Manclark nodded to Edwards. 'You got elephants, let's play polo.' To which Edwards is reported to have replied, 'Buy me a drink, and we can play.' So a partnership was formed that would lead to what is fondly known as the 'biggest' sport in the world. Polo players tend to be wealthy, and of an adventurous type. There weren't many polo ponies in deepest Nepal, but there were an abundance of domesticated elephants used for logging.

The following spring, a telegram arrived at Tiger Tops. It read: 'Have long sticks. Get elephants ready. Arriving 1st April. Regards James'.

Was this some big joke? Edwards pondered, noticing the date. But he couldn't afford to doubt the crazy Scotman's intentions, and so prepared a field at Meghauly and carefully picked the elephants. The first game was between Scotland and Nepal, and within two years, eight nations were competing for the World Cup. The rules are similar to horse polo, but one change had to be made after the first tournament.

Originally light footballs were used, but the elephants, who are surprisingly fleet of foot, seemed to enjoy stamping on the balls and bursting them. Standard polo balls were then introduced, and this made it much more skilful. It was much harder to hit the ball. In addition a rule came in permitting the elephants to kick the ball towards the goal. It is, though, still a foul for them to pick it up with their trunks.

In many ways it's easier than horse polo, because each elephant has its keeper, the Mahout, tucked in a position just behind the ears, to steer and drive the elephant. The mahout has a very close relationship with the animals, spending many years bonding with them. So any elephant polo player is a guest in a sporting threesome. Your job is to connect with the ball and get it towards your opponents' goal. The first thing I learned was treat your elephant and your mahout with the utmost respect, or they may not 'understand' which way you would like to go.

As Torquhil said, elephant polo is now played to raise funds for their welfare and awareness of their plight in Asian countries, where many domesticated elephants have been left redundant as they are no longer needed for logging. At the World Cup there are strict rules to stop any mistreatment of the elephants. All matches end by noon, so they don't get too hot, and they never play more than two matches in any one day.

I arrived after six hours on a bus, around mountainous hairpin bends on the road down from Kathmandu. I was to make my debut playing for the Duke's Chivas team and there was pressure on me not to let this team, with its illustrious past, down.

Torquhil's love affair with the sport had started in 2001, and as captain of the Scottish team he had lifted back-to-back world titles. The walk of out the tunnel at Wembley must be spine tingling, and the stroll down the steps from the long room at Lords awe-inspiring, but the journey to the field of play across swamps and through the jungle on the back of one of these magnificent beasts ahead of the 27th elephant polo World Cup was out of this world.

The teams were then led out for the opening ceremony by a band of locals playing their wood pipes with huge grins. They called themselves the Rolling Bones. They could hardly play their instruments for laughter as I strutted in my jodhpurs in front of them, recording a piece to camera for *Breakfast*.

Then came the draw, to see which elephants we would each be riding on. You toss a coin and then each side takes it in turns to choose their favourites. Elephants of all shapes and sizes were standing in line. Ideally you should end up with two smaller and faster elephants in attack, and two big bruisers in defence. They may be slower, but these centre-backs are huge and not to be messed with.

I was drawn on a smaller attacking elephant, which at least was easier to climb on to. My mount dropped to its knees and a teammate gave me a leg up; a shove so hard I nearly went over the other side.

Once in place, I then grabbed the rope in front of me with all my might to stop myself tumbling down the elephant's trunk as it rose from its knees. I tucked my own knees under the rope, which was tightly strung across the hessian seat, and held on tightly.

The mahout who fed and cared for my elephant was next

to jump on. He kissed the beast near one eye, before nonchalantly climbing up the trunk and into position. Soft words were said which I didn't understand and for a moment the telepathy was such I felt I was encroaching on a Valentine's night meal for two.

The mahouts and the elephants decided where we went. All I had to do was hold on and give instructions on where the ball was, which way to turn and when to speed up or slow down. At first it's a challenge letting go of the rope with one hand so that you can swing your mallet and hope to hit the ball. It's easier said than done when you're straddling a small bungalow, but the sticks are long enough to reach the ground as long as you lean over far enough. An elephant doesn't run, it lumbers like a juggernaut with a flat tyre, and on the first few forays down the wing I was convinced I would fall off. I kept asking politely and then in exasperation for the mahout and my elephant to slow down. Such requests fell on deaf ears. My partners had played this enough times to know what they were doing and they knew best because after a few minutes, I was loving the speed.

I was just dragging my carcass back up the elephant's powdery dry skin into a sitting position, when I stopped in my tracks, paralysed by anticipation. I had just hit the ball, but not very far. It was still nearer to my stick than anyone else's and now I was aware of two defending elephants thundering towards me with ears flapping and trunks pointing. I was about to be the sliver of cheese in an elephant burger, the jam in a giant grey tusker sandwich, and there was nothing I could do but wait. I braced myself and patted my poor little defenceless elephant, who didn't seem at all bothered about the impending collision. The impact never happened. Well it did, but these creatures are big sofites really and it was like being squashed by two large cushions. The elephant scrum also happened in slow motion, as the warm, soft hide smothered my leg.

Like in any sport, when you get through your first tackle, the adrenalin is pumping and I was soon tangling my sticks with the best of them. I even got away at one point and had a clear run at goal. It was then that I was distracted by the thousands of screaming school children on the touchline and behind the goals, and sensing my lapse in concentration, another elephant stuck out a foot to kick the ball away from the goal line.

The school kids were dressed in uniforms that wouldn't look out at place at your poshest private school, and are bussed in from hundreds of miles around to cheer for the teams. They told me this was the region's FA Cup final, their Wimbledon, their Grand National, and at this point their high pitched screams added an extra spurt to our charge. I lifted back my stick, and inspired by the chance to run off into the jungle with my gold and black shirt pulled over my head in celebration, I connected cleanly with the ball, despite the speed we had built up. It was a proud moment. I looked up, hoping to see the ball flying between the sticks and towards the baying crowd, but saw nothing until I looked down to see my shot rather apologetically trickling along the grass towards the goal line.

To this day I still think it was going to go in, until I was cheated out of glory by my own elephant.

As if to say, 'call that a shot you novice buffoon?' he flicked the ball off course with the end of his trunk. To make matters worse he made it look like it was an accident. The mahout uttered a few chuckled words to his partner in crime and we were veering away from the goal again.

It was dusty, sweaty and exhausting, but completely exhilarating. After a while, I forgot that I was up on an elephant and purely focused on fighting my opponents' sticks for the ball. It was a battle of courage: who dares lean over the furthest, wins and who dares poke his or her stick in where it most hurts succeeds on this bumpy rollercoaster.

The American team were left jumping up and down on the touchline, furious that they had been knocked out in the semi-finals. Even though I did eventually score a goal to tell my grandchildren about, it wasn't to be the Duke's year and a team from England won. I felt that I had played my part in sporting history, and been given a unique insight into one of the world's more bizarre events. But if I needed proof of the real power that elephant polo has, it was to come in the late afternoon.

A two-hour drive through the jungle followed, in an open-top jeep. We were hot on the trail of a tiger, we were told. Fresh footprints and panicking monkeys in the trees above told us that Shere Khan was not far away. We had to cross a swirling river before finally arriving at a state-of-the-art school, which had been funded by the proceeds of the elephant polo World Cup. It was far smarter than any of the 50 or so houses that made up the village. On the grass in front of the elegant building, a class of 30 students were practising tai chi as part of their morning PE lesson, all dressed to the nines in their maroon and grey uniforms.

The headmaster told me that without the money from elephant polo, the school would not have been built. This is why the World Cup is held in such high esteem here. What's more the empire that Jim Edwards created has helped fund the building of medical centres for the villages. Perhaps his greatest gift has been in the fight against disease. The malaria that was once a plague here is virtually gone.

The celebratory post-match scenes in the river that you have to cross (by elephant of course) to get back to the Tiger Tops lodge from the pitches, were a powerful reminder of how this sport has brought an area back from the brink and brought nature and people together. Football and rugby stars are famous for their communal baths as they soothe their mud-scarred skin, but none of them will have had the pleasure of sharing those soaks with an elephant. Yes, after elephant polo there is the communal bath. A chance for players and the mahouts to wash, scrub and massage the elephants in the murky water, and we didn't need a power shower either. Every so often the wonderful creatures lifted a trunk and sprayed us all around.

Back at the ranch, there was just time to see the winners lift their cup aloft before it was time for me to leave this extraordinary sporting experience. Sadly, though, it was the last World Cup founder Jim Edwards ever saw. The 2009 tournament was held in honour of its creator, who had died during the summer. His legacy, though, is here to stay and among those who have tried their hand at the sport, which has spawned similar competitions in Sri Lanka and Thailand, are horse polo stars such as the Mexican Antonio Herrera; Sir Edmund Hillary, the conqueror of Mount Everest; the Beatle Ringo Starr; and the comedian Billy Connolly.

It still courts some controversy. The conservationist Dame Daphne Sheldrick, who has worked with the animals for 50 years, declared that 'elephants are not designed to play polo – nor should they'.

I understand this viewpoint and indeed in other parts of the world some tournaments and matches have been stopped after protests over the way elephants were being treated. However what I saw with my own eyes in Nepal was nothing but love and care for the elephants. I didn't see any evidence of the elephants being prodded or forced to do anything against their will, and they genuinely seemed to enjoy the social interaction and sense of play. They would often let out a triumphant snort after kicking the ball or making a run down the wing. Perhaps it was their way of letting us know that they are the real stars of the show.

I was saddened in the summer of 2012 to hear that the dominant bull with the most impressive tusks of all, Shamsher Gaj, had died. The legend of the jungle, a gentle giant, he was so majestic and calm that he had been promoted from the field of play to become the umpires' elephant. So his demise was painful for all that had grown up with him. He was attacked by a rampaging wild elephant, who had thundered into camp. His distraught mahout did all he could, but he was no match for the ferocious intruder, and in the prime of his life, Shamsher was so badly wounded that he failed to recover from his injuries. His passing was mourned with almost the same respect that was given to Jim Edwards, the great godfather of the sport. Jim would have wanted it that way.

As for Torquhil, the Duke of Argyll, he may no longer be captain of the Scotland team, but he is still involved in promoting the welfare of elephants and is one of the leading figures in the sport.

The World Cup continues to go from strength to strength. Although on rare occasions 12 teams from all over the world have competed, the tournament is now restricted to eight finalists, who all pour money into elephant welfare and conservation, and which has helped enrich the lives of people who live in Chitwan. For more information contact WEPA, the World Elephant Polo Association.

MORE TALES FROM AROUND THE WORLD

The jockey stood tall in the sand, but still only came up to my knees. I couldn't see his face, as he was sheltering from the sun under a blue cap. But this diminutive racer has nothing to shy away from. The impact they have had on one of the most popular sports in the Middle East has been huge and even dwarfs the impact of the elephant polo in Nepal.

I have been on some strange foreign assignments over the years, for BBC World and BBC *Breakfast*. We will come to the reason for the tiny jockeys in the desert shortly, but it still doesn't win the prize for my strangest trip.

BEARD LIFTING

There was the case of the record breaking star, Antanas Kounas, from Lithuania. He has dominated his event for the last decade in the way that Bjorg did in tennis or Schumacher did in F1, just untouchable for a period of time.

The reason you may not have heard of this icon, though is that he's a world champion beard lifter. I don't mean he can lift the fallen whiskers off a barber's floor. No, he keeps smashing the world record for the strength of his Rumpelstiltskin-length beard, which measures over 50 centimetres. In 2010 he broke his own record again, lifting a Chinese lady weighing 63.4 kilogrammes clean off the floor using just his beard, which he'd wrapped around her. He had to hold her for a tear-jerking five minutes. He can lift more, but that was the official one, recognised by the *Guinness Book of Records*.

Antanas doesn't need a tow rope to get a broken down car off the road, because in 2002, he pulled an army jeep with five passengers a whole 42 feet. That's almost three tonnes attached by straps to his chin forest, which he hasn't shaved for over 25 years. He claims it's his neck and back muscles, combined with a strong spine and stamina, that have enabled him to have such hair strength, and he's now using his hairy fame for political muscle too, to get recognition for the Lithunian region of Samogita, which he is proud to be from.

I had been getting a series of emails in Lithuanian inviting me to film a feature with him and it was suggested I come to Frankfurt to see him compete in the latest round of the world beard lifting championships. I hadn't got to the stage of asking someone senior at the BBC whether this was feasible when I heard the devastating news that some whiskers had been trapped in a door and he was out injured for several weeks. He would miss the trip to Frankfurt and I never got to meet him. At least his injury made a change from the usual broken metatarsals!

ICE CRICKET

Broken metatarsals were a worry lurking at the back of my mind as I slipped and shuffled onto the uneven crease at what was a World Cup of cricket. I had misjudged a bouncing ball in the week of my sister Louisa's wedding and am still there on the photos with a fighter's black eye.

The ball I was now about to face on the slippery wicket seemed even more of a challenge than the one spun my way by Shane Warne in the nets at Southampton. It seemed more of a cricketing conundrum than trying to oust Alistair Cook in a net session at Lords. Although my first ball at the England batsman had been wider than a whale – 'you are beyond help,' he had remarked – the rest were on target, even if he had swatted them away like drunk flies. That cricketing experience, like Warne's spin, was at least predictable compared to the lottery of a delivery I was now facing.

I wasn't sure if I would still be standing by the time the ball bounced in front of me...I wasn't sure how the ball would react at all when it came into contact with the sheet of ice that we were playing on. I was in Latvia for the World Cup of ice cricket. It was early March and the tournament I played in was the idea of British cricket fan Julian Tall. Ice cricket had first been played 200 years ago by English adventurers in northern Scandanavia. There is an 18th-century painting in the British Library showing as much. It surfaced again over 20 years ago in St Moritz, but this version was played on a carpeted area lay down on the ice on a frozen lake in the Alps.

In 2005, Tall, the Estonian Cricket Board, and another Briton, Jason Barry, took the idea further and started the first tournament to be played actually on ice and with frozen stumps and bails. The ice is a real leveller, and it's the only form of cricket Australia have never won. It's like cricket has gone to Narnia with the crystal white trees lining the boundary and the odd inquisitive wolf poking its nose out of the forest to see what all the fuss is about.

Of course when I went over to report on the new sporting phenomenon for BBC World, it was the warmest winter for 20 years and the lake on which the tournament is normally played was melting. It was only getting down to -2 degrees Celsius and not to the usual -20. Luckily the outdoor ice rink in Riga is one of the biggest I have ever seen, and so play could commence alongside bewildered skaters who must have wondered why grown men and women were chasing balls on their bellies.

The stumps were made out of ice and spiked shoes were optional. On one hand they enable you to grip as you run, but it's like tiptoeing in high heels, with short stuttering steps. So the more effective teams wore full-body ski suits, and would launch themselves onto their fronts to slide for the ball. This technique also proved quicker than running between the wickets.

There is a purpose to the event, which brings together the main cricketing heavyweights from New Zealand to South Africa, and from India to Pakistan. Ice cricket is helping to spread the sport to the countries of the old Soviet block, some of which don't yet appreciate the intricacies of the game and don't have suitable conditions to play in. 'It's a very strange game,' said the captain of the Latvian team. He wasn't referring to ice cricket either, just the sport in general. In fact there were so few locals who knew how to hold the bat that the Latvian team included myself and a TV reporter from India to make up their numbers.

We were playing Ireland, and my first swing for the ball caused my feet to disappear from beneath me. In a second, I was on my back on the ice. A couple of attempts later and it was away to slip, quite literally, as I slid legs first to safety at the far side.

I was eventually caught for five and we were soundly beaten, but having enjoyed the game, the Latvian hosts said they'd been won over. 'I like it better than baseball,' announced one of my new Latvian friends.

It may look silly from a distance, like penguins dancing on ice chasing an orange ball, but the teams take this seriously. Just as has happened on grass, the Indian team and Australians started sledging each other during the tense final few overs, with the Indians complaining they never got the cut of the ice or the rub of the green. They won with a controversial catch that only made matters worse, until the power of beer refreshed the smiles and they were all friends again. In the end the Indians didn't make the final and instead the trophy went to an English cricket team from Brighton.

Another ice cricket tournament is today played on a frozen lake just outside Tallinn, in Estonia, and another in an old Soviet missile factory that has been converted into two huge ice rinks. The stumps are now standard wooden ones that spring back. With more tournaments and more summer touring teams from the UK going to play on the ice in the Baltic states, it seems that this kind of 'sledging' in the game is here to stay. For more information check out www.icecricket.co.uk or www.balticexperiences.com

ROBOT CAMEL JOCKEYS

It's back to the desert now, a world away from the ice of Latvia. The warm air whipped up a flurry of sand, as the jockey stood there motionless, after winning his latest race. No expression, no celebrations, no emotion, not a flicker...for this jockey was a robot.

I shouldn't have been too surprised. This after all was the desert near Abu Dhabi, where the past and the future and different cultures and religions have been thrown into the melting pot to create a fascinating blend of contradictions. The chemical reaction from this eclectic mix has erupted into a plume of opportunity, ambition, wealth, and skyscrapers that aims to be higher, bigger and better than anywhere else on earth.

It was 2007 and its ambition to be the new capital of world sport was growing: with the building of Sports City and the Palm resort. I had attended the launch of the A1 grand prix motor racing series, which was the brainchild of one of the ruling Maktoum family members. I had been to the city's ski slope, which is the biggest indoor ski centre in the world. It's situated just yards from the sand dunes, where the temperature is often over 40 degrees and where many of the local population will never see real snow.

So in this land of the unexpected, it wasn't that strange to see a robot jockey, no bigger than a thermos flask, stood there in front of me. Weighing three kilograms, he – or it – had arrived earlier in the day in its owner's 4x4. Like dozens of others it had been carefully lifted out of a box, and complete with stables colours, in this case blue and gold, it was lined up on blankets in the sand. The cap, also in the team colours, shielded its blank face from the sun.

It was the latest meeting at the Al Wathba camel race track, about 45 kilometres from Abu Dhabi, where the great and the good of camel racing were gathered. It's a huge part of the culture in the United Arab Emirates and is one of the region's most popular sports. A successful racing camel will fetch millions of dollars at auction, and there are reports that at the Al Dhafrah camel festival in February 2010, one man alone spent £4,000,000 on just three camels.

So you can see what big business it is, and this is why in 2006 I was standing on the spotless white railings by the track, looking up a manicured grass slope to a sparkling palace of a building where sheikhs, dressed in their bright white robes, were flicking through their programmes. Down in the stable areas, dozens of camels were being prepared for the next race. The robot jockeys were tightly strapped into position on the animals' backs. Then a trainer lifted a remote control handset out of another box, and started moving a lever to make sure the jockey was ready. With the touch of a button, the robots sprung into life. The metal arms of these gadgets, powered by a hand-drill motor, started spinning furiously. The snake-like whip in its hand whirred round and made a flicking noise on the fidgety camels' hides. It was like being in a sci-fi movie set in the days of Lawrence of Arabia.

The sight of the camels roaring down the home straight

through a veil of dust is a powerful image, one which dates back centuries, but it's so surreal when you see the pint-sized machines on top, all twirling their flexible canes. Then cast your eyes to the right, and over the railings, another race is unfolding. A herd of 4x4 cars jostles for position, as they keep pace with the camels which can reach 30 kilometres per hour.

The sheikhs shout to their drivers while leaning out of the passenger window, frantically tapping at their handsets to get the clearest signal over to their robot jockeys. Bumper to bumper, side to side, they weave in and out of each other in a contest that's just as enthralling as the camel race itself. There is noise, there is speed and there is a storm of excitement. I could see this sport was thriving again and it's down to the new robot jockeys.

'It's much better now, the robots are great – they keep going and don't tire as much,' I was told. As much as what? This is where the story turns from a bizarre and funny tale about robots on camels, to a story of broken families and heartbreak and the real reason I went all the way to the UAE. The former camel jockeys had been children. Some as young as four. Behind the comical facade of the robots is a harrowing story of child welfare and human trafficking.

It's no exaggeration to say the robots have saved lives. For decades children were bought by owners to race on their camels. Poverty in parts of Africa and in Asian countries like Pakistan would push families to send their children abroad to earn a living, and many were sold into camel racing. Not only would they miss out on their childhood but these young jockeys were risking their lives being tied onto the camels. Reports from international agencies said the children were being treated like slaves by their employers who 'cared more for the camels than the children'. To make the camels go faster, children were often given little to eat to make them much lighter. Some fell off and were injured and some were even killed.

International pressure grew on the UAE, and other Middle Eastern countries, and in 2005 they introduced a ban on anyone under the age of 18 being used as a camel jockey. Thanks to the robots, the camel racing fraternity were happy to embrace the change.

'The use of robots is successful here in the UAE,' said the head of the camel racing association at the Al Wathba racetrack. 'All child jockeys were sent back to their country after the investigation by the United Nations children's charity UNICEF. Robots have many good characteristics, they are practical and they are cheap, everyone can buy one.'

The robots cost just a couple of hundred dollars and don't need feeding, clothing, medical care or housing. I arrived in Dubai shortly after the ban had been imposed, and was happy to report that at the camel race meeting I attended, only robots were being used, apart from a handful of adult male jockeys, who were proving to be heavy and slow.

I had been shown grainy footage of small children strapped to the camels taken several years earlier, and I could see the misery and pain etched on their bleak faces. In contrast Abdul was radiant like the desert sun. With the most handsome brown eyes looking out from beneath his neatly-cut fringe, he was six years old and was preparing to go home. He had been sold by his grandfather into camel racing when he was four. He'd broken both legs and so when the ban came in, he had been taken to a refuge set up to nurture child jockeys back to full health as they got ready to go back to their childhoods.

We sat on the garden bench outside the refuge as Sharla Musabih, the founder, explained the work they do. 'Now children like Abdul can have a life again,' she added, with quiet, intense passion.

Abdul wasn't the only one to go home. More than a thousand child jockeys were sent back in the year that followed the ban, with UNICEF reporting that 97 per cent were able to find their families again.

The robots have proved to be a mechanical solution to a very human problem. 'Everyone is happy again,' added a trainer, as he strapped his blue rider onto another camel. 'The owners like the new jockeys and the price of camels is soaring again.'

The United Arab Emirates has since said it will give £4.6 to former the former child jockeys who were employed in the country. The money, it says, will ensure they receive the salaries owed to them and compensation for losing their income. It will also go towards education.

In 2010, the BBC reported that some camel racers in the UAE were ignoring the ban and still using child jockeys at their meetings. Anti-Slavery International had issued pictures of 10-year-olds on camels at a prestigious Abu Dhabi competition in February of that year. However racing officials said that these young riders were Emirati children, who had their parents' consent. The situation continues to be monitored.

MORE SPORTS IN ODD PLACES

It was time for the grounds man to get his revenge. For years the players had moaned about the grass being too long, the pitch being too boggy (like a vegetable patch, one striker had sneered). For far too long, he had taken a shovel load of stick, so on this sunny evening in the Scottish town of Dunoon, it was time for David to strike back.

With spade in hand he attacked the pitch with all his might, hacking, smashing and ripping up the soil. Several hours later he had sent for reinforcements, calling on his friend with a digger and craters were now appearing around the penalty spot. From there to the centre circle there wasn't now a blade of grass to be seen.

For good measure he would dig all night, and then add 10,000 litres of water. It was paradise, every grounds man's fantasy. He could sell the lawn mower and the rotavator and forget about which seed to sow this month.

It was 2006, in Scotland, and from across the north sea, a new kind of football had arrived on these shores. We will come back to our grounds man in a moment, but this was one of many sporting challenges that has popped up in the most unusual place. From extreme ironing on the sides of mountains, and at the bottom of the sea, to playing rugby and hockey at the bottom of a swimming pool.

OCTOPUSH

Underwater hockey, otherwise known as Octopush, has become a global phenomenon and was one of the first sports I profiled on my Saturday morning *Breakfast* slot.

It was invented as early as the 1950s by a group of sub-aqua divers in Southsea in Hampshire, who got bored of just swimming up and down the lanes to keep fit. The club wanted to stop its members abandoning the sport during the winter months, when it was too cold to dive in the sea, and so underwater hockey was born. It soon spread to South Africa where spear fisherman used to it to hone their skills when they couldn't get out onto the ocean. It's now played in over 40 countries worldwide.

It is a supreme aerobic exercise, because while all other sports allow competitors to breathe as they play, in Octopush the action takes place underwater. Every so often you have to opt out and grab some air through your snorkel on the surface before diving back down to do battle.

·You have your swimming cap, flippers, mask, snorkel and stick. This is only the size of a spatula and is carried in a special glove which protects your fingers. The idea is to get the puck, which weighs around 1.2 kilograms, into your opponents' goal, at the bottom of their end of the 25-metre pool. Only six players are allowed on each team at a time.

When I joined the Bournemouth team, I couldn't believe how physical it was down there. It was a scrum of arms, legs, flippers and sticks through a sea of bubbles and I had to come up for air every 30 seconds. Those that play regularly must have gills because they could stay down for over a minute, maybe even two.

The real skill, however, is not how long you can hold your breath, but judging when to dive; when to make that move to tackle your opponent, to pass the puck, or shoot. I found I was far more effective with short sharp bursts, when I had full lungs to call on.

Not only does it keep your body fit, but Octopush also claims to make your mind more alert too. The sport has developed to such an extent that Great Britain's women were crowned world champions in Portugal in 2011. For more information check out the website of the British Octopush Association, www.bguwh.co.uk

SWAMP SOCCER

Back to our muddy swamp that had once been a football pitch and Andy the groundsman had used enough water to fill several swimming pools to get the stage ready in Dunoon for Scotland's first ever swamp soccer World Cup.

The sport might have some roots in the north east, where it's said soldiers and athletes included running in a bog as part of their training because it is so physically demanding. The idea was taken a step further by a man called Jyrki Vaananen in Finland, nicknamed the Swamp Baron, who created the world's first swamp soccer world championship in 2000. It was several years later in Iceland that football fanatic Stewart Miller met the Swamp Baron in a bar and was quickly sucked in. He could see that Scotland could have a great future in the sport, and so in 2006 he brought swamp soccer to the UK. A year later and I was on my way to Dunoon.

It was Easter Day and my family and joined the crowd of 600 to see a warm-up match between a local side, including yours truly, and a team representing the rest of Scotland. The sun was shining, which gave the pitch a deceptive crust and hid the quagmire beneath. But as we tried to run out for the national anthems, I saw my white trainer disappear as the thick brown sludge advanced past my heel, past the top of my foot, until it reached just below my knee.

As I tried to move, my whole body tipped forward and foolishly I thought I could stop myself with my hands. They vanished in the bog as well. Eventually I squelched my way upright again and, lifting my leg, discovered that my shoe was still down there. My first top tip is to make sure you tie your laces tightly.

We have often seen non-league clubs embarrass the fancy-dans from top teams on muddy pitches and likewise swamp soccer is a real leveller. Forget free flowing football: this is up and under, and you might only get one touch, before you are slopping around again. The best tactic seemed to be tip-toeing like a sneaky fox making off with the chickens. It's case of running as if you are on hot coals, because the moment you stop, you get that sinking feeling. The small, light girl on our team was easily our best player as she could skip around like one of those water boatmen you see on ponds.

There are six players on each team and due to the physically exhausting effort it takes to run through thick mud, there are only 12 minutes in each half. The modern playing surface is roughly the same size as a five-a-side pitch, and there's no offside rule.

Eventually as the pitch became more churned up, thicker boulders and clumps of mud made it easier to get around and to get hold of the ball. The Rest of Scotland took a one-nil lead...a couple of simple passes and a shot as our keeper slipped while trying an impossible dive. By half time there was hardly a speck of clean skin left on show – it was as if we had been dipped in chocolate, the sludge dripping from ear lobes and nostrils.

'It's good to develop your close control, and you really have to work to run,' said one player who was also a coach with the Scottish FA. 'There's fit guys and then there's me,' said his teammate 'Me, a bald fat bloke who can get out and have just as much fun as everyone else,' he said.

Stewart Miller, the organiser and referee on the sidelines (who was still as clean as a whistle) was grinning from ear to ear.

'We are taking on the rest of the world here, teams from Germany, Finland, Estonia, Belgium and Iceland. We are never going to win the proper World Cup, but we might be able to win this one,' he chortled in his Lanarkshire accent.

In the second half a flying melée of bodies resulted in the ball pinging off an outstretched boot for the Rest of Scotland's second goal, but the match wasn't over. I was sucking my feet through the treacle towards the corner flag, when from behind an unstoppable force pushed me face-first into the dark mass. The hulk who'd tripped and created a tidal wave through the mud protested his innocence, but it was a penalty. My chance had arrived, and the best bit about swamp soccer is the set pieces.

Kick offs, corners, throw-ins, free kicks and penalties are taken by dropping the ball onto a foot. So with the ball in my hands, I balanced my weight on my left leg, planted like a tree in the soil, and swung back my right peg as I released the ball from my clutches. As if in slow motion, I connected as cleanly as you can in such conditions and the ball flew into the net. Delirious with delight, I spotted my daughters behind the goal. Surely Lucy, Isabel and Sophie would want to share this proud moment with their old man? Surely we would dance around in one big Bushell embrace?

But alas, the crowd parted as if I had the plague. The girls ran back aghast from the swamp monster trying to embrace them and it was only then, with firm ground beneath my feet again, that I too noticed the stench, the waft of wet warthog steaming off my sullied body.

So I was left to celebrate my consolation goal in a 3-1 defeat with the giant who had flattened me for the penalty. It would be several showers later that I finally returned to my original form. I had a few little scratches which I hadn't felt at the time, but my skin was like the proverbial baby's bottom, as smooth as the day I was born. Plus I felt as if I had run a marathon. Running in mud really is a punishing exercise. I had also never seen a crowd laugh so much at a football match. Swamp soccer was here to stay.

The World Cup outgrew its home on the Western Isles and moved to Edinburgh before finally settling in Glasgow and Dublin so that it can accommodate the thousands who attend.

It's planned to alternate between the cities every year. From 24 teams in 2006, the tournament is now held over several days with around 100 sides from 20 countries battling for the golden cup. The sport is spreading around the world as well. In 2011, swamp soccer arrived in China and the inaugural match in Beijing drew a crowd of 20 thousand people. Turkey, known for its famous mud baths, was next to embrace this sport.

Scotland did realise Stewart Miller's dream, lifting the Swamp Soccer World Cup in its inaugural year, 2006. They have never managed to repeat this feat as other countries to have triumphed include Russia, Belgium, England and Germany, who beat the English – yes, you've guessed it – on penalties. Despite the powers of the swamp, some things never change.

To find out more, visit www.swampsoccer.co.uk

KABADDI

Take a deep breath and get chanting. I am not talking about standing on the Kop or at the Stretford End, but the sport that crosses playground tag with yoga.

I realised how big Kabaddi was at the Asian Games in Doha in 2008. It was the one sport that had sold every ticket; it was the one sport that everyone was talking about. I had the honour of going to a training session with the reigning world champions, India.

I was told to take a deep breath, start chanting the word 'Kabaddi' and then make my move. Opposite me were seven athletes. They had the upper body muscles of Louis Smith but the legs of rugby players. They smiled menacingly as I danced on my toes. Seconds later I was upside down, being dangled by my legs like a prize fish. I had just experienced what it's like to be the raider. In Kabaddi, two teams compete with each other for points, scored by touching or capturing players from the opposing teams.

It is a team sport that requires both skill and power and combines the techniques of wrestling and rugby. There is evidence that the game is 4,000 years old, and was originally meant to develop self-defence skills. It was primarily a game played in India and Bangladesh, but it has now spread to all parts of the world including the UK. A demonstration match was held in 1936 at the Berlin Olympics, which is when the sport was officially recognised. The first national championships were held nearly 20 years later and it made its debut at the Asian games in 1990.

I found it fast and impulsive. There would be a tense build-up, and then the sudden burst of an attack and chanting would only last a few seconds, before I was tackled and lifted off my feet, which caused me to break my Kabaddi chant and pause for breath. This meant my go was over.

It's such a simple game to pick up and cheap. You don't need any equipment, nor a massive playing area, which is why it became so popular across rural India and then all over Asia. I say it's simple, but I had still better explain how it works. There are 12 players on each team, with seven on court at one time, and the other five in reserve. Each team takes it in turns to attack and defend on a court which is 12.5 by 10 metres. It's divided into two halves and the team winning the toss goes first. They send a 'raider' who enters the opponents half chanting the word 'Kabaddi, Kabaddi, Kabaddi...'. The word is said to mean 'holding hands' in Tamil.

The aim of the raider is to enter the opposing teams territory and touch any, or all of the opposing players before then trying to get back to their own side, without being caught and while still holding that breath and chanting 'Kabaddi'. Anyone the raider has touched is out. However the aim of the other team is to stop the raider getting back in the same breath. They have to stop him or her returning, until they are forced to take another breath. If the raider breaks the chant or stops for a breath then they are also out. They also go, if they are forced over any of the boundary lines. The winning team is the one with the most points and a match usually consists of two 20-minute halves.

Now there are various forms of Kabaddi. There's the form called Surjeevani, which is played under the Kabaddi Federation of India, and in this one players can come back into the match, the duration of which is fixed. In the Gaminee type of Kabaddi, players do not come back on and so when all the players of a team are out, the game is over. In the Amar version of Kabaddi, which is the one that has spread far beyond India to Canada, England, New Zealand, USA, Pakistan and Australia, players do not leave the field at all. If a player is touched the other team simply wins a point. There are stoppers and raiders. Every time a stopper prevents a raider from getting back to their starting point, the stopper scores a point. On the other hand, every raider that goes in, tags and returns to his or her starting position again, also gets a point.

There are other variations too. In the version played on a rectangular court, you do hold your breath and chant, whereas circular Kabaddi is fought out on a 35-metre round pitch and there is no chanting or breath holding in this form.

It was in this type of Kabaddi that the England women's team astonished the world in 2012 and reached the semi-finals of their World Cup in the Punjab, before eventually losing to India. So it wasn't just the England cricketers who made headlines there in 2012. This was an England team though that only formed three years ago and some players only got their first taste of Kabaddi six months before they were representing their country. Many of the team came from a rugby background, while Ashley Hunter reckons her experience as a pig farmer also helped her adapt to the game.

'It's a very respectful sport. It's skilful and tactical,' she said, 'but there's a lot of upper body grappling going on as well. It's a lot more than a game of tag. My friends think I go off to do some kind of Indian dancing, and they get a shock when I show them clips of what it's really like on YouTube.'

Rosie Haigh, the England captain, also came from a rugby background. 'It looks nasty at times, but it's not really painful, apart from the odd bruises. We were mobbed in India. It was incredible,' she explained.

Anyone old enough to watch TV in the 1980s and '90s might remember it being on Channel Four when it had a cult following, and its revival in the UK is now well underway. It was originally brought to the UK by Indian and Pakistan-born players around 30 years ago, and there was an explosion in the number of clubs during the two decades that followed. The first World Indoor Kabaddi Tournament was held in Birmingham in 1993, and there are now nearly 20 major clubs.

Back in Doha, the Head Coach of the Indian National team which has dominated the World Cup events, J Udon Yakumar, was chuckling in despairing frustration. 'Your reactions are poor' he said to me, 'You need to be like lightning or you will get caught. We say Kabaddi, Kabaddi, because it's like yoga. We are not breathing for 30 seconds during the raids, and so are doing Yoga while also having the tackling skills of rugby.'

The best technique seemed to be to dive head-first over the challenges and then I would try to reach my starting line with a forward roll. That was my theory, but in practice I was too slow and predictable for the World Champions. It really did have all the excitement and simple guilty pleasures of playground tag and it's true, you don't get hurt, because every time I was tackled, I would let out my breath, and then the opposing team would put me down very gently before any real damage was done.

For more information visit www.kabaddi.org or www.kabaddiuk.com

WIFE CARRYING

The moment you mention wife carrying, there's a snigger, a titter, and a flick of the eyebrows. Well, it is one of the world's daftest events. However like any great sport, it is steeped in history and there is a dark and mysterious story behind how it began.

The man who is said to be responsible is a chap called Herko Rosvo-Ronkainen. Legend has it that he was a robber, a villain, living in a forest in Finland in the late 1800s, and along with his gang he would raid villages, stealing food and sometimes men's wives. The women were picked up, kicking and screaming, and thrown over the backs of the robbers. This carrying position is the most common one still used in wife carrying today, although now it's usually the men screaming as they stumble down the course.

It is also said that Rosvo-Ronkainen would hold competitions in the forests, to see which men were the strongest and fittest, and so worthy of taking part in the raids. That competitive element was revived when Finnish historians decided to create a cultural event to remember the man who must have given marriage guidance councillors nightmares.

So Finland staged the first Wife Carrying World Championship in 1992. The Finns have also given the world the mobile phone throwing world championships and the sauna world championships. In this the winner is the person who can literally sweat it out the longest.

I wonder what Herko would make of the sport that has made his name famous around the world. He would be horrified to learn that the women now actually volunteer to take part, but he might well approve of the fact that the women don't have to be the wives or the girlfriends of the man doing the carrying. They can be a friend's wife, a stranger's wife ('Even better!' shouts Herko) or how about racing with an aunty, a mother-in-law or Grandma? Anything goes, as long as they are 17 or older.

Of course it is an advantage carrying your real other half. The championship's official website offers some top tips to entrants, and advises that at the heart of the race is the woman, the man and their relationship. For a start, this is up close and personal. How can it be anything else, when the woman has her nose pressed against the man's buttocks and her legs spread-eagled around her partner's neck?

I don't know if something has been lost in translation, but the official website also says: 'Intuitive understanding of the signals sent by the partner, and becoming one with that partner, are essential, and so too sometimes is whipping.' Do be aware of the new Jockey Club rules on the use of the whip though...

It also recommends: 'It is possible to train for the wife carrying competition everywhere in the middle of the daily routines: in the bath, in the supermarket, in the playground, or in the bodybuilding centre. Wife carrying is good for your relationship.'

Maybe life is very different in Finland, but I know there would be only one outcome if I tried lifting my partner Emma onto my back in the middle of Asda.

It is easy to mock, but this sport has expanded from its

motherland in the Finnish city of Sonkajarvi and become hugely popular around the world, with competitions all over Finland and in Central Europe, Australia, North and South America and now also the UK. It has its own section in the *Guinness World Records* book and is funded by sponsors queuing up to be associated with the event, which annually pops up on television sets in all parts of the world.

There are strict rules. For the distance race, the length of the course is just over 253 metres, and the surface changes from sand to grass and to gravel along the way. The track has two dry obstacles and a water one, the depth of which must reach a metre. This means the wife, who is going backwards and can't see the oncoming dunking, must be warned of the point at which she should take a deep breath.

There is also a minimum weight for the wife. She must be at least 49 kilograms. If her weight is less then she must wear a heavy rucksack to make up the difference, preferably without the packed lunch still inside. By the way, don't be put off if you are at the other end of the scales. One of the most wonderful alternative sport athletes I have met on my travels is Ireland's Julia Galvin. We'll find out more about her later.

Julia became a regular at the world wife carrying championships, and yet in her first year she weighed in at 132 kilograms. Julia is larger than life in so many ways, oozing warmth and infectious laughter, and has now been competing in wife carrying since 2003 with Irish strongman champion Paul Roberts. Such is her outlook on life that when she was asked by her rivals if she found it difficult competing with the 49kg ladies, she had one simple answer. 'Think of the beer'. The prize for winning the race is the wife's weight in beer, so winning with Julia, is like hitting the jackpot. For me, Julia epitomises why I think these events deserve to be recognised.

'I've had the great honour of representing Ireland in Finland,' she said. 'I know I will never go to the Olympics, but I am so proud to represent my country. I could stay at home and criticise the efforts of other sports people, and never participate myself in life and games, but I know through my positivity, I can get more out of life and also enrich the lives of others. I have shown that despite my sciatica and size, I can get involved and compete at world championships, and this can inspire others to do something, to get them more active. If I can do this, maybe you can too.'

In 2007, after many trips to Finland, Julia's perseverance paid off. She parted with regular carrying partner, Paul (although I hasten to add they remain very good friends) and teamed up with the former champion Margo Uusorg, from Estonia. It made sense; the Estonians are to wife carrying what Brazil are to football. They have dominated the event for years, and are famous for coming up with new ways of carrying while jumping the obstacles. Margo and Julia came in 29th out of 44 couples, a personal best, in front of 8,000 spectators. Before this, she had come last in every other year she had entered. She was ecstatic to have made the top 30.

Julia was a star attraction when wife carrying made its mark in the UK, in August 2012 at the World Alternative Games in mid-Wales. There was an extra incentive here too, because the couple to complete the course with the heaviest wife also won a prize.

I last saw Julia at the Llanwrtyd Wells post office asking if I knew of any strong Welsh men. She found one, in the form of Jamie Leigh Redwood: 6'5" and 23 stone. He was a former Welsh strongman champion from the valleys. They came last, but won gold for having the heaviest wife.

Now don't think this sport is just about taking part. Anyone who has competed in a woolsack race at a country fair will know that carrying something that weighs at least 49 kilograms at speed and over distance requires fitness and technique. It was at the World Alternative Games that I had my first taste of this sport. Not in the actual race, as I don't think I would have qualified. However, I did train with hopeful Karen Perkins and quickly realised how there's no room for embarrassment or politeness. It's head against the buttocks and away you go. Once Karen's legs were wrapped around my neck, I got a good grip, but never got into the rhythm we wanted. There was a lot of swinging going on as I lurched from side to side. If I am honest I don't think Karen felt particularly comfortable, and it's a good job we didn't try the water ditch as we would have both gone under.

At least Karen could cling onto my belt, the only equipment that can be worn, but every tug on the belt dragged me back and I could feel my knees wobbling. It's not that Karen is large either; had we entered for real, she might have needed a rucksack containing some tins of baked beans to get to the minimum wife weight of 49kg. We maybe should have tried the sprint event, because the distance for this is just 100 metres.

There is a lack of sentimentality in this sport, which shows how hardcore it still is. The penalty for dropping the wife into the sand, gravel or water is a 15-second penalty. Note the compassion there for the poor lass in the rules. Some of the athletes do train for months, and one of the first things that struck me was how fit the leading couples were. Many are keen runners, cyclists, and extreme sport enthusiasts who see this as a new and novel challenge. The world record over the longer distance is 55.5 seconds, held by Margo Uusorg and his regular partner Birgit Ulricht.

There are many more peculiarities about this sport. While

the winner gets their wife's weight in beer, the loser has to make do with a tin of dog food. In the UK race, the loser also gets a Pot Noodle.

Wife carrying is now firmly established in the UK running calendar. Indeed, the UK race was named as the country's top adventure race in 2012 by *Runner's World* magazine.

Two couples didn't make it to the start line that year, since they – or rather the wife – became pregnant before the event. It seems all the training really had brought the couples closer together, and it's claimed it may even have a positive effect on fertility, according to the organiser Robert McCaffrey.

The country's longest-established wife carrying event, the UK Wife Carrying Race, has taken place every March in Dorking, Surrey, since 2008. The UK race has many differences from its Finnish ancestor. In the original event, couples run against the clock, one after another, but in the UK, all the couples go at the same time, meaning it's often a scrum of flailing arms, legs and buttocks over the obstacles.

The 380-metre UK course is not flat, like the one in Finland. Carriers have to tote their 'wives' uphill to the halfway point, a climb of around 10 metres overall, before running back downhill to the finish line. Hay bales are used to provide hurdles, but the course does not feature a pool, like in Finland. Instead, volunteers with water pistols and buckets of water soak the competitors as they near the end.

Until 2013 the UK Wife Carrying Competition had seen men carrying women, a man carrying a man and a woman carrying a woman, but never in the world of wife carrying had a woman carried a man, until my *Breakfast* business colleague Stephanie McGovern and I decided to enter the sporting history books. Yes, in freezing conditions on 24 March 2013, Steph carried me. I was the heaviest wife of any of the 30 couples competing, but Steph survived my repeated fidgeting in the saddle to complete the course and set the record straight – all in the name of Comic Relief. The race in Dorking has seen the full spectrum of carrying styles: the piggyback (popular, but tiring and not very fast); the bridle (almost impossible to keep up for long); the Fireman (across the shoulders); the shoulder ride (precarious but surprisingly swift); and of course there is the Estonian hold, in which the 'wife' hangs upside down on the man's back with her legs over his shoulders. There is even the Dorking hold which is even more up close and personal, with the wife's face in the man's private area, but for many reasons, Steph and I went for the piggyback hold and I salute her reserves of mental and physical strength. We came last against a field of very serious athletes who used this as part of their marathon training, and so we got the wife carrier's wooden spoon, a Pot Noodle and tin of dog food, but Steph would have made our thief, Mr Rosvo-Ronkainen, very proud.

It all means that it shouldn't be too long before Great Britain knocks Estonia off the top of the rankings and boasts a world champion.

More details can be found at www.wifecarryingrace.com

HUSBAND DRAGGING: A WIFE' S REVENGE

Many women reading this chapter will have been left horrified. Did Emily Pankhurst and her heroines suffer in vain? Well, thanks to the Australians, some equality has been restored. In 2010, New South Wales held the world's first husband dragging world championship. Fittingly it runs alongside the Australian wife carrying event and is a chance for the women to get their own back. It was designed to depict a typical Aussie weekend, when – as the organisers say – a lady often has to drag her bloke out of the pub.

Husband dragging involves women pulling their men along a slippery surface away from a makeshift bar. She then makes him complete household duties. The husband cannot be kicked or punched, but must act as a dead weight while being pulled. It was worth it for the winners, Emma Mellows and Jacabe Woods, as they took home $1,000, which hopefully didn't go on divorce proceedings.

15

THE WEIRD
AND
WONDERFUL

We've already explored countless bizarre, painful, novel and fascinating sports – but now it's time for the seriously weird ones. If you've ever wondered why anyone would want to snorkel in a bog, have their shins kicked or charm a worm, read on...

JUST PLAIN ODD

BOG SNORKELLING

People often ask, of all the sports and activities I have tried, which has been the strangest, and which have I least looked forward to.

Often it's the build-up to filming that's far worse than the day itself, and that was certainly the case ahead of my dip into a Welsh peat bog to get my first taste – quite literally – of the world famous phenomenon that is bog snorkelling.

I remember the day so clearly. I was on holiday on a sunny

beach in Tenby, on my partner Emma's 40th birthday. What more could my lovely girlfriend want on her landmark birthday than to jump into a smelly, murky, scorpion-infested bog? It's testament to Emma's patience that she entertained the idea of celebrating with the creepy crawlies. Imagine how gutted she was when her daughter Lara woke up with a cold and didn't fancy a trip to chilly mid-Wales. So along with other willing guinea pigs Andy Pieser- Peppin and his son Barnaby, I headed up to the town of Llanwrtyd Wells.

The smallest town in the United Kingdom, it has certainly punched above its weight over the last 30 years. The green mound that overshadows the town was once a volcano, and has shaped the community's history. There are several mineral water springs in the area, and in 1732, a frog helped cure the local vicar, the Reverend Theophilus Evans, of scurvy. Believing his days were numbered, he was trudging through the local park when he noticed a healthy-looking frog wallowing in the sulphuric spring water. Despite the foul smell, he sampled the water himself and his scurvy was cured. Word spread, and once the railway opened in Victorian times, thousands of visitors flocked there every day to drink the special water.

Those days are now long gone. But the volcanic spirit in the town continues to erupt, and the area's connection with what lies beneath is not diluted. In a way, history has repeated itself. People don't flock here to drink the water now, they come to snorkel in it, and at the same time enjoy the healing powers of sport.

Before they tapped into the bog, it was all about the horse. During the 1970s, the town was in decline and desperate to do something to get tourism flowing again. The owner of the Neuadd Arms at the time, Gordon Green, overheard a heated discussion after a few pints at the bar. Was a man equal to a horse over a certain distance? We are not talking a sprint here; a horse would easily win that. But over a marathon course? Would the horse tire over the mountain paths sufficiently for the human to catch it?

So the town's first sporting event, the Man vs Horse race, was born and now attracts hundreds of runners from all over the world every June. They come with one aim, to beat one of a number of horses and jockeys over moorland, bridges, hills, rivers and rocky footpaths, and a distance of 22 miles. On the event's 25th anniversary, Huw Lobb beat the horses, in a time of 2 hours 5 minutes and 19 seconds, and the achievement was bettered in 2007 when two runners beat their equine challengers by a full 11 minutes. The winner still gets 1,000 guineas and a trophy.

So the touch paper had been lit, and over another few pints in the pub, the locals wracked their brains for the answer to their next question: 'What else have we got that will bring the tourists back here?'

'We've got the bog...' piped a voice from the back. Of course, they had plenty of bogs. Surely people would fall over themselves to swim in the murky sludge.

The next morning, as their hangovers kicked in, the sensible part of their brains mocked such a ludicrous suggestion, but it was all they had and so they drew up the rules for the bog snorkelling world championship.

You can't see the bottom of the bog and it's no more than a metre wide. Plus its only 60 yards long. But the organising committee decided this still wasn't enough of a challenge and so they banned competitors from using their arms. Instead you have to propel yourself up and down with flippers on your feet, while keeping your face submerged for the full sulphuric experience. It's the same technique that is used in the sport of 'fin swimming', which can give you so much more power through the water once you master the technique.

In the bog the locals were to strike sporting gold. They had tapped into an age when people in boring office jobs wanted something different to tell their colleagues about on a Monday morning. It started in 1986 and now over 25 years on, thrillseekers come from across the world.

The event, held over the August Bank Holiday weekend, is now covered in national newspapers, and TV networks around the world. Indeed the first person I met on arriving in the middle of nowhere, up on the moor, was a former American tennis player, now reporting with NBC. 'We are fascinated by this,' she told me. 'It's one of those alternative sports you have compared to the Olympics that make Britain the quirky and wonderful place that it is.'

I was only too happy for her to go first, as we crossed the rickety wooden bridge that took us to the edge of the bog. Due to demand there are two bogs in use now and between them on the grassy plateau were a dozen people in bright yellow and orange raincoats. It was August, yet it was 10 degrees, cloud was clawing the peaks all around and the sand of Tenby seemed a million miles away.

I had been warned about Weil's Disease by concerned family and friends. It's the disease that is carried in rats' urine and can be transmitted in water. But they haven't had a case here in all the years they've been bog snorkelling, so don't use that as an excuse. We may have been stupid enough to be stripping off, but rats are known for their intelligence, and why come to a place with no food.

Given the cold and the constant threat of rain, most competitors wore a wetsuit, but Barnaby did not, letting the cloak of peat water chill his bare skin. Rather that biting than the leeches or water scorpions, although to be fair the scorpions here are totally harmless. Far more dangerous is your imagination as you slip your toes into the brown water.

It seemed to take a lifetime for my flippers to come to rest on the soft bottom. This was the only time I would stand because already I could feel my feet sinking into the mud. I soon had a face that fitted in, as my guide, the Irish bog snorkelling champion Julia Galvin, had dropped in beside me and was rubbing black gold into my face.

The whistle blew and I plunged my head into the gravy, with a mini-camera strapped to my forehead to give the viewers tucked up in their warm, cosy beds an idea of the gloom. We were in a twilight world of murk. The claps of encouragement from the small crowd gurgled and bubbled in and out of earshot, and as the cold around my cheeks became soft and soothing, the peace that swallowed me every time I ducked under was surprisingly pleasant. My instinct was to recoil, to grit my teeth in disgust, but in reality the wetsuit was doing its job and I had reached halfway without any of my fears taking control.

On the return leg, my flippers were flicking like a dolphin's tail and with the right action, I was soon hearing the call to the line. As the last wave of weed and silt crossed my goggles, I lifted my face from the gloom, and touched the splintered side of the wooden bridge that marked the end. The skin on my face felt wonderful, as if I had just spent £30 on a health spa treatment. I had been in the water for four minutes and two seconds. Some distance off the world record at the time, held by Dan Morgan with a time of 1:30.06. But bog snorkelling embraces the Corinthian spirit, in which taking part is recognised, and so everyone gets a medal.

Having said that, as techniques have improved, so the times

have tumbled, and in the summer of 2011, Andrew Holmes from Halifax became the first person to snorkel the distance in less than 90 seconds. It's now estimated that bog snorkelling and its associated events earn the town of Llanwrtyd Wells a cool one and a half million pounds every summer. Bog snorkelling has even been added to lists of the top 100 things to do before you die.

There is now the bog snorkelling triathlon as well. This is a proper test for any long-distance athlete. A run up the hills and then down the rivers, over seven and a half miles, followed by two lengths underwater in the bog. Then, dripping with ooze and stinking of mud, you have a 19-mile mountain bike ride, including almost impossible climbs and breathtaking descents. Dan Bent from Surrey, who holds the world record with a time of 2 hours 21 minutes and 5 seconds, is a seasoned triathlete, and said it was one of the hardest events he has ever done.

It doesn't end there. For the locals at the Neuadd Arms bog snorkelling has become a bit mundane, so now they hold the world mountain bike bog snorkelling championships as well. It is a bit of a mouthful, especially if you angle the snorkel wrong and swallow the sludge above your head. You ride on a bike with a special lead-weighted frame and water-filled tyres, so there is no buoyancy. You sink to the bottom of the bog and try to pedal for 45 yards along the matting at the bottom of the trench, with just the tip of your snorkel poking out.

I have yet to tackle this challenge, so maybe we could all give it a go together one year. For more information, go to the www.green-events.co.uk website.

Someone who turns up every year is Julia Galvin, the Irish champion who splattered me with mud and whose life has been transformed by the lure of the bog, just like that Reverend all those years ago.

In 1997 Julia was in hospital with excruciating back pain caused by sciatica. She'd had a couple of minor accidents and had suffered a twisted spine. 16 painkilling tablets a day and what she says was indescribable agony aren't conducive to sport, but a physiotherapist advised her that swimming was the best remedy. It was hard, though, because Julia couldn't swim and was daunted by the thought of getting into the local pool with people happily swimming around her.

One Friday evening, at her lowest ebb, Julia was flicking though the *Guinness World Records* book and stumbled across bog snorkelling. For the first time in what seemed like a long time, a smile broke out across her face. The smile became a chuckle when the next morning Julia saw bog snorkelling featured on the TV news and thought it must be fate.

Julia told her dad there and then that she would be a world champion bog snorkeller. It would be her sport. He assumed it was the medication and humoured her, but the next day she hobbled to a swimming pool having booked a private lesson. Those first steps towards glory were taken in just 10 centimetres of water. Swimming had terrified Julia, but the bog was a new world where she could be who she wanted to be, where she could achieve and succeed and where she would never be out of her depth. Just standing in the shallow water, gradually venturing deeper week after week, Julia got used to her new environment. She felt lighter and as she spent more time in the water, her spine became less painful.

Three months later Julia was able to throw away the crutches, dispense with the medication, and was pain free. She could swim lengths of the pool like everyone else, and the next step was a snorkelling lesson in the sea. She trained hard with the snorkel, driven on by what she had seen all those months ago and making use of the Irish bogs near her home. And so it was that in 1999, she entered her first world bog snorkelling championships in Wales.

She stunned officials and the rest of the field by finishing second, and five years later came back to take the world title in the mountain bike bog event.

News of her success spread and her story was told in newspapers around the world. Bog snorkelling had saved her. It had reached out and touched her, when no other sport or activity had the power to do so. Julia says she owes a lot to the *Guinness World Records* book and it's the same book that inspired her to branch out into wife carrying.

During the summer of 2012, Llanwrtyd Wells's claim to be the world capital of unusual sports was strengthened when it held the UK's first World Alternative Games. It was a celebration of weird sports from all over the world, spread over three weeks, and showed the locals how far they had come since that initial meeting in the pub.

To mark the games, water from the volcanic springs was carried down to the town's fountain in a chariot attached to two mountain bikes. Once again the water flowed through the centre of the town, just like it had done in Victorian times. The same water that had given the frog such a healthy complexion, and which had nursed the Reverend back to good health, now symbolised the sports which had got people flocking back again in the 21st century . It had helped save an Irish lady's life. And in 2010, Julia Galvin was made a Dame by the region she represents.

WHIP CRACKING

It was Nessa from the TV series *Gavin and Stacey* who first described Barry Island in South Wales as 'cracking'. You can buy mugs there with the phrase printed on them and Ness will never realise how right she was. The place is now quite literally cracking – to the sound of the whip. Yes, it is the home of whip cracking, to which Ness would probably say 'don't mind if I do'.

It helps explain why I was in a hall near Barry Island one October evening in 2009, holding out my arm in fear. A distinguished man with a bald head and Sean Connery goatee beard was clutching a bull whip. 'Keep still, very still...' purred Pete Gamble in his deep, late night radio presenter's voice. I was frozen to the spot, for the tip of the whip would be lashing towards my arm at 750 miles per hour. A flick of his wrist, and the snake was unleashed. An enormous crack exploded as the tentacle wrapped itself around my arm. Amazingly, though, I hadn't felt a flicker. Pete had been so precise and accurate with his weapon that he had made the whip crack before I had been lassoed.

I had been right to trust this man, for Pete had just returned from America with a gold medal. Along with his whip cracking colleague Major Horton (he's not an army major; that's his Christian name) from Wolverhampton, they had just stunned the Americans in their own back yard. Pete had become International Champion in Freestyle Performance and had to beaten the seven time Guinness World Record holder and former world champion Adam Winrich in the process.

Earlier I had met these two champions on the seafront at Barry Island. You could hear Pete and Major before you saw them. Crack, slam, bang – bouncing off the arcade windows, and then off the sea wall. Children, a man with a dog and two policemen who weren't sure whether they needed to take any action stood transfixed, trying to fathom out why two men dressed in cowboy gear were acting as if they were on the ranch, rounding up the steers.

Ever since humans began domesticating animals, whip cracking has been around. It's the technique that helps humans train and control, and it is the art of producing a cracking sound through the use of a whip. It was the Australians who first turned it into a competitive sport, and its growth down under was matched by its presence at rodeo events in the US. Cowboy films and later the *Indiana Jones* movies helped give it a new lease of life. Now, thanks to Pete and Major, it's growing in the UK too, a century after the sport almost died out completely.

You will need a lot of nerve and accuracy and are judged on speed of your routine as well. Back at the sports hall, Pete and Major got a training partner to hold out strands of spaghetti in both of his hands. It was if they were playing a game of darts, only instead of going down from 501, they were cutting the spaghetti closer and closer to their brave mate's fingertips.

'It's the same satisfaction you get from hitting a golf ball,' Pete explained. 'Getting a golf ball to go exactly where you want it to go, the same as when you hit a squash ball and make it go right into the corner. It's that same feeling of "yes", of getting it spot on, in the back of the net, you are controlling something, and it's very mechanical.'

The most common training technique is to hook a paper cup on a stand and then try to cut it in two. If you manage to slice it clean in half with the end of your whip, it's three points. As a beginner I had to wear safety goggles, given the danger if I got the action wrong. I tried to remember the advice I had been given on a trip to George Hall in Essex. I had put on the gold chains and the rings for a darts lesson with the diamond geezer, Bobby George. He had told me: 'Throw where you are looking and look where you are throwing,' with a cackle of his Sid James laugh. I don't know if he was taking the Michael with that advice, but I have never known anyone crack up in hysterics as much as he did during the subsequent interview.

But what would Bobby have made of whip cracking? A bend of the elbow, the drawing back of the wrist…and as I visualised a viper jabbing towards its prey, I shot my arm forward. But the spring in my elbow had obviously jammed, because there was no crack, no explosion, just a limp ripple of rope.

'Guide the whip with your thumb', Major Horton advised. 'Keep it straight, and just imagine you are throwing a javelin or a dart.'

Ah – that did the trick, as I pulled the trigger again. This time – *kerpow!* – the energy flowed down my muscles and transferred into the stick of the whip. The line of lightning coiled back on itself in a split second, and the lash fired right through the cup for a clean strike.

Once you start, it's hard to stop, and we were soon all having a go. 'I go back to the days of the cowboys,' explained the Major, 'and more recently Indiana Jones, after that I was hooked'.

Major attempted to break the world record of 257 cracks a minute, and while I counted at least ten more than that, the record was never verified by Guinness. The children around us who had come for a taster session thought it was crazy and loved the part when they made a 'big noise'

I left our new whip cracking friends in the dark on Barry seafront, but there was a snap and crackle in the air as they were now adding fire to their routine to put on a spectacular show.

Four years on, whip cracking continues to grow. The UK whip crackers have now reformed as the Sport, Performance and Circus Whip Cracking Group. There are now 78 members who meet regularly and there are British champions in all the sport's whip cracking disciplines.

What's more, there is now 'Extreme Whipcracking', in which you get recognition for cracking whips in an unusual positions or places. Todd Rex, a Californian film stuntman, once cracked a whip in each hand while doing a backwards flip out of a tree. Pete, meanwhile, is on a mission to crack whips on all the mountain ranges in Wales.

For more information on whip cracking see www.whipcrackuk.co.uk

NURDLING

If you and a bunch of mates went out into the street with long sticks and started throwing bricks around, banging dustbin lids, shouting and screaming, you would probably get arrested for rioting. Yet this is what happens in a traditional rural sport which is still being kept alive in Dorset.

It is called nurdling. Now don't get confused here. The word 'nurdle' can mean a run in cricket (scored by gently nudging the ball into empty areas of the field). It can also mean a wave-like blob of toothpaste applied on a brush – this has actually been at the centre of a legal row between two major toothpaste companies.

But that couldn't be further from the sort of nurdling that goes on down country lanes near Weymouth and which local historian, Albert the Tall, says dates back centuries. There are references to the sport in Roman times, and more recently in Dorset in 1583 and 17 years later in Cornwall. Its revival came in the 1970s.

This is a world of droves, of grunting sticks, offenders and of grouting poles – and beyond all that mystery, it's basically a great way of adding fun and variety to a Sunday stroll along a country lane. Rugby and hockey players tend to be skilled nurdlers.

I thought the old man was drunk when he approached me at the campsite bar on the Dorset coast in the Summer of 2007. 'Hey, I know you – you're that man off the telly. You think you've tried all the sports? Well you haven't covered nothing unless you've got your grunting stick out and are banging your fender...' was roughly how his pitch went.

You don't ignore comments like that, especially as he had a sunshine yellow smile and a bit of blackberry stuck to his middle tooth which made him look like a witch. 'It's nurdling, that's what you wanna do, speak to Albert the Tall.'

So a few months later, having tracked down the mythical Albert the Tall (who is really Bill Crumblehome, a skilled potter) I arrived one Sunday lunchtime at the nurdling site in Upwey on the edge of Weymouth.

My dog Basil had come along with the promise of an afternoon sniffing the bushes along a country lane. Basil was half-lurcher and had once harboured sporting ambitions as a racing dog, until we had to break it to him that his mother had run off with a black Labrador and his bloodline had been polluted.

On this occasion, though, Basil needed persuading to climb the cobbled steps to the kick-off point, because of the strange banging noise coming from over the hedge. It was a metal clanging followed by a medieval bear roar and a guttural 'nurdle ho', which merged into a collective clashing of what sounded like dustbin lids. That's exactly what they were. To nurdlers this is a beautiful sound; as Albert said, 'the sound of nurdle on fender is rather like cricket's evocative leather on willow.'

But this is far more primeval than cricket, even if fielding skills do come in handy. You have two teams of so-called drovers. Both teams have one nurdle each. This now tends to be a wooden block, rather than a stone, and is the size and rough shape of a grown man's fist. In the match I played in, one was white and one was red, and both were about the size of a bar of soap. Recycled wood is the favoured material these days, as new timber is often grown too fast and is nowhere near as resilient. Stone can cause too much damage and is only rarely used.

Imagine the nurdle is a ball, and the aim is to get this object to the other end of the track or footpath you have chosen for the contest. It needs to be a defined right of way, which is called the nurdlynge alley. It can be five miles long, but is more commonly around one and a half. You can't run with the nurdle, so it's up to your team mates to advance up the course so that you can then throw it on to them. The teammate that receives it now waits until he or she can throw it on, and so the pass-and-move tactic continues.

It's like a continuous line out in rugby, but with a scrum going on at the same time, because all the action takes place along a narrow footpath or lane and you are allowed to get physical. Each team member has a fender, which is a galvanised dustbin lid, and this has two purposes. One can be to attack. You can intercept the opposing team's nurdle by knocking it off course into the rough, or any place where time might be lost. This can only be done while the nurdle is moving. Then there's the art of defence, when you need to shield the passage of your own team's nurdle. It all means that in mid-air you get the gladiatorial clashing of metal on metal. Gloves are essential, as fingers don't make a good sandwich filling.

Albert the Tall explained: 'It was once used to train armies in battle. It got them to practise using their shields to defend themselves. It's said that centuries ago, teams often used the severed heads from vanquished enemies as their nurdles.'

There is one more piece of equipment to deal with before we can get stuck in. As well as a fender, you are armed with a grouting pole. This is a stick made up of a broom handle with a spoon attached. The purpose of this instrument is to help a drover retrieve their nurdle from the rough or the bushes.

I thought I had slipped into a medieval dream as I donned the blue team's hessian sack shirt and on the command of 'nurdle ho' from the two team captains, the battle commenced. There was a frantic race into position and the first hurl of the nurdles followed along the bramble-framed lane. It was narrow and I was shoulder to shoulder with a bearded man whose natural whiskers didn't match his gingery wig, which was worn to make him look even more like a character from the middle ages.

We jumped together into the air as the red stone raced up from the sea of autumn gold, across the white paper sky and into sharp focus just two feet away from the deflection of my dustbin lid. You have to watch its trajectory because there are no helmets, and just as I thought I was about to smash it into the thicket, an arm and giant metal hand slapped my ear, his fender crashing down on top of mine, scraping my head and bringing the nurdle to a stop on the pathway.

My assailant stooped and, picking it up with the awe of King Arthur pulling the sword from the stone, bellowed in a victorious rallying call, 'nurdle ho!' It seemed you had to shout this every time you hurled the nurdle further along the line.

Once it was gone he was in pursuit flanked by fellow members of his clan. I was left to stroke my throbbing ear, and picking myself up from my knees could see that already the match was 100 metres down the lane.

It only stops when a nurdle is lost in the bushes, and there was a small consolation for the loser in this early battle. My opponent's ginger wig had snagged on a bramble, and was wafting in the breeze. I couldn't release it either and so set off on the chase.

It was fast, furious chaos, it was raw and it was fun. Tactics were key. A close unit working its way up with short sharp throws seemed to work best, while all the time remembering to block your opponent's brick on the way.

'I play rugby and a bit of hockey and it was a good work out,' said one new drover. 'It was more fun being mean to the other side and knocking them off course than worrying about our own bit of wood.'

A member of the Weymouth ladies' hockey club added, 'Hand-eye coordination was obviously key plus you have to be quite fit.'

Apparently there isn't always a winning team, but there is normally a losing team – which I ended up on. Crossing the finish line first doesn't mean a win. It is more like gymnastics, and so points for style are added up during the event and the final fling is important too. We all got a trophy and it was reassuring to know the next time I hear the smashing of dusting lids and lots of shouting, I won't predict a riot.

For more information go to Albert the Tall's nurdling site, www.crumbleholme.plus.com/nurdling.htm

SHIN KICKING

Many footballers can claim that they have been tackled by Robbie Savage. The former Wales combative midfielder, now BBC pundit, added steel to any team he played for. But how many professionals can claim to have been kicked on the shins by Mr Savage – indeed kicked so hard that it brought tears to the eyes? Not only that, but kicked on stage in front of hundreds of people – and with straw down their trousers?

This was one time that Robbie could kick as hard as he could and be applauded by the crowd, rather than getting a yellow or red card. Needless to say he enjoyed his chance to get his own back on a sports reporter, and to be fair to him, I had asked him to give it his all. It may not be allowed in the beautiful game, but there is one sporting tradition that is all about putting the boot in to your opponents.

Shin kicking, which is also known as 'purring', has been described as an English martial art. There's a hint of sumo wrestling and a smattering of karate, but any kick above the knee is a foul. It may be a quaint English tradition, but there is nothing quaint about competing, for it can be brutal.

As I climbed the grassy bank rising to the top of Dover's Hill in rural Gloucestershire, it was the sound which disturbed me first of all. Not the bleating of the bewildered sheep scattering to avoid me, but the strained grunting that was coming from over the brow. It was the weirdest of noises...the sound one would imagine a water buffalo would make if it had got stuck doing a crossword while on a packed commuter train. It wasn't necessarily a yelp of pain, more a guttural throat belch; a forced expression of frustrated effort.

Normally people climb this hill for the wonderful panoramic view of the Cotswolds, but on the green plateau about 200 metres down from the ridge on the other side were two men in white coats, performing what looked like a bird of prey's mating dance.

It was the way they were circling with their arms entwined and feet dancing from side to side before thrusting in and out. I then realised their booted feet were sometimes making contact with flesh and bone – and suddenly one of the men was down, writhing for a moment, clutching his ankle, only to spring to his feet again. And so the ritual was repeated.

I was alone, but this is normally a spectacle witnessed by hundreds of people. Bear baiting and cock fighting may have gone from British culture, thank goodness, but shin kicking is alive and yes most definitely kicking. The sport has actually been practised on Dover's Hill near Chipping Campden since the early 17th century. The competition was one of the highlights of the Robert Dover Olympicks, which were established by lawyer Robert Dover in 1612.

This lawyer got the blessing of King James I to transform an existing Whitsuntide fair into a series of games, modelled on the ancient Olympian ideals of strength and endeavour. Other events included a cross between stick fighting and fencing, and a sack race. These games, with shin kicking as their showpiece, were a landmark in British sporting history.

In their bid to host the Olympics in London in 2012, the British Olympic Association said, 'An Olympic games in London in 2012 will mark a unique anniversary. It will be exactly 400 years from the moment that the first stirrings of British Olympic beginnings can be identified.' A direct reference to the Cotswold Olympicks, with shin kicking at its heart.

By the 1830s it's said that over 20,000 people would gather on Dover's hill for the annual shin kicking contest, and early English travellers had also spread the sport to the USA.

'It was vicious in those days,' secretary Francis Burns told me. 'There were a lot of inter-village rivalries and lads used to harden their shins with hammers, and were allowed to wear iron capped boots.' There are also reports of local farmers hardening their shins to get themselves ready for competition by going into the fields and smacking their legs against fence posts. Such brutality meant that by the 1850s shin kicking was outlawed.

It had always struggled to compete with boxing and

wrestling, which had introduced codes of practice and rules at an early stage. In contrast, shin kicking had gained a reputation for being wild and barbaric and in the more refined society of 19th century Britain, there was no place for it any more.

The Cotswold Olympicks suffered their own demise. The parish of Weston Subedge wanted to enclose the land and so the venue was gone. Dover's Hill also fell quiet. No more grunts and groans, no more white coats.

The games were gone, but not forgotten. The Festival of Britain in 1951 provided an opportunity for historians and enthusiasts to celebrate and recreate bygone past times. By now the modern Olympics were firmly established in the sporting psyche and when it became clear that this unique Cotswold event had played such an important role, the games and shin kicking returned. In 1963 the games were formally reintroduced, and the crowds have been flocking back ever since.

It's not as brutal now though. For a start, steel toe capped boots are definitely banned. People must wear soft shoes like trainers, and they can stuff as much straw up and down their trousers as they like to cushion the blows. This was reassuring as I strolled back to the green cauldron that would be the venue for my first shin kicking bout, against a local pub landlord and defending world champion.

'We never had broken bones,' I was assured by Francis Wilson. 'Not since last year anyway...' chipped in my opponent with a hearty alehouse laugh. 'No broken bones,' reassured Wilson, 'but there are some bruises.'

I had brought along my football shin pads thinking they were the answer, but was swiftly informed that they were banned. So with glee, I began stuffing a barnful of straw up my trousers and down the top of my jeans as well. Despite the itchy texture, it felt like cotton wool with the protection it would hopefully give me in the minutes ahead.

Competitors still wear the white coats, said to be worn by shepherds in the area at the time the sport started rather than anything to do with this sport being considered insane. Then there's the stickler, who's the umpire, also in a white coat, with a stick in hand to intervene if the contest gets out of hand. No kicks above the knee are allowed and a scoring blow must happen in mid-kick; i.e. you can't sweep your foot along the ground into your opponent's shin. A kick is not enough, though. You have to strike with enough force to bring your rival down to the ground. It's usually a best of three contest.

Against a former champion, I danced, dodged, ducked and dived, but unlike in a boxing ring, there is nowhere to hide as you are linked arm in arm, and as I ventured a foot out of defence for a tentative strike, whack, in it came like a cobra's tongue, catching me on edge of the shin and like a pack of cards. Down I went.

The expectation of pain was worse than the mild ache that followed. Encouraged by my own bravery, I jumped back up, desperate to get back into the contest and conscious too that I was being filmed for my *Breakfast* report. After another minute of shadowing, posturing and gesturing, I managed a flick to his shin, but I doubt he felt it because he refused to flinch and instead responded with a kick that had me hopping away, clutching my limb as if I had been shot. For no other reason than the chance to call it a day I rolled down onto my side and his victorious arms went up. I was out in the first round, and my shin kicking career was over.

Maybe you need to have been born and bred in these parts. In 2012, a 23-year-old stonemason from neighbouring Worcestershire was the last man left on his feet to claim the world title. Zac Warren had only entered to prove doubters at work wrong. Previous champions have claimed that local cider has seen them through and it seems now that shin kicking is here to stay. No longer is it seen as a thuggish pursuit for the riff raff; it's a historic British tradition that attracts thousands of people every year.

There are reports of a similar sport in Lancashire, called 'Clog Toe Pie'. It may sound like a hearty dish for a winter's evening, but it was essentially shin kicking with clogs on. It's said that it was very popular amongst miners and that they would grapple with each other wearing nothing apart from their clogs. Let's hope the 'below the knee' rule still applied.

The Shin Kicking Association of Britain is campaigning to make it an Olympic sport, just like in 1612. They came up with 10 reasons – well, actually nine, as they couldn't think of a tenth. They say that if judo fighters are allowed to break bones at the Olympics, then shin kicking should be a shoo-in. They claim the man who started the modern Olympics got his idea from them, and joke that there's no need for a 'dope' test, because if anything stupidity is encouraged.

The shin kicking world championship takes place every spring at Dover's Hill in Gloucestershire. It happens on the first Friday after the Whitsuntide bank holiday and for more information visit the Shin Kicking Association of Great Britain's website.

WORM CHARMING

The former policeman fiddled away furiously with his wood, but still the worm wouldn't rise. Rocking back and forth, he beat a stick against the pitchfork with increasing speed and precision. I looked around. We were alone on a playing field in Cheshire. Others were coming, but before they could get there, the man, whose distinguished beard was dancing above the handle of the pitchfork, looked up at me slowly and said: 'This is it, this is how you charm a worm.'

A couple of weeks later and I was sitting under the restaurant roof at Wimbledon, overlooking the outside courts. It was pouring with rain and it was before the days of the roof, so I didn't have much action from the day before to look back on. I ran through the day's sports news and speculated on the day ahead with my distinguished guest, the interviewee from heaven, tennis coach Nick Bollettieri. He is TV platinum; always warm to listen to, and with lashings of humorous insight from his days nurturing some of the world's best players. You ask him a question and off he goes with wonderful stories, and great knowledge, all delivered in his big screen voice. You might have guessed then that this is a man who is never lost for words. However, I might be able to claim a first.

After our tennis chat, it was time to move away from the sport to a different kind of activity that was taking place on that wet Saturday. The weather may not have been good for tennis, but it would be ideal conditions for a new world record in worm charming. 'Did you say what I thought you just said?' Nick asked, as the report on the world worm charming championship began to roll.

His ears hadn't deceived him and he sat there in silence, eyes fixed on the small monitor screen just below the camera. 'Is this for real? Do they...?' He paused mid-sentence and began shaking his head, smiling at the quirkiness of the British sporting summer.

Nick was so taken aback by what he had seen that he vowed to get his grandchildren having a go in the back garden. Little did he know that a version of the sport had already been going for many years in the USA.

It's not like rugby union and rugby league, both hatching out of the same egg, though. Worm charming in the UK and 'worm grunting' across the Atlantic are not directly related.

Let's deal with the American version first. The official video promoting the 2007 worm grunting festival in Florida begins with gladiatorial music and a quote from Charles Darwin in 1891.

'It may be doubted whether there are any other animals which have played so important a part in the history of the world as the earthworm.' Little could Charles have imagined that one day they would also be taking part in a sport.

Grunting normally begins before sunrise, when the tapping can be heard. It rises in inflexion and the only way I can describe it is like a wildebeest who's been for a vindaloo and yet the next morning still has to get away from the lions. The stomach-wrenching sound from the grunter on the block accompanies each tap of the wooden stake on the pitchfork as they aim to entice as many worms as they can out of the ground.

The video continues to pay tribute to the power of the worm, informing us that one acre of land equals one million earth worms. Indeed that one acre of worms can recycle or recompose 10 tonnes of fallen leaves in one year. I bet you also didn't know that there are approximately 2,700 different kinds of earthworms, and that they all have 16 hearts. They might not want to start worm charming in South Africa. The world's largest earthworm was found there, at 22 feet long.

It might seem a shame then that despite the worm's hero status in the States, and the good that they do for the soil and plants, that the whole point of worm grunting is to take them away from their homes, so they can be used as fishing bait, and also as food. Oh yes, worms are very good for you. They are 82 per cent protein and it's claimed that eating earthworms can reduce cholesterol.

In America, the roots of worm charming are in business. The Revells have made a living out of it for decades now. Ever since they were married, Guy and Audrey, known as the King and Queen of worms, say they love working out in the forest, grunting away day after day, sometimes 16 hours at a time, collecting the worms in their sacks. In fact it's now claimed that Mr and Mrs Revell, from Florida, have collected enough earthworms to reach the moon and back. They count every one. Not surprisingly then they have become the Posh and Becks of the worm world, greeted like superstars when they turn up at the worm grunting contests which have grown up on the back of the commercial business that provides fishermen with essential tools for their trade.

On the other side of the pond, at a village school in Cheshire, there is also a worming academy. This one, though, developed completely unaware of the grunting in America and can genuinely claim to be more 'charming'. Charming because there doesn't seem to be any grunting, for a start. Tap dancing, clarinet playing, yes – but no bellowing. And charming because the worms are always retuned to where they came from and are never intentionally harmed in the process. In the UK the big difference is that worm charming didn't start as a business on which people's livelihoods depended.

It was in July 1980 in the village of Willaston near Crewe that deputy headmaster John Bailey came up with a novel idea for the school fête. He had noticed that if you tapped the top soil, like a bird, earthworms would rise. He had also seen fishermen use this trick and thought – tongue firmly in cheek – that it would make an interesting variation to the lucky dip and bash the rat stalls. Plus he probably didn't fancy being the teacher nominated to get a soaking in the stocks yet again. So for 10p a go, the good folk of Cheshire became the first in the country to entice worms out of the ground.

The stall was a hit and so local policeman and parent Mike Forster was charged with making a competition out of it, which would raise money for local charities. The village community association got to work and a regulatory body of control was formed. The International Federation of Charming Worms and Allied Pastimes held their first meeting and drew up the 18 rules that are still in force today. You might ask what the allied pastimes are by the way; well best not, as I was told they include indoor hang gliding, underwater Ludo and ice tiddlywinks.

We may scoff, but the Chief Wormer Mr Forster proudly boasts that all these years on, the rules have been translated into 33 different languages across the world. It has proved a challenge for some. Other cultures don't have an equivalent and have had trouble embracing the concept. For instance in the Tibetan booklet, it takes 4 pages of script just to explain what worm charming is. In the Russian guide book, it is translated into worm conjuring which at least gets across the magic of this story.

If you ever have a wet afternoon and want to improve your language skills, do look at the various translations on the website of the IFCWAP, which is www.wormcharming.com. You will wonder how you ever lived before being able to explain the 'no water' rule in Korean.

To save time and make life simpler I will now just pick out the highlights of those 18 rules in English.

1. Each competitor gets a plot 3 metres by 3 metres
2. Lots are drawn to decide who gets which plot

3. You get 30 minutes to charm away
4. Worms must not be dug from the ground. Any digging means instant disqualification. Only vibrations can be used
5. No drugs are allowed. In worm charming water is said to be a banned stimulant and like any liquid is strictly prohibited
6. Any form of music is allowed to charm the worms out of the ground
7. A normal sized garden fork can be used and stuck into the ground and vibrated by any means to encourage the worms to the surface
10. A piece of wood, smooth or notched, may be used to strike or fiddle the handle of the garden fork to assist vibration
11. Some competitors who may be squeamish and don't wish to handle the worms may appoint a second team member to do so. These act like a golf caddy, and are known as a gillie
12. Each competitor can only collect worms from their plot
13. Worms must be handled carefully and collected in damp peat and placed in the container provided by the organisers. They are then counted before being returned to the ground, either 30 minutes after the competition is over, or later in the evening when any hopeful birds have left for their nests
14. The winner is the person who collects the most worms in the half hour period. In the event of a draw, there is a sudden death play-off plot, with five more minutes of charming

The only tie break so far came in 2003, when the Windsor family (Richard and Rodney) and Lee Clark with Robert Oltram both raised 157 worms. In the play-off pitches, the Windsors won the worm shoot-out, getting just one more than their rivals.

Now there must be something about the clay rich soil of Cheshire, because this has always been the most successful place for worm charming. Other parts of the country have tried to start their own championships and not fared quite so well. At a competition held in Lincolnshire, no worms at all were charmed.

Yet in Willaston, where it started, in the very first year a staggering 511 worms were tempted out of the ground in just half an hour. It was a stunning success for local farmer Tom Shufflebottom, and his name would become legendary in worm charming and grunting circles all over the world.

The record seemed like it would stand forever. Normally a couple of hundred would be enough to win you the famous worm trophy, and once the world championship was won with a paltry total of just 43. However in 2009, worms the world over froze on the spot, all because of a nine-year-old girl called Sophie who was to make headline news.

Before I tell Sophie's story, let us twang together for a moment and consider the various methods that people have tried over the years.

TWANGING – the most common and most successful method. This is simply flicking (no digging) the garden forth back and forth at high speed, and often fiddling with it, which means beating the fork frantically with a wooden stick to create a wave of vibrations.

TWICKLING – to get more rotational movement in the ground, by getting a circle of vibrations going, created by hitting the fork from different directions.

TWEAKING – If you are squeamish and don't like the worms, long handled garden forks can be used and touched with a larger stick from distance, therefore just tickling the top of the fork to create a softer vibration. Your gillie will then need to collect the worms.

TWACKING – think of a musical tuning fork. This method involves lying the fork on the ground, and then beating the handle, so that that fork end vibrates just above the soil, creating a humming effect, which seems particularly attractive to worms. Maybe they are actually musical. Twacking became a recognised technique by accident. A competitor got so angry because he hadn't charmed a single worm that he threw his fork down onto the soil in disgust. He then noticed that at the fork end several worms started to appear.

Others have built rain simulators, which mimic the sound and feel of raindrops on the ground. They have also tap danced to Irish jigs, bounced on space hoppers, and one year someone brought a pony along. It was taught to hoof and rake the ground, but when it came clear that it would tread on and kill any worms that it had charmed, the pony was given a red card and went onto the banned list.

Music has become a popular method, second only perhaps to twanging and fiddling. Saxophones, violins, and drums all have to be options and there are no prizes for guessing the tunes chosen: 'Raindrops Keep Falling On My Head', 'The Green Green Grass of Home', Handel's 'Water Music' and the '1812 Overture'.

I decided to go for the musical approach when I went along to see the Chief Wormer and some of his academy stars in training for the 2007 championship. My grandparents Bill and Olive had lived in the neighbouring village of Wistaston and my Uncle David and Aunty Sue still live in Crewe, and so they came along for moral support.

As often is the case, I couldn't make the actual event

because it was on a Saturday, when I am normally in the studio presenting. So that's why I attended a training session some days before. While David and Sue used a homemade device that involved a stamping wellington boot, my cousin Alison and son Bradley employed the space hopper technique with limited success.

I watched from afar, working out my approach and stroking my chin in a way that suggested I was hatching a brilliant idea before getting out my clarinet, on which I can play two tunes. One happens to be 'Stranger on the Shore', and I thought the high notes of this Acker Bilk classic would have the worms calling 'encore' as they wiggled their hips clear of the soil.

I filled my lungs with air and began...and it started to work. There's one, I thought, and another, and my eyes widened as five, maybe 10 worms appeared, inching their way into the sunshine. In my excitement, my lips slipped, and suddenly there was a screech. I had got my embouchure all wrong and it was downhill from there. I sounded like I was strangling cats, and when I finished just two worms had made their way fully out of the ground. The others had gone back down under, clutching their beating hearts. I had no plan B and with the twangers looking on smugly, I was out of the reckoning.

By the way you might think it's strange that there was a training session, but half an hour of twanging leaves you dripping with sweat and with your arms dropping off. It's the intensity of the movement that burns off those calories, a bit like a drummer on a 33-inch vinyl that's suddenly turned up to 45. 'You have to be fit for an attempt on Shufflebottom's record, so we build up our strength, speed and stamina, by putting in the hours beforehand,' Mike Forster chuckled.

My failing just went to prove that in this sport, the early bird doesn't catch the worm. You see I had got carried away too quickly, thinking I was heading for a high score. But to count, a worm must be fully out of the ground. They are sensitive little things and it doesn't take them much to put them off. My sisters Jane and Louisa will know how they felt, having also suffered my clarinet playing.

You won't be surprised then to hear that 'premature worm grasping' is something of a problem for the sport's governing body. Apparently according to the IFCWAP, children under five and women over 40 are the most at risk from this. Symptoms include reaching down too early to pull the worm out, before it's clear of the soil. The dangers are pretty obvious. Either the worm reels back in terror or even worse, the poor creature is split in two.

The sport prides itself on treating the worms humanely. Their welfare is the priority to the committee. Mike Forster was once accused of organising a worm hunt, and so called in the RSPCA. They monitored proceedings and concluded that the sport could continue, because thanks to the measures that were in place, everything was being done to ensure the safety of the worms.

For instance, once a worm is out and collected by the gillie, it is taken and counted by the officials and then put into a huge trough of rich peat, containing the worm's favourite food. They work their way down into this until they reach the soil, and the trough stays in position until all the birds have gone to bed that night. Education is key to the humane treatment of worms and so to cut down on the amount of 'premature worm grasping', the IFWCAP now runs a worming academy.

The highlight of this is the worm charming simulator which has a plastic worm which can be tugged out of its hole with a piece of string. It's so instructors can show people how to handle worms with the upmost care and attention, and this has been taken to W.I meetings, local playgroups.

If you think all that is hard to believe, even more incredible was the achievement of Sophie Smith, the 9 year old girl from Cheshire who in June 2009, smashed Tom Shufflebottom's record, of 511, that had stood for 29 years.

Sophie and her Dad, Matt, who acted as her gillie, used the traditional twanging method. Onlookers remember the speed and intensity with which they hit the handle of the garden fork with a metal bar. They hardly stopped for air, and 30 minutes later amid a mountain of worms which were being collected by the organisers, it became clear something special had happened.

Not only had she beaten the record, but she had smashed it with a final score of 567. Sophie was front page news in the UK, and went live on national radio in America. Even more staggering when you consider it was the day after Michael Jackson died. She was in the news in Japan too, and after earning her place in the *Guinness World Records*, became a young ambassador for the sport. Her secret? 'Sheer determination', and it's likely her record will stand for a very long time.

The annual world championship now attracts interest far beyond the worming hotbeds of the UK and America; there are competitions as far afield as Australia, the Philippines, Portugal, Holland, Thailand, Italy and India.

The Japanese are especially keen, and British worm charming now appears in a comic which teaches children English. Why is there such interest? It seems it's that old chestnut again: a fascination with the quirky pastimes that make Britain unique.

Sophie is by no means the youngest competitor to take part. That honour must go to Evie May Benbow who entered, with a bit of help from Mum and Dad, aged just five weeks. They attached a stick to a fork, and then to her cradle so that when she moved or giggled or cried, the cradle would rock and the vibrations would fall via the fork into the soil. It had limited success and 19 worms were charmed, but Evie is still learning her trade.

Worm charming has come a long way since it was a whimsical school fête idea. There are now other competitions around the UK which are run under licence from the IFCWAP, but the village of Willaston remains the capital and final word must go to the former policeman Mike Forster:

'It puts the area on the map, and raises money for good causes. It brings people together, like all good sport does and when all we hear is bad news, this brings some fun back into people's lives. It fulfils the basic human need for enjoyment.'

I remember Ken Dodd once saying we all need to exercise our 'chuckle muscle' once a day or we lose it. That's one area of the body that worm charming is guaranteed to work on.

The world worming championship are held every June and booking a plot will cost £5.

www.wormcharming.co.uk

16

THE NEXT
BEST BITS

I hope you have seen that there really is a sport for everyone and a chance for us all to get involved. We shouldn't be embarrassed if at first we find something difficult, but instead should enjoy the adventure along the way. The biggest thrill comes from reaching the end of a learning curve, and everyone has to start at the bottom. Along the way you may push your body to limits you never thought it had, or you may just enjoy the freedom that playing a sport gives you.

As I mentioned at the start 'play' shouldn't be seen as a dirty word, suggesting that we are not taking a sport seriously. Whether it's Lewis Hamilton getting into a go-kart for the first time, or Mark Cavendish getting on his new bike at the age of 12, it all begins with a chance to play. It is a natural instinct that is in all of us, which child psychologists believe is essential to preserve. It helps us to interact with the environment around us and how to communicate better with others. I am sure 'playing' at being 1970s Leeds United football icon Tony Currie every evening after school on the Yorkshire estate where I lived helped me interact with the youngsters around me. One other lad was Benny from ABBA, and another someone out of *Coronation Street*, and we would meet in our imaginary soap opera. Whether it was actually kicking the ball or riding my bike (pretending it was his flash '70s footballer's car) I was in dreamland and didn't notice the fresh air, exercise and interaction I was getting.

In this age when we are becoming more insular, hooked on our video games, phones and electronic tablets, the role of play has never been so important, and yet of course it has become harder and more dangerous to let our imaginations loose on the streets.

So the new, weird and wonderful sports that have emerged over the last seven years have helped combat this by re-introducing their own sense of play, while at the same time getting people fitter. Hundreds of activities later, there are still many more to come: some that haven't even been conceived as yet.

I believe there is a new sport in all of us. I spent a day off a couple of years ago visiting a school in Ashburton in Devon. As an experiment we gave a class a blank sheet of paper and asked them to get into groups and to design a new game or sport. The response was staggering. I couldn't hear myself think when I came back into the class an hour later. There were at least eight new game ideas on the table.

Ask yourself how many games have you made up in the car or the park with the kids. Along with primary school friend Peter Haynes, I came up with swing cricket. It's so simple to play. You take a lightweight football down to the swings in the local park. You take it in turns to swing and once you are into your rhythm the game can start. The bowler has to try to get the ball past your legs and into your lap. You have to kick it away. Before the game begins, you agree the scoring. For instance, when I play now with my kids in our local park, if the player on the swing kicks the ball clear of the soft landing area around the swings, it's a single. If they get it as far as the roundabout, it's a four, and if they can kick the ball past the bear-shaped dustbin without it bouncing, it's a six. Of course if they kick the ball into the air, it can be caught.

There is a simple card game which I came up with for a friend's football-mad son. I called it the Freddie Football Game and it's for two people. Deal all the cards out face down to both players like in a game of snap. Then the youngest player goes first and turns over his or her first card. The idea is to get a run of three cards in ascending order. So if the first card is a low number it's a good start. For example let's say Freddie turns over a four. He then turns over another card, and if it's higher than a four he keeps going, but if it's lower then Freddie is 'tackled' and the turn switches to another player.

Let's say in the example here that Freddie's second card is a seven. That means overall he's drawn a four, and now a seven, and can keep going. If his next card is lower than a seven, he is tackled and the go is over, but higher, and it's a great run up the wing and he's in a shooting position. So let's say it's a jack next. He has then got three cards ascending in a row and can say 'shoot'. The opposing player then turns over their first card. If that card is a picture card, then it's a save. If it's not a picture card then it's a goal to Freddie. Play resumes again with the other player setting off on a run of their own.

The only other rule is that if Freddie had a seven and then turned over another seven, and so had two matching cards, this would be a foul and so regardless of where Freddie was in the sequence, he could say free kick, and the opposing player would have to turn over a picture card to stop a goal.

It's proved a popular game among friends and family for long train journeys and at airports or on a rainy day at home, and shows how straight forward creating your own game or sport can be. By unleashing our imaginations we can further unlock the possibilities of play.

There will be sports out there which I don't even know about yet, maybe ones, still in people's imaginations, or on the back of an envelope which I look forward to profiling. They may soon be unusual sports which have a dedicated following, that engulf people's passions and energy every weekend, that have their own world champions, their governing bodies, and that ability to change people's lives.

Some future ones which I have been contacted about recently include tambourelli (which is growing in the South West), horse-ball, stone skimming, bat and ball, white water rafting and surf boat rowing. There was also the call about the annual 'Chap Olympics' which includes bicycle jousting and cucumber sandwich discus. What's more I have always been fascinated by the annual cheese rolling event which has become known all over the world, but which so far, I have been unable to attend. It attracts thousands of spectators to Cooper's Hill in Gloucestershire to watch hardened souls run and tumble down a steep hill in pursuit of a rolling piece of cheese.

At the other end of the spectrum, there are more established sports, such as rugby sevens, and croquet still on the list. Expect rugby sevens to feature a lot more in the media over the next four years as it will be part of the Olympic programme at Rio 2016. Kite surfing was also due to feature, until the International Sailing Federation reversed a decision to include it and restored windsurfing to the programme instead. Nevertheless, kite surfing remains a ghost I have to lay to rest after getting the award for the most difficult sport I have tried. To see for yourself visit www.britishkitesurfingassociation.co.uk

In the meantime, I will keep searching the horizon for new sports and activities that reflect the rich diversity of British life. I will keep trying to give unheralded British sporting stars like four-times world sidecar champion Tim Reeves and back-to-back PWC world champion James Bushell the recognition they deserve. There are undoubtedly more incredible athletes out there with skills and bravery in pole climbing, sledge hockey or air racing that are as yet unnoticed.

At the same time, are there further bizarre sports we should salute, which can help turn around and save people's lives, as in the story of Julia Galvin? She is proof that the wife carriers, the worm charmers and bog snorkellers who have helped make Britain unique and get coverage across the planet have their place alongside the elite as well.

The response to my Saturday morning features has been so positive, especially from those I was most worried about: the athletes and professionals themselves. But far from seeing these reports as an attempt to belittle and undermine what they do, they have said they show the all en-compassing power of sport, and also highlight how hard they have to work, and how super human they truly are.

It was Dame Kelly Holmes who said to me: 'Sport doesn't have to be at the elite end all the time. It's about taking part and having a go at something. If you get involved in a new sport or activity, you will get the fun element, and you will enjoy it and think, oh, I will now give something else a go. It can be any form of activity, as long as you are getting the heart rate going and actually feel like you are doing something for a purpose'.

I must just give a final mention to someone who has taken this spirit to the extreme; king of bizarre sporting challenges,

Ashrita Furman from New York. In 2004, he set a new world record for the fastest 100 metres on a space hopper, with a time of 30.2 seconds. It's one of 431 official Guinness World Records that he's set since 1979. He currently holds 148 titles, ranging from tiddlywinks to hopscotch. What's more, this non-athlete is now the world record holder for the most world records held by an individual at the same time. Not bad for a health store manager in his mid-fifties who says 'I am not a natural athlete, but am trying to show others that our human capacity is unlimited if we truly believe in ourselves.'

ACKNOWLEDGEMENTS

The past seven years wouldn't have been possible without the support of so many people and I would like to thank all my colleagues past and present at the BBC, including: Alison Ford, Nick Dickson, Julia Barry, Katie McDougall, Adam Bullimore, Peter Salmon, Barbara Slater, Richard Burgess, Adrian Hobart, Lisa Kelly, Kelly Crawford, Victoria Bartlett, Sally Watson, Jim Lumsden, Richard Burgess, Kim Barrett, Ian Moss, Nick Parrott, Phillipa Shaylor, David Kermode and last but certainly not least Jonathan Squires. There are so many people who have helped in so many ways, and it's impossible to list everyone here: the day editors, the producers, the incredibly talented picture editors, and hope i have thanked you all personally. Despite what anyone says the BBC is the most fantastic and creative place to work.

Special mention must go to the cameramen/editors who have had to put up with my at times bizarre ideas (and new ways of using a go-pro) most often: Kevin Saddington, David Varley, Ian Da Costa, Simon Monk, Dave Painter, Trevor Adamson,

Chris Marlow, Simon Oliver, Errol Young, Don Slater and Andrew Blake...and apologies to those who I haven't mentioned and who I have been lucky enough to have worked with more recently.

Most importantly I would like to thank my wonderful parents, Mum and Dad, plus my sister's families, Jane, Louisa, Glen, Dominic Ian, Ben, Sam and Evie, who have seen me leave family occasions when a new sport had to be filmed. Thanks to the support of the Carters, Matt, Lucy, Tilly Ted, Wendy and Alan, and of course to the very brave Emma (maybe no longer harbouring bog snorkelling aspirations), Roly and Lara, so patient as I spent many an evening burning a hole in the dining room table as steam rose up from my fingers. I hope you agree it was worth it and thanks for being such a part of my own 'best bits'.